797,885 Books
are available to read at

Forgotten Books

www.ForgottenBooks.com

Forgotten Books' App
Available for mobile, tablet & eReader

ISBN 978-0-282-27074-2
PIBN 10207449

This book is a reproduction of an important historical work. Forgotten Books uses
state-of-the-art technology to digitally reconstruct the work, preserving the original format
whilst repairing imperfections present in the aged copy. In rare cases, an imperfection in
the original, such as a blemish or missing page, may be replicated in our edition. We do,
however, repair the vast majority of imperfections successfully; any imperfections that
remain are intentionally left to preserve the state of such historical works.

Forgotten Books is a registered trademark of FB &c Ltd.
Copyright © 2015 FB &c Ltd.
FB &c Ltd, Dalton House, 60 Windsor Avenue, London, SW19 2RR.
Company number 08720141. Registered in England and Wales.

For support please visit www.forgottenbooks.com

1 MONTH OF FREE READING

at
www.ForgottenBooks.com

By purchasing this book you are eligible for one month membership to ForgottenBooks.com, giving you unlimited access to our entire collection of over 700,000 titles via our web site and mobile apps.

To claim your free month visit: www.forgottenbooks.com/free207449

* Offer is valid for 45 days from date of purchase. Terms and conditions apply.

English
Français
Deutsche
Italiano
Español
Português

www.forgottenbooks.com

Mythology Photography **Fiction** Fishing Christianity **Art** Cooking Essays Buddhism Freemasonry Medicine **Biology** Music **Ancient Egypt** Evolution Carpentry Physics Dance Geology **Mathematics** Fitness Shakespeare **Folklore** Yoga Marketing **Confidence** Immortality Biographies Poetry **Psychology** Witchcraft Electronics Chemistry History **Law** Accounting **Philosophy** Anthropology Alchemy Drama Quantum Mechanics Atheism Sexual Health **Ancient History** **Entrepreneurship** Languages Sport Paleontology Needlework Islam **Metaphysics** Investment Archaeology Parenting Statistics Criminology **Motivational**

THE LIFE OF

MAJOR-GENERAL

SIR ROBERT MURDOCH SMITH

K.C.M.G., ROYAL ENGINEERS

BY

HIS SON-IN-LAW

WILLIAM KIRK DICKSON

WITH PORTRAITS, MAPS, AND OTHER ILLUSTRATIONS

WILLIAM BLACKWOOD AND SONS
EDINBURGH AND LONDON
MCMI

The design on the cover represents the sword of honour presented to Sir Robert Murdoch Smith by Nasr-ed-Din Shah in 1885.

PREFACE.

I DESIRE to express my cordial thanks to the many friends of Sir Robert Murdoch Smith's who have helped me with information and advice in the preparation of this volume. Above all, my gratitude is due to Sir Frederic Goldsmid, who has not only allowed me to make use of his published writings and supplied me with many interesting documents, but has most kindly revised the proofs of the chapters relating to Sir Robert's Persian services. The chapters on the Halicarnassus and Cyrene expeditions have been read in proof by Dr A. S. Murray of the British Museum, to whose good offices I am also indebted for the loan by the Trustees of the Museum of several illustrations from the Catalogue of Greek Sculpture. Among others who have helped me my special thanks are due to Sir Juland Danvers; to Mr G. S. Mackenzie, C.B.; to Mr Sidney Churchill, now British Consul at Palermo, formerly on the staff of the British Legation at Teheran; to Dr

C. J. Wills; to Mr J. J. Fahie; to Mr C. E. J. Twisaday, of the Indo-European Telegraph Department; to Mr D. J. Vallance, Curator of the Edinburgh Museum of Science and Art; and last, but not least, to my wife.

W. K. D.

3 DARNAWAY STREET,
    EDINBURGH, *August* 22, 1901.

CONTENTS.

CHAPTER I.

EARLY YEARS. CHATHAM.

A many-sided life—Birth—School-days at Kilmarnock—Glasgow University—Enters Royal Engineers—Life at Chatham—Selected for the Crimea—Naval Review of 1856—Introduction to Sir John Burgoyne—Dog stories—Return of Crimean Sappers—Boating adventure—Ordered to Halicarnassus . 1

CHAPTER II.

THE FINDING OF THE MAUSOLEUM.

The Halicarnassus expedition—Letters to Sir John Burgoyne—Murdoch Smith's share in the work — Commencement of operations at Budrum—"Smith's Platform"—Discovery of the Mausoleum—Excavation of the remains—Discoveries of sculpture — Rhodes — Turkish life — Friendliness towards England—Myndus—A Turkish festivity—Wrestlers—Continued work at the Mausoleum—Finding of portions of the chariot group 19

CHAPTER III.

FURTHER WORK AT HALICARNASSUS.

Expedition to Mughla—Melassa—Travelling in Ramazan—A hospitable Pasha—A khan at night—The British uniform in Turkey—Report on the Mausoleum—Murdoch Smith's restoration of the building—Visit of the Viceroy of Egypt and of the French fleet—Temple of Hecate at Lagina—Labranda—Letter from Lord Clarendon—Further excavation of Mausoleum—Keramo—Excursions round Budrum—Visit of the Pasha—The Turks and the Indian Mutiny—Christmas at Budrum 63

CHAPTER IV.

CNIDUS.

A severe winter—Work at Cnidus commenced—Excavation of tombs—Daily routine—Snake-charming—Quarantine troubles—Discovery of Odeum—A sailor's letter—The Sappers' triumphal arch—Discovery of the lion tomb—Embarkation of the lion—Visit to Constantinople—A run home—Athens—Antiparos—Corporal Jenkins—A Greek bridge—Visit of Prince Alfred 105

CHAPTER V.

THE CYRENE EXPEDITION.

Garrison duty at Malta—Dumaresq's monkey—Murdoch Smith proposes the Cyrene expedition—Letter from Sir John Burgoyne—Start of the expedition—Landing at Benghazi—Supposed bloodthirsty intentions—Despatch to Lord John Russell—Journey up country—Commencement of work at Cyrene—Temple of Dionysos—Relations with the Arabs—Mohammed el Adouly—Temple of Apollo—Finds of sculpture—Visit of H.M.S. *Assurance*—A narrow escape—Amateur sorcery—Exploration of the Cyrenaica—A Scotch Turk—Teuchira and Ptolemais—A serious disturbance—Attack on the castle at Ghegheb—A feat of endurance—Unruly negroes—An awkward incident—Excavation of the Augusteum—Imperial portraits—Fever—Arrival of H.M.S. *Melpomene*—Trouble with the Arabs—A blackmailer—Friends in need—Embarkation of the statues—Success of the expedition . . 143

CHAPTER VI.

THE PERSIAN TELEGRAPH.

Employment at the War Office—Appointed to the Persian telegraph staff—Telegraphic communication with India—Colonel

Patrick Stewart—Telegraph convention of 1862, Persia—The *chapar*—Persian characteristics—Major Bateman Champain—Making of the line—Murdoch Smith's troubles—*Mudakhil*—The line completed—A political hitch—Murdoch Smith becomes Director—A diplomatic triumph—The racecourse incident—The convention of 1865—Visit to Beluchistan and to India—Later history of the telegraph—A telegraph muddle—Formation of the Indo-European and Eastern Companies—Later conventions—Efficiency of the telegraph—Lord Curzon's estimate of its effect on Persia . . . 198

CHAPTER VII.

LIFE IN PERSIA.

Teheran in the 'Sixties—Dr Wills's visit to Murdoch Smith—The Major's dervish—"Ashes on my head!"—Teheran festivities—"She Stoops to Conquer"—Legation buildings—Marriage—The *Corps Diplomatique*—Mrs Murdoch Smith's illness—Visit to Europe—Paper at United Service Institution—Chaparing adventures—Persian justice—St John and the lioness—Starving soldiers—The saddle and the Prince—The "transit of Venus"—The Falckenhagen concession—Pole-shooting—Russian influence—*Tanzimat*—Murdoch Smith's relations with the Persians—The Mukhber-ed-Dowleh—Administrative methods—A polyglot world . . 242

CHAPTER VIII.

WORK FOR THE SOUTH KENSINGTON MUSEUM. LATER YEARS IN PERSIA.

Purchases for the Science and Art Department—M. Richard—The Persian collection at South Kensington—The Shah's interest in the Museum—His presents—Domestic trouble—Illness—The telegraph and the War in Egypt—Interest in commercial enterprise—The Karun River question—Death of Mrs Murdoch Smith—The tragedy at Kashan—A dark time—The Afghan Boundary Commission—On the brink of war—The Shah's sword of honour—A change of fortune—Estimate by his chief of Murdoch Smith's services to the telegraph 281

CHAPTER IX.

THE EDINBURGH MUSEUM. MISSION TO PERSIA IN 1887.

The Edinburgh Museum—Reception in Edinburgh—Lighthouse cruise—The Queen's book—Death of Sir John Champain—Appointed Director-in-Chief of the Indo-European Telegraph—The Jask affair—Mission to Persia—Presents to the Shah and his Ministers—The Karun River—Visit to India—Reception by Lord Dufferin—Settlement of the Jask question—Journey to Teheran—Mr Cecil Smith's archæological work—Reception at Teheran—Audiences of the Shah and his Ministers—Extension of the telegraph conventions—Presentation of band instruments to the Shah—The diamond snuff-box—Arduous ride to Ispahan—The Zil-es-Sultan—Return to Teheran—Farewell to Persia—Mr Nicolson's despatch—Letter from Lord Salisbury—K.C.M.G.—Retires from the army 304

CHAPTER X.

LIFE IN EDINBURGH.

Amalgamation of Indian and Indo-European Telegraph Departments—Murdoch Smith resigns Directorship—Returns to Edinburgh—Work at Edinburgh Museum—Additions to the Museum—The Shah's visit in 1889—A picturesque ceremony—Continued interest in Persia—Papers on the Karun River—The Board of Manufactures—Edinburgh friendships and occupations—Speech on art—Effect of the Reformation on art and manners in Scotland—Domestic life—Holidays—St Giles's Cathedral—Character—The last years—The end 329

APPENDIX.

REPORT ON THE MAUSOLEUM 353

INDEX 369

ILLUSTRATIONS.

PORTRAIT OF SIR ROBERT MURDOCH SMITH IN 1898 . *Frontispiece*
    From a photograph by Mr R. S. Webster, Edinburgh.

PORTRAIT OF LIEUTENANT MURDOCH SMITH, R.E., IN 1856 *To face p.* 8
    From a coloured photograph by Mr Alexander Stanesby.

VIEW OF BUDRUM . . . . . . „ 20
    From *Travels and Discoveries in the Levant*, by permission of Messrs Vincent Brooks, Day, & Son, Ltd.

PLAN OF HALICARNASSUS (BUDRUM) . . . „ 26
    From *Travels and Discoveries in the Levant*, by permission of Messrs Vincent Brooks, Day, & Son, Ltd.

THE CHARIOT GROUP OF THE MAUSOLEUM . . „ 60
    From a block lent by the Trustees of the British Museum.

MAP OF THE COAST OF CARIA . . . *Between pp.* 64 *and* 65
    By permission of Messrs Vincent Brooks, Day, & Son, Ltd.

THE ORDER OF THE MAUSOLEUM . . . . *To face p.* 92
    Lent by the Trustees of the British Museum.

THE LION OF CNIDUS . . . . . „ 120
    Lent by the Trustees of the British Museum.

MAP OF THE CYRENAICA . . . . . „ 146
    From *History of the Recent Discoveries at Cyrene*, by permission of Messrs Vincent Brooks, Day, & Son, Ltd.

PLAN OF CYRENE . . . . . . „ 156
    Lent by the Trustees of the British Museum.

BUST OF THE EMPEROR ANTONINUS PIUS, FOUND AT CYRENE „ 184
    From a photograph by Messrs Mansell & Co.

ILLUSTRATIONS.

MAP OF PERSIA . . . . *Between pp. 204 and 205*

PORTRAIT OF COLONEL SIR JOHN BATEMAN CHAMPAIN, K.C.M.G. . . . . . . *To face p.* 214
    From a photograph by Messrs Window & Grove.

VIEW OF TEHERAN . . . . . " 244
    From a photograph by Ghassem Khan.

PORTRAIT OF H.E. THE MUKHBER-ED-DOWLEH, K.C.I.E. . " 276
    From a photograph by the London Stereoscopic Co.

PORTRAIT OF MRS MURDOCH SMITH . . . " 294
    From a photograph by Messrs Elliot & Fry.

PORTRAIT OF H.R.H. THE ZIL-ES-SULTAN, G.C.S.I. . " 324
    From a Persian photograph.

SKETCHES IN TEXT OF LETTERS . . {*pp.* 38, 50, 52, 59, 84, 90, 115, 121, 122, 123, 124, 127}

DIAGRAMS TO ILLUSTRATE REPORT ON MAUSOLEUM {*pp.* 355, 356, 357, 358, 361, 363, 366}

MAJOR-GENERAL
SIR ROBERT MURDOCH SMITH.

CHAPTER I.

EARLY YEARS. CHATHAM.

A MANY-SIDED LIFE—BIRTH—SCHOOL-DAYS AT KILMARNOCK—GLASGOW UNIVERSITY—ENTERS ROYAL ENGINEERS—LIFE AT CHATHAM—SELECTED FOR THE CRIMEA—NAVAL REVIEW OF 1856—INTRODUCTION TO SIR JOHN BURGOYNE—DOG STORIES—RETURN OF CRIMEAN SAPPERS—BOATING ADVENTURE—ORDERED TO HALICARNASSUS.

WRITING to Lord Salisbury in December 1887, Sir Robert Murdoch Smith said: "During my long connection with the Indo-European Telegraph, it has always been my earnest endeavour, while striving to maintain the efficiency of the special department intrusted to me by her Majesty's Government, so to act as to allay the suspicions and gain the confidence of the King, Government, and people of Persia." The words may be taken as summarising what he regarded as the main work of his life. To have brought the English telegraph in Persia into a state of high efficiency, to have conciliated Persian feeling towards England, to have extended and consolidated British influence in that country, and to have conducted with conspicuous success an important mission to the Court of Teheran,— these achievements alone would have entitled him to an honourable place among the men who during the reign of Queen Victoria worked for the Empire. But they formed only a part of Murdoch Smith's many-sided lifework. He was a zealous and efficient officer of Engineers. He was a great archæologist. As a young subaltern he played an important part—a part the importance of which has never been duly recognised—in the expedition which secured for the British Museum the magnificent sculptures of Halicarnassus and Cnidus. At his own risk and expense he organised and carried out the adventurous Cyrene expedition of 1860-61, which opened a new field of archæological research, and added fresh treasures to the national collection. During his residence in Persia he devoted practically the whole of his leisure to the acquisition for the Science and Art Department of the collection of Persian antiquities and works of art now shown at South Kensington—the finest collection of the kind in Europe. His work at the Edinburgh Museum of Science and Art, during the last fifteen years of his life, was of itself sufficient to give him a claim to remembrance as a valuable public servant. No apology is needed for an attempt to preserve some record of a life so busy, so useful, and so honourable.

Robert Murdoch Smith was the second son of Dr Hugh Smith, medical practitioner in Kilmarnock, and Jean his wife, daughter of Robert Murdoch, farmer at Pennymore, near Ochiltree. He was born in his father's house in Bank Street, Kilmarnock, on the 18th of August 1835. There were five other children, three of whom, Hugh, Jeanie, and David, lived to grow up.

Dr Smith came of an old Seceder stock—Auld Licht Anti-Burghers; there is a tradition that one of his forebears was drummed out of Ayr by the town authorities for refusing to take the burgess oath. Needless to say his family were brought up in the old Scotch way, and well drilled in the national virtues of industry and thrift. At an early age Robert was sent to school at Kilmarnock Academy. The rector, Mr Harkness, was a teacher whose methods would scarcely commend themselves to "My Lords" nowadays; they were, however, effective in turning out both good scholars and good men. Speaking at the opening of the new Academy buildings at Kilmarnock in February 1899, Sir Robert described the Academy as he knew it fifty years before. "How vividly," he said, "I can recall the familiar old school, and more especially the Latin class-room, where, for seven years, I sat at the feet of the learned and accomplished rector, whose methods of imparting a knowledge of the classics were, as some of you may remember, simple and effective—those, in fact, of the teacher immortalised by his pupil Horace as the *plagosus Orbilius*. His special horror, I well remember, was the perpetration of a false quantity in Latin, which never failed to rouse his ire as if it were a gross personal insult that could only be wiped out by the immediate castigation of the offender. As false quantities were his special horror, parallel passages to those we happened to be construing were his special delight. He had a fine literary taste, and an amazing number of apt quotations at his fingers' ends from all the great poets—Greek, Latin, and English. With these he expected us boys to be as familiar as himself. In this exorbitant expectation, thanks to iteration and to the simple methods I have already referred to, he was not altogether disappointed. There was always a certain grim humour which, on the whole, I think we rather enjoyed, in the situation of a culprit smarting from the effects of some peculiarly heinous and unmusical false quantity being called upon to quote *ore rotundo* Shakespeare's opinion of his lamentable condition :—

> 'The man that hath no music in himself,
> Nor is not moved by concord of sweet sounds,
> Is fit for treasons, stratagems, and spoils,
> . . . . . .
> Let no such man be trusted.'

Or, under similar circumstances, to be made to exclaim with Solomon, as if he entirely agreed with the sentiment, 'He that spareth his rod hateth his son'; or, with the great lexicographer, 'Yes, rod, I still revere thee for this thy duty.' On the whole, the liveliness and amusement thus afforded to the many quite counterbalanced the temporary inconvenience to the few; and had the total abolition of the ferula been put to the vote, it would have been lost by an overwhelming majority."

To the end of his life Sir Robert was a believer in the old-fashioned Greek and Latin schooling as the best of all mental drill, and it may be added that he was never converted to the theory that the instructor of youth can dispense altogether with the judicious help of Father Stick.

The four years after leaving school were spent in study at Glasgow University, in teaching, and in private study. The son of a country doctor with little money and no special influence, Murdoch Smith knew that he must look to his own efforts for advancement in the world, and set strenuously to work to qualify himself to make the best of his chances in life. At Glasgow he attended the classes of Greek and Latin, Chemistry, Natural Philosophy, and Moral Philosophy. The last he soon deserted, with a lack of interest in speculative questions which remained a lifelong characteristic,— a somewhat unusual characteristic in a Scot. His main interest was the Natural Philosophy class, taught by Professor Thomson, now Lord Kelvin, then a young and recently appointed professor. Lord Kelvin remembers him well as a zealous and distinguished student. He took a high place in the class, working far into the night in order to reach the high standard of mathematical knowledge which was requisite in order to derive full benefit from the professor's lectures. He fully appreciated the eminence of his teacher, and was one of the old pupils who in 1896 gathered to do honour to the veteran professor's jubilee. Outside of university work he devoted himself diligently to the study of modern languages. French and German he thoroughly mastered, and acquired a working knowledge of Italian and some acquaintance with Arabic.

At last, in the summer of 1855, his chance came. The country was in the midst of the Crimean war, and there were plenty of vacancies in the army. In August 1855 the first open competitive examination for commissions in the Ordnance Corps took place. Murdoch Smith went up for the examination and passed first out of some 380 candidates, the second being C. W. Wilson, now Major-General Sir Charles Wilson, K.C.B., K.C.M.G., late Director-General of Military Education. On September 24, 1855, he was gazetted to a lieutenant's commission in the Royal Engineers, and on the 15th of October he joined the R.E. establishment at Chatham.

He had now found his work and place in the world. His surroundings at Chatham were thoroughly congenial, and his career in the service was a success from the very beginning. He threw himself with keenest zest into the work, the amusements, and the society of his new world. His journal and his numerous home letters record days full of work well done and pleasure keenly enjoyed, — study and parades, regimental duty and regimental dances, his first levee, his first visit to Aldershot. Colonel Sandham, his commanding officer at Chatham, soon formed a high opinion of his character and capacity, and he made many friends among his comrades of all ranks.

To Dr Hugh Smith.

BROMPTON BARRACKS, *January 8th*, 1856.

Yesterday I had the distinguished honour of being chosen and booked for the Crimea. There are four companies to go out, and the captains were allowed to choose their lieutenants, one to each company. Capt. Cox of the 24th Company chose me, passing over all my seniors. The four seniors were to have gone, but he urgently requested to get me, and my name is up to the Horse Guards accordingly. He says that the 24th is to go in spring, although the whole plan may be changed before that. My being chosen has caused no small amount of talk among the rest of the lieutenants. He asked me yesterday if I was willing to go, when I told him I felt only too proud of the honour, and thanked him for it. . . .

I am going to a ball at Col. Sandham's to-night. It is to be a large one I believe.

Sir Harry Jones is expected here to-day. We have invited him to dine to-morrow evening. I am vice-president of the Mess this week and will be president next.

To Jeanie Smith.

BROMPTON BARRACKS, *January* 21, 1856.

. . . Speaking of the Crimea, the whole affair is countermanded, and I am as uncertain now as the day I joined whether I may ever be there. I fear it will be a bad look-out for us if the war stops. But I don't believe it will.

I have been very busy for the last ten days writing a report on the state of the R.E. Widows' Fund. Sandham asked me to do so as a particular favour. I had all the accounts and papers to go over since the year 1785, which was no small task. I finished my report this morning, and when I took it to the Colonel he said I had given "a very lucid statement of the state of affairs." I have been getting over head and ears in work since I came back. . . .

We are to give a grand ball on the 5th. The mess-room and ante-rooms are all to be decorated, and for music we will have two military bands—our own and the Marines. . . .

My bun, shortbread, oatmeal cakes, and all were not long in disappearing, which shows how they were relished by the English. The whisky is also a very great favourite.

BROMPTON BARRACKS, *March* 13, 1856.

Three hundred men and eight officers left this for the Crimea on Tuesday morning. I got up and went with them to the station. The parade was before 5 in the morning, when of course it was quite dark. The scene was quite striking, all the men in heavy marching order and with their haversacks and calabashes as well. After the roll was called and the inspections made, when the word "Quick march" was given, the band struck up the Grenadiers and the men gave quite a deafening huzza. All the way down the men's wives who were left

LIEUTENANT MURDOCH SMITH, R.E.
1856.

were continually rushing into the ranks to bid their husbands good-bye, comrades were shaking hands, &c., and whenever we passed a group of people another shout was raised all along the column. The band went with them to Southampton to play them through London, and by this time I suppose they are all sick in the middle of the Bay of Biscay. . . .

To Dr Hugh Smith.

BROMPTON BARRACKS, *April* 25, 1856.

Strange to say, I had just returned from the grand Naval Review when I got your letter asking if I had been there. I had not the remotest idea of going, as I knew it was of no use without a ticket, so I was much surprised when I came home at night on Monday to find a telegraphic message from Tom Gillespie offering me a ticket for the review. . . . It was an invitation card from the Royal Mail Steam Packet Co. to one of their ships at Southampton. I slept at Gordon Square, getting up at four in the morning to be off by the five o'clock train. . . . I got down in time to get on board the *La Plata*, certainly the most magnificent steamer I ever saw. . . .

On board everything was provided for us in grand style—breakfast, dinner, &c. It must have cost the Company an enormous sum, as there must have been six or seven hundred at least on board, and we were all the guests of the Directors.

We had a splendid view of the whole affair, which was really grand. The ships were arranged in two columns parallel to each other, the one headed by the *Duke of Wellington* and the other by the *Royal George*. You may have an idea of the number of ships from the fact that each column was twelve miles long, and this exclusive of the gunboats, nearly 200 in number. The movements, however, are necessarily so slow that it does not form so attractive a spectacle as a military review, which one's eye can take in and so far understand. The day was very fine, and the sail down Southampton Water and past the Isle of Wight was beautiful. We passed close under Osborne House, which has a very fine situation. I got to Southampton again between 9 and 10 in the evening, and was very fortunate in getting a train, by which I arrived in London about three in the morning. . . .

THE HUTS, CHATHAM, *May* 6, 1856.

For the last three days I have been sitting all day on a district court-martial. . . . We have tried 6 prisoners, and as we are not yet dissolved, I don't know how much longer we will have to sit. I should certainly not like to be a judge. It is one of the most tedious things imaginable sitting all day over a case as we had the other day when trying a sergeant of the 8th for embezzlement.

I have just finished a report on the degrees of elevation of the Enfield rifle for different distances. Colonel Sandham wanted it done for Sir John Burgoyne, and after a good deal of trouble I got it done, and gave it in yesterday. He has given me another employment to-day which will last as long as I am here. It is to assist in remodelling the men's schools, which they attend every morning till breakfast-time. The men are at present without any arrangement or prescribed course of study, so that beside a man busy with square or cube root or some such thing you may find another deep in the mysteries of simple addition. It is proposed to get them properly classified, and let them go on regularly as in an ordinary school. . . . All these employments are over and above my usual regimental and professional duties, so that I am busy enough.

To Jeanie Smith.

THE HUTS, CHATHAM, *May* 17, 1856.

We have had rather a great week here. On Wednesday we had the half-yearly inspection by our chief, Lieut.-General Sir John F. Burgoyne, G.C.B., Bart., Inspector-General of Fortifications. We have good reason to be proud of such a member of our corps. He got his commission in the Royal Engineers in the end of last century,[1] and distinguished himself in almost every battle and siege throughout the long wars with Napoleon. His breast is literally covered with medals, stars, crosses, orders, &c., and although he must be nearly 80 you would not think he was much above 50. . . .

On Tuesday evening, the night before, Colonel Sandham asked me to his house to meet Sir John. There was a large party of bigwigs, but only three or four subalterns besides myself. Sir

[1] Sir John's first commission was dated August 29, 1798.

John's son-in-law, Captain Wrottesley, introduced me to him, and I had a long conversation with the old General. He was very affable, asking me about Glasgow College, what I had studied there, &c. . . .

To Dr Hugh Smith.

THE HUTS, CHATHAM, *May* 23, 1856.

I have just been appointed by the assistant adjutant-general to take command and charge of the 23rd company Royal Sappers and Miners during the absence of its captain, who goes to-morrow to Hythe School of Musketry preparatory to becoming instructor of musketry for the Sappers and Miners. Lempriere, the captain of the company, may perhaps be known to you as the owner of the famous dog "Sandie," that was wounded at the battle of Inkerman. He is about the most general favourite of any man I ever saw. He will be at Hythe till about the end of August, till which time I shall have command of the company. You may imagine my astonishment when it was read out in orders on parade on Wednesday, considering that subalterns are almost never in command, and I am about the most junior officer here. . . . I am exceedingly glad of the appointment, as it may be of use in the way of bringing me forward. . . .

It was about this time that Captain Lempriere was commanded to take "Sandie" to Windsor, as the Queen wished to see him. "Sandie," alas! was no courtier, and misconducted himself woefully in the royal presence, to the utter discomfiture of his master.

Sir Robert used to tell another dog story of the Chatham days. A brother officer who shared his quarters in the Huts owned a fine retriever, which unluckily developed the habit of sheep-worrying. On one occasion the dog, having been caught in the act, received a tremendous thrashing. That night he disappeared, and next morning turned up at the door of his owner's quarters wagging his tail and evidently highly pleased with himself. On going out his master was disgusted to find that a dead lamb had been deposited at his doorstep. The dog thought that he had been punished, not for killing lambs, but for *failing to retrieve them*. It was thought better to risk the death of an occasional lamb than to spoil a good retriever, and so he received no further punishment.

To Dr Hugh Smith.

THE HUTS, CHATHAM, *June* 14, 1856.

I am getting on very well with my captain's duty. I am glad everything has gone on all right as yet, and I hope it will continue so. It gives me much more work to do than I had any idea of, but I have learned more of the internal economy, so to speak, of soldiering than I ever did before. . . .

THE HUTS, CHATHAM, *July* 19, 1856.

Last week I was member of a committee for trying some new pontoons invented by Mr Forbes, engineer of the North Staffordshire Railway, formerly a sergeant-major of the Sappers. One of the days the wind and tide carried off one of the rafts, and as it had no anchor on board it was swept away with its crew down the river, and I have no doubt would have reached Sheerness but for the timely arrival of a cutter with an anchor which we had despatched after it. In the afternoon it came on a violent thunderstorm, and as the men had no shelter and no food since the morning, Tyler, one of ours, and myself took down their dinners, greatcoats, and a barrel of water to them in one of our boats, which of course they were very glad to receive. They got back all right at night when the tide turned.

We had a grand day to-day in the barracks, on the occasion of the return of the companies of Sappers from the Crimea. We all paraded in full dress, and were drawn up in line at open order to receive them. Our band met them at the station and marched them up to "Auld Lang Syne," "See the Conquering Hero Comes," "Home, Sweet Home," &c. The streets were decorated with flags, mottoes, &c., and the populace cheered the men most lustily. When they came into the square they were formed in line the same as we, and facing us. One can't imagine a nobler sight than they presented. They were all great, broad, burly fellows; for, alas! their companions less sturdy than themselves had all fallen victims to the hardships they had to undergo. When they had formed we gave "General salute, Present arms," the band playing "God Save the Queen." They then returned the compliment in a similar way. When they had done so we gave them three times three, and loud as our cheer of 1000 men was, when their commander, Major Nicholson, gave the word, "Crimean Sappers, three cheers," we were thrown quite into the shade by the thundering cheers they gave in reply. It was splendid to see them with their weather-beaten faces and great shaggy beards, and breasts covered with medals. When the Queen saw them at Aldershot she was so pleased with their appearance that she asked some of the officers to dine with her the same night at the Pavilion. We have now so many men here that besides the barracks and huts, tents had to be erected for 200 more. . . .

At Chatham much of Murdoch Smith's spare time was spent in boating, and he used often to say that one of the most useful things he learned at that time was to sail a boat. Throughout his life boating remained one of his favourite amusements. On one occasion he had a somewhat narrow escape.

To Dr Hugh Smith.

THE HUTS, CHATHAM, *July* 25, 1856.

I write this to keep you from being alarmed should you see my death in any of the papers, as Col. Sandham has sent notice of it to headquarters in Pall Mall. On Wednesday night three of us—Wynne, Festing, and myself—were up at Rochester with a pair-oar outrigger. We spent the evening at Capt. Moorsom's, and started early, about half-past ten, to catch the tide before it turned, and as we had five or six miles to pull. It was a beautiful clear night, although there was no moon, but about ten minutes after we started we saw frequent flashes of lightning in the distance, which we saw were gradually gaining on us. We pulled hard to get home before it should reach us, but on it came, and in two or three minutes it had overtaken us. It was now a perfect calm, but so dark that I could not distinguish Wynne, who was steering, while I pulled stroke. Suddenly we heard the whistling of a breeze, and before we had pulled two strokes down came such a hurricane as I have never witnessed. We gave ourselves up for lost, as the boat we had was one of those light racing gigs, not two inches out of the water, and which the catching of a crab would upset even in a mill-pond. Fortunately the wind was dead down the reach in which it caught us, otherwise the first gust would have capsized us. We tried to run into the mud, but found it impossible. We were driven more than a mile in this way, pulling away all the time as hard as we could to keep the boat upright. We were speculating on how to save ourselves should we upset, as a single false stroke would do it, and the wind was like to blow the oars out of our hands. We were drifted most miraculously on the mud under Upnor Castle; but being low tide, we had a long way to drag the boat through the mud, which took us above the knees at every step. The storm was terrific, almost a *thick* darkness, and the thunder just over our heads. We got in, however, in safety to the quarters of Gorton of the 84th in the Castle. We spent the night with him, as the storm did not abate all night. As an outrigger was found upset in the creek we were all thought lost, and when we came back we found boats despatched to search for us, &c.

The entry into Upnor Castle was effected under the guidance of E. R. Festing, now Major-General Festing, C.B., Director of the Science Department of the Victoria and Albert Museum. The ship-wrecked subalterns slipped past a sentry, having first observed with satisfaction that owing to the lightning he had unfixed his bayonet. On reaching the quarters of their involuntary host they found that he had gone out to dinner, and, covered with mud as they were, they were regarded with great suspicion by his soldier-servant, who made no small difficulty about admitting them. On Gorton's return he found the man awaiting him. "There are three queer-looking men in your room, sir," he said; "they *say* as how they know you." The "queer-looking men" were recognised and made welcome for the night. Next morning they returned to Chatham, to the delight of Colonel Sandham, who was much distressed at their supposed loss. They received, however, a severe wigging for turning up after they had been officially reported drowned.

By this time Murdoch Smith had been noted by the authorities as a likely man for special employment. From the beginning of his career he had been brought under the special notice of Sir John

Burgoyne. At the time of his entering the service his examination papers had been submitted to Sir John, and, as we have seen, Colonel Sandham had taken an opportunity of introducing him to the General. Writing home in July 1856, he says: "Sir John Burgoyne, it seems, has got impressed with some sort of good opinion of me. One of our fellows, a friend of his, who had been calling on him the other day, told me that Sir John had been speaking to him about me. He did the same thing once before, I can't make out how or why."

He had been recommended for employment first in connection with the delimitation of the Russo-Turkish frontier in Asia, and then with the Oregon Boundary Commission. Ultimately, in October 1856, he was selected to command the detachment of sappers which accompanied Mr C. T. Newton's archæological expedition to Asia Minor.

CHAPTER II.

THE FINDING OF THE MAUSOLEUM.

THE HALICARNASSUS EXPEDITION—LETTERS TO SIR JOHN BURGOYNE—MURDOCH SMITH'S SHARE IN THE WORK — COMMENCEMENT OF OPERATIONS AT BUDRUM — "SMITH'S PLATFORM" — DISCOVERY OF THE MAUSOLEUM—EXCAVATION OF THE REMAINS—DISCOVERIES OF SCULPTURE — RHODES — TURKISH LIFE — FRIENDLINESS TOWARDS ENGLAND — MYNDUS — A TURKISH FESTIVITY — WRESTLERS — CONTINUED WORK AT THE MAUSOLEUM—FINDING OF PORTIONS OF THE CHARIOT GROUP.

AMONG the national treasures preserved in the British Museum, few are better known to the public than the contents of the Mausoleum Room. These priceless remains of ancient sculpture and architecture are for the most part the result of excavations in the neighbourhood of Budrum, the site of the ancient Halicarnassus, in the southwest corner of Asia Minor. The magnificent tomb of Mausolus, Prince of Caria, erected in the fourth century B.C., when Greek art was at its zenith, ranked as one of the seven wonders of the ancient world. Many pieces of sculpture which were believed to have formed part of its decoration were built into the Castle erected in the fifteenth century at Budrum by the Knights of St John, but the Mausoleum itself had entirely disappeared in the middle ages, and its very site was unknown.

In 1846 Lord Stratford de Redcliffe obtained from the Porte authority to remove some of these sculptures from the castle walls, and thirteen slabs in low relief, forming part of a frieze, were sent to England and placed in the British Museum. Nine years later, in April 1855, Mr C. T. Newton, then British vice-consul at Mytilene (afterwards Sir Charles Newton, Keeper of the Department of Greek and Roman Antiquities in the British Museum), visited Budrum. He returned in the spring of the following year, and spent six weeks in exploring the place and in small experimental excavations. As the result of these visits Mr Newton submitted to Lord Clarendon, then Foreign Secretary, a memorandum suggesting that a firman authorising the removal of further sculptures should be obtained, and that the sum of £2000 and the services of a ship of war should be appropriated to carrying out this purpose, and to searching for the site of the Mausoleum. He also recommended that an officer of the Royal Engineers and four sappers should accompany the expedition.

These suggestions were carried into effect. The ship detailed for the service was the steam corvette *Gorgon*, Captain Towsey, and Murdoch Smith was placed in command of the Engineers' party. The detachment consisted of Corporal William Jenkins, as senior non-commissioned officer, Corporal B. Spackman, as photographer, and two lance-corporals, Patrick and Francis Nelles, one a smith, the other a mason. Mr Newton had suggested in joke that

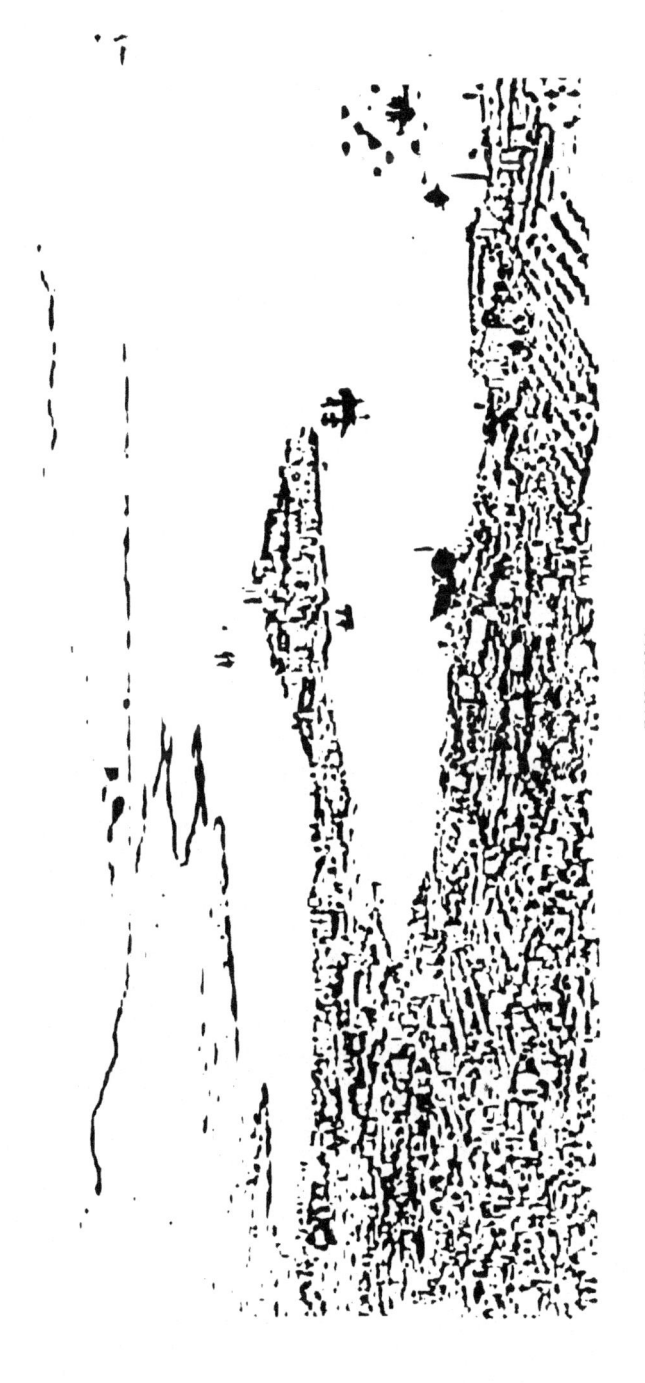

BUDRUM.

it was desirable that some of the sappers should be able to speak Greek. The omniscience of the Corps, however, was not at fault. The Nelleses had been born in Corfu, and both possessed the required accomplishment. Among those who spent some time with the expedition were Mr G. F. Watts and Mr Val Prinsep.

After a few days' leave spent at home Murdoch Smith joined the *Gorgon* at Spithead on October 13, 1856.

The archæological results of the expedition have been very fully described and illustrated in Sir Charles Newton's *History of Discoveries at Halicarnassus, Cnidus, and Branchidæ* (Day & Son, 1862); and *Travels and Discoveries in the Levant* (Day & Son, 1865); and in the official papers presented to Parliament at the time. (*Papers respecting the Excavations at Budrum*, 1858, and *Further Papers respecting the Excavations at Budrum and Cnidus*, 1859.)

During the whole of the expedition Murdoch Smith kept up a regular correspondence, private as well as official, with Sir John Burgoyne. He kept copies of his letters to Sir John. When he went to Persia these were left at home, and he believed that they had been lost. In the early summer of 1900, when he was seriously ill, I had occasion, while in search of some business documents, to turn out the contents of a box of papers in his room in the Edinburgh Museum. At the bottom of the box was a packet of documents which proved to be the missing letters. Sir Robert was delighted with the find, and during the month of

June, when it seemed for a little while as if he were convalescent, he took the utmost pleasure in having them read to him, and in talking over the old days in Asia Minor. He often spoke of preparing them for publication. They give an interesting and complete narrative of the work of the expedition from month to month, besides some vivid pictures of life on the shores of the Ægean in the years which immediately followed the Crimean war. "I never thought they were so good," he once laughingly said. They certainly are notable productions for a subaltern of one-and-twenty.

In an article on Murdoch Smith's career contributed to the *Royal Engineers Journal* of September 1, 1900, Sir Charles Wilson says: "It is scarcely too much to say that the success of the excavations was largely due to the intelligent insight and skill with which they were conducted by Smith, and his friends have always felt that he received scant credit for his work in the elaborate publications of his chief." Many of his brother officers thought so at the time. Murdoch Smith certainly thought so himself, although he never cared to raise the question. From the letters now printed, and from his report on the Mausoleum, which was included in the papers presented to Parliament in 1858, and is printed as an appendix to this volume, it will be seen that it was he who first pointed out the actual site of the Mausoleum, and that it was his report with its accompanying drawings which provided the key to the restoration of the building. On his drawings all subsequent reconstructions in detail have been based. One letter (pp. 119-133) describes a piece of work which he used to recall with great satisfaction, the embarkation of the great lion of Cnidus, which was carried out under his direction in circumstances of no small difficulty. A comparison of the letters with Sir Charles Newton's publications shows how fully Sir Charles Wilson's observation is justified. The narrative portions of the letters are now printed almost in their entirety, the passages omitted relating chiefly to personal matters connected with the Engineer detachment. The letters printed contain a good deal of minute description and technical detail, and the chapters of the present volume relating to the expedition have thus been expanded to a length somewhat out of proportion to the general scale of the work, but it is thought that the value of the letters as archæological records is sufficient to justify the disproportion.

To Sir John Burgoyne.

BUDRUM, *November* 26, 1856.

MY DEAR GENERAL,— ... On account of the state of the weather we did not get the stores on board the *Gorgon* at Spithead till the 17th, when we weighed anchor. After a very favourable passage we arrived at Gibraltar on Saturday the 25th, and remained there till the following Monday. From this we had very fine weather all the way to Malta, which we reached on Monday the 3rd November. As we remained there three days I reported our arrival to Col. Harness, by whom I was introduced to Sir William Reid.[1] Before leaving Malta we got the photographic apparatus which had been sent by the *Indus*.

We arrived at Smyrna on the 11th, and finding that Mr Newton had not arrived, I went the same afternoon by the Austrian packet to Constantinople to meet him. We left together immediately after my arrival, and reached Smyrna on the 15th. Mr Newton brought with him a vizieral letter authorising us to carry on the excavations at Budrum and Cnidus. We weighed anchor the following morning and entered the harbour here on Tuesday the 18th.

The Bey, who is very obliging, was kind enough to let us have some rooms in his *konak* for the use of our shore establishment. . . . We have three rooms and a storeroom, besides the use of a large courtyard at the back. One of these rooms we had set apart as the photographic one, fitting it up with a dark chamber, shelves, &c., for the use of Corporal Spackman. Another is used as a kitchen and barrack-room for the sappers, and Mr Newton, Mr Stanhope, Mr Prinsep, and myself occupy the third. All the tools and materials which we landed were placed in the storeroom, and I appointed Corporal Jenkins storekeeper. We pitched several tents in the courtyard to be used as required, and the ship's carpenters have been on shore since our arrival fitting up the rooms with tables, &c.

The object of the expedition, as explained to

---

[1] Colonel Harness was then Commanding Royal Engineer at Malta. Sir William Reid was Governor.

me by Mr Newton, is to excavate at places where Hellenic traces have been found, and discover as much as possible of the ancient city. The principal points are the Mausoleum, the Temple of Mars, the Temple of Venus, the Palace of Mausolus, and the Rock Sepulchres. The site of the first of these and its restoration have been the subject of much discussion among archæologists. Captain Spratt gives it the position marked in the chart, while Dr Ross, a German, places it on the platform marked Temple of Mars. As none of the places have been excavated it remains to be seen which or whether either of them is the true position. Their chief guides in fixing its position are the accounts left us of the city of Halicarnassus and of the Mausoleum by Pliny and Vitruvius. The latter author says that there was a broad way (*platea*) running from one end of the city to the other, and in this street, halfway up the heights, stood the Mausoleum; and Pliny gives certain dimensions of the building.

Regarding the Palace of Mausolus and the Temple of Venus, Vitruvius mentions that they occupied the two *cornua* of the arc in which the city was built, and that the palace was in such a position that Mausolus could see the whole town from it.

The remains of the ancient city are to be seen in many parts of the town. First of all there is the wall, almost the whole circuit of which can be easily traced. There is also part of an outer wall to the N.E. of the town. In both instances the wall occupies the ridge of the hill, and at almost every change in its direction remains of towers are to be seen which seem to have stood in the place of the modern bastions. Those of a theatre are on the summit of the hill on which the city was built. It is in a good state of preservation. On the large platform marked Temple of Mars are pieces of Greek walls, one corner of which is still entire and is built of large blocks of grey marble. On the platform marked Mausoleum some lower parts of Greek wall are visible. A Byzantine monastery, the foundations only of which remain, has evidently been built on the site and of the material of the more ancient building. Large pieces of marble columns and other parts of architecture lie on the surface of the ground or are built into modern Turkish walls and houses in the neighbourhood.

Another part of the town where a great quantity of marble fragments are visible is on the rising ground a little to the north of our *konak*. Several fluted columns, still entire, and apparently in their original position, are marked "Doric Portico" in the chart. Mr Newton supposes them to be the remains of the Agora. In many other places marble pilasters, pieces of columns, cornices, bases, &c., are to be seen in modern walls. In the Castle of St Peter especially are such remains and inscriptions to be found. This, however, from want of time I have not visited, and Mr Newton has not yet got authority to carry off the Hellenic marbles which it contains. At Kisalik and other places are a great many tombs which, if time permits, we purpose exploring before going to Cnidus.

PLAN OF

HALICARNASSOS

(Budrum.)

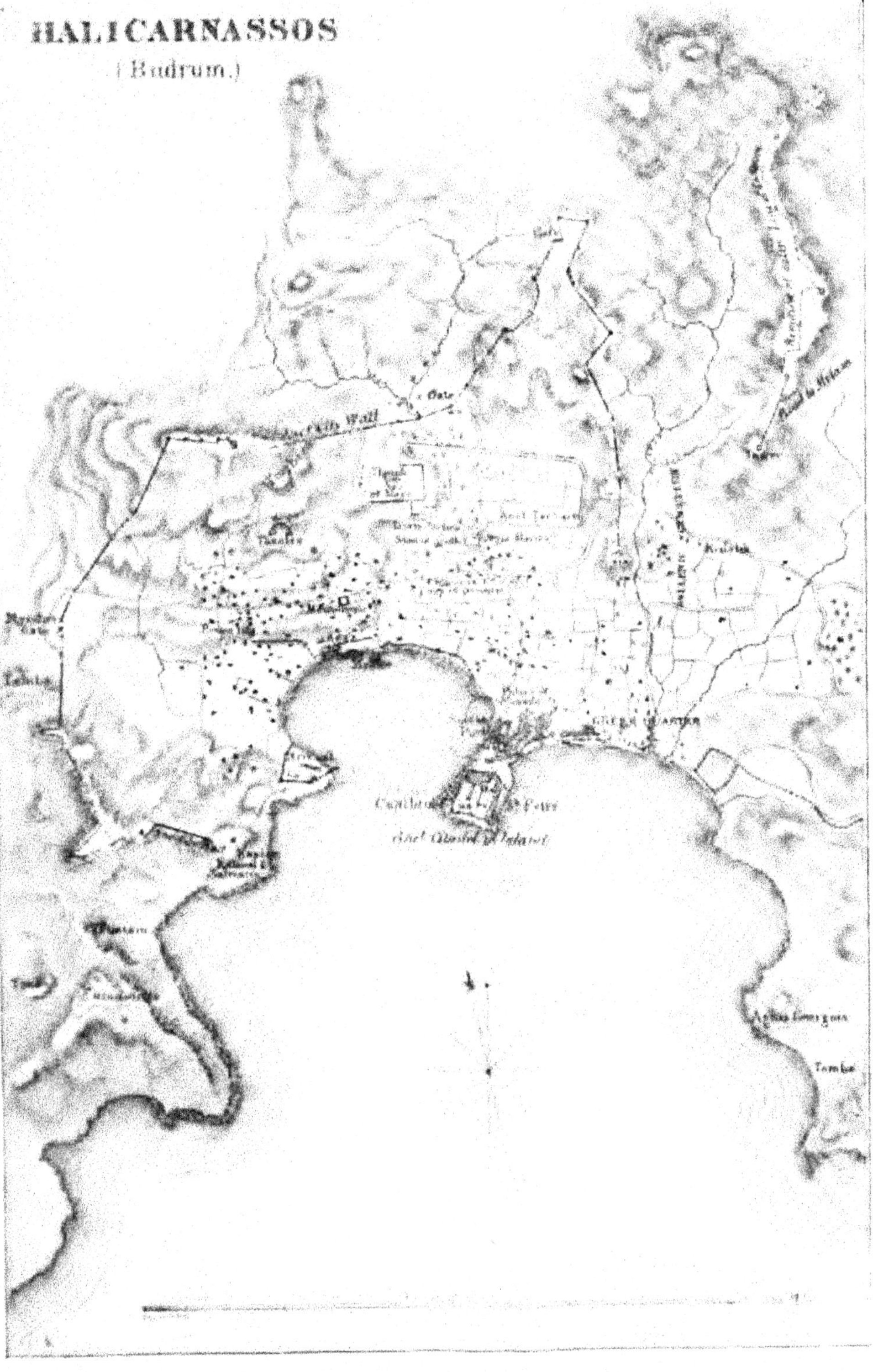

We commenced active operations on Monday with a party of 45 sailors from the *Gorgon*. The excavations were made in the field marked in the chart [Chiaoux Field]. Mr Newton dug part of this field last year. Two barrow-loads of small lamps were discovered about 3 feet, and some walls of doubtful age, the foundations of which were from 6 to 7 feet, below the surface. During the day I was employed making a plan of the field, in which I enter every day the position of anything that is discovered.

The mode of excavating which Mr Newton has found most economical is to dig a trench to a certain depth and carry this forward, always throwing the earth behind, thereby covering the part already dug. The depth of the trench depends of course on the depth at which one meets with the older soil, or the foundations of ancient buildings. On account of the nature of the work it is impossible to allot a certain portion to each workman, so that Mr Newton has in former instances found it more expedient to divide the party into pickmen and shovellers than to furnish each man with a pickaxe and shovel. By this arrangement every man has a certain amount of rest and the work is carried on continuously. It greatly facilitates the superintendence of native workmen, as there can be no stopping on the plea of taking rest.

The country here is exceedingly beautiful and the climate fine. During winter, however, there are frequently violent storms. In the cultivated parts of the country fig-trees are thickly planted in the fields. There are no roads, properly speaking, and there is only occasional communication with Rhodes and

Smyrna by means of the caiques. The nearest post is at Rhodes, which is 60 miles distant. Captain Towsey of the *Gorgon* has written to the consul at Rhodes requesting him to take charge of our letters, so that communications from England should be addressed to his care and not to the consul's at Smyrna.

The conduct of the sappers has been very good ever since they came under my command. The two brothers Nelles are of the greatest service on account of their being able to speak Greek. Patrick Nelles speaks some Turkish also, and as a smith he is an excellent workman. I paraded them with kits, &c., this evening and found everything correct.

The great obstacle in the way of getting on is the difficulty of getting the Turks persuaded to allow allow us to dig in their fields; seeing a ship of war and so many people coming to the place, they imagine that they can obtain the most extravagant prices for the right of digging in their property. They have also raised the price of everything to four or five times its value since our arrival. . . .
—I am, my dear General, yours most faithfully,

R. M. SMITH.

BUDRUM, *December* 23, 1856.

. . . We continued the excavations in the field of Chiaoux where we commenced, but found nothing very remarkable with the exception of the terracotta figures and lamps which I mentioned. Just before leaving it, however, we found an inscription bearing the name of Ceres. As several fine pieces of cornice were found in the next field, Mr Newton supposes that both they and the inscription belonged to a temple of Ceres which must have stood in the neighbourhood. We uncovered a good many foundations, which, however, were not of a very decided character.

On the 1st of December we filled in and removed to the place marked Mausoleum in the tracing of Captain Spratt's chart, which I enclosed in my last. . . . Almost all round the platform are the remains of a Byzantine monastery, the walls of which are of very coarse masonry and averaging 6 feet in thickness. Most of the foundations were evidently of the same date as the walls of the monastery, and probably were interior walls of the same building. The one along the roadside, and the other at right angles to it, running in towards the middle of the field, were of much finer masonry and to all appearance of Greek construction. In the middle of the field the rock appeared close to the surface, thus accounting for the total absence of foundations found in other parts of the field. It sinks very rapidly, however, so that in that part of which the enclosed is a tracing we followed the walls to a depth of 10 or 12 feet before we again reached the rock. In one place we discovered some fragments of Greek mosaic of very fine quality, and pieces of a fine kind of painted plaster, the colours of which were in a remarkably good state of preservation. We trenched the field in various directions, but found nothing that pointed it out as the site of such a building as the Mausoleum.

On the 8th we left this field and commenced in one to west of the Doric portico, between it and the theatre. We got a party of Turkish workmen by way of trial, and have since found them very expert and trustworthy. They are very careful of the tools, and seem to put their whole heart into whatever they are engaged in, working as well without as with an overseer. After digging two days and finding nothing we removed to the field of Hadji Captan, where we are still at work. It lies on the south side of the main road leading through the centre of the town, and is nearly south-west of the theatre. In the afternoon of the same day on which we commenced our excavations we found the half of a marble statue about 3 feet below the surface. Close beside it we afterwards found the other half. The style is very bold, and Mr Newton at once remarked its resemblance to the Lycian Marbles brought to the British Museum by Sir Charles Fellows. It is a female figure in an advancing position, the drapery falling backwards as if from the rapid motion. The folds are very deeply cut. It was found under a mosaic pavement of later date. As this pavement was evidently in a good state of preservation we did not continue the excavations by breaking it up, but commenced uncovering it, removing the earth to a distance. This occupied us till the 16th, when we commenced washing it. Fortunately it was near the surface, its average depth being not more than 3 feet. A number of the patterns, at first very indistinct, were afterwards brought out by means of "holy-stoning," an operation with which the sailors were of course well acquainted.

Corporal Spackman has been employed every day taking photographs of the different designs, some of which are very beautiful. The difficulty of getting a view not in perspective was overcome by erecting movable scaffolding on which the camera could be fixed so as to look straight down on the part to be photographed. It consists of two sheers with a cross frame into which the camera fits, and a guy at each end to keep the whole steady. The height of the camera from the ground is 15 feet. Mr Stanhope and Mr Prinsep are colouring a set of photographs, so that we shall be able to bring away a facsimile of the whole pavement. I made a plan of the field, including a plan of the pavements, showing the different walls and rooms. I am now making a separate plan of each room, showing the borders of every different pattern and design. This will give the scale of the photographs, and by numbering them and putting corresponding numbers on the plan their relative positions will be at once seen. If possible we shall bring away some of the best designs, but I anticipate great difficulty in it as they lie very near the rock, which I fear will prevent us from undermining them. Our intention is to lay coatings of plaster and lime on the mosaic to preserve it, and undermine it until we are able to introduce wooden frames by which it may be lifted. . . .

About 2 feet below the surface of the ground we came upon the mouth of a well which I have marked in the plan. At a depth of 12 feet there is a passage 6 feet high and $6\frac{1}{2}$ feet wide running horizontally for a distance of 40 feet, where it is blocked up. While cleaning out the well we discovered in it a marble head, a photograph of which I enclose with the others. On the second day of our excavations we also found the pedestal of a statue bearing an inscription, most of which, however, was broken off. I need not enter into the description of the pavement as the photographs will show its character. The colouring, which of course they do not show, is very fine. In the rooms which we have not yet photographed there are designs of Atalanta and Meleagros, Bacchus, Europa, the four seasons, and heads symbolical of different towns, besides a variety of ornamental patterns. In the passage are the words ΥΓΙΑ, ΖΟΗ, ΧΑΡΑ, ΕΙΡΗΝΗ, ΕΥΘΥΜΙΑ, and ΕΛΠΙΣ[1] surrounded by a wreath.

January 1, 1857.

Since writing the above I have had no opportunity of sending letters to Rhodes, so that I now continue the account of our operations till the present time. . . .

After trying different methods of lifting the pavement, we now do it by first laying on it a coating of plaster of Paris, and then placing on this before it sets a piece of canvas, which again is coated with plaster of Paris. When the whole has set we undermine it and raise it on a frame. The rock fortunately is very soft, so that it can be cut by the pickaxe; still, however, the process is very slow.

[1] Health, Life, Joy, Peace, Cheerfulness, Hope.

On the 27th we commenced digging in another place. As I happened to point it out as the probable site of the Mausoleum it goes by the name of Smith's Platform.[1] It lies on the rising ground a little to the north of the Pasha's palace, which you will see marked in the chart. From the number and appearance of the marble fragments, and its central position, I was always of opinion that the Mausoleum must have stood in the neighbourhood, and since we have commenced our excavations there, every day brings additional proof of its being the actual site. As you are aware, the building was broken up by the Knights of St John for material with which to build the castle. Now we have found several architectural fragments which correspond with others still to be seen in the castle. For instance, there is a stone in one of the walls with exactly the same ornament on it as there is on the large cylindrical one in the castle, a photograph of which I send with the others. Several pieces of immense Ionic marble columns are lying on the surface of the ground, and in the course of our excavations we have found small pieces of the cornice and the frieze. Should we find any more of the frieze, and should it correspond with that already in the British Museum, the proof of course would be complete. All that can yet be said is that the site seems remarkably promising. We are still occupied lifting the pavement. The only other place that Mr Newton intends exploring is Ross's

[1] When it turned out that this *was* the site of the Mausoleum, no more was heard of " Smith's Platform."

Platform, marked Temple of Mars in the Chart. When that is done we are to go to Cnidus. . . .

The sappers are going on very steadily indeed. Corporal Jenkins is quite invaluable in an expedition of this kind, as he seems acquainted with almost everything. He has learned enough Turkish to speak to the workmen, who all entertain the profoundest respect for him, and never speak of him but as the "usbashi" (captain). Regimentally the detachment continues quite correct. We parade with arms and accoutrements every Sunday morning, and I inspect the kits every three or four weeks. . . .

The Turks continue very civil and obliging. The Greeks we have as little to do with as possible, as deceit and theft seem part of their very nature. They keep continually prowling about and stealing everything they can lay their hands on. . . .

I have just received the sad intelligence of my father's death.

BUDRUM, *February* 3, 1857.

. . . We have been busy continuing the excavations in the place to the north of the *konak* which I mentioned in my last. At that time there was good reason to suppose that we had eventually hit upon the true site of the Mausoleum, but now I think the matter is placed beyond a doubt. The ground unfortunately is covered with Turkish houses, which the proprietors are very unwilling to part with. Our space is consequently much contracted, and there is some difficulty in getting room for the displaced earth. We began in several places, and although we found a number of fragments, there was nothing of importance. We at last came upon the right clue in taking down an old wall filled with pieces of fine Parian marble. In digging below the foundations of the wall we found the rock artificially levelled, and afterwards a little to one side we got a point at which from being level it suddenly became quite perpendicular. Following this face, we found that the rock formed a kind of wall running nearly north and south. The face is roughly tooled as if with a pickaxe. About 8 feet below the upper levelled surface we came to a pavement consisting of large stones very well squared and jointed. The average dimensions of these paving-stones are 4' × 3' × 1', the 1 foot being the depth as they lie on the rock, which is cut level to receive them. They seem to have been clamped together with iron, as the clamp-holes still remain although the iron has disappeared. Iron seems to have been used for such purposes, as we found pieces of it in the course of our excavations completely corroded. Both on the surface and at various depths we discovered pieces of fine Ionic marble columns. These pieces are in general pretty entire, being in their original lengths of about 4 feet. From measurements of different ones the diameter near the base seems to be about 3' 4", and the diminution or tapering about 1 inch in a length of 4 feet. There are 24 flutes in the circumference, and the depth of each is about $2\frac{1}{2}$ inches. They are very beautifully finished and of the finest Parian marble, so from this fact and the dimensions given above you can form an idea of the splendour of the original building. One of the best of these pieces, measuring nearly 5 feet in length, we have packed and transported to the beach ready for shipping. It is the part of the original column next the base, as seen from its suddenly flattening out at one end. To preserve the fluting we got wooden fillets made to fill up the flutes, and then bound them with hoop-iron. Although we are well supplied with stone trucks, &c., we can only use them for transporting light weights on account of the state of the roads. In moving such things as this piece of column we have used a kind of sledge, which is drawn along on planks by means of tackle. A small ship's anchor was brought on shore, to which to attach the fixed block. This is, of course, a tedious operation, but to make use of any kind of wheeled carriage it would be necessary to make a road, which could only be done at great expense and labour.

Besides the columns, we found in the same place, and still continue to find, pieces of different parts of the building. We have already got the different mouldings of the base, and the capital, including two or three volutes entire, several pieces of the architrave, and a great many fragments of frieze and cornice. The sculpture of the frieze is very fine, and the cutting of the cornice, and, in fact, of all the mouldings, is remarkably beautiful. From the great difference in the relief of the pieces of the frieze which we have found, it would appear that the Mausoleum had at least two friezes—one, part of which is in the British Museum, and another of much higher relief, and probably considerably larger. Most of the fragments we have discovered are of detached legs, arms, &c., of men and horses, but we have a few pieces in which the sculpture is attached to the body of the frieze itself. On many upper mouldings traces of the colouring, chiefly light blue and red, are to be seen. All these, like the columns, are of the finest marble.

At a corner of the rock on a level with the lower part on which the pavement rests, we found the entrance of a subterranean passage which evidently had been used for sepulchral purposes. On entering we saw that it was cut out of the solid rock, the original tool-marks being quite perfect. It is about 3 feet wide and of varying height. At places where we have cleared it out it is about $6\frac{1}{2}$ feet high. In the middle of the higher platform rock there is a modern well, the sides of which contain pieces of marble and architectural fragments. In pursuing the passage it was found to run close past the side of the well, into which we made an opening. About 30 feet past the well the passage seemed closed up, but Corporal Jenkins cleared out some of the earth, and it was found to go on after taking a sudden turn to the left. I got enough cleared away to enable me to crawl through, and Jenkins and I went on exploring. After this obstruction the way was so clear that we could almost walk upright, and we went on, turning sometimes to the right and sometimes to the left, sometimes going straight onwards and sometimes circling round about. The most of the way the passage was, as at the entrance, cut out of the rock, but at some places where the rock seems to have failed it was formed of masonry. The construction of the arch, if such it can be called, is very simple. The wall on each side consists of only two courses of very large stones about 2½ or 3 feet thick, and on these the two stones forming the arch are laid, their ends resting on the upper course and on each other in the middle of the passage overhead thus: All along at various intervals on each side are small holes, which seem to have been for the purpose of holding small lamps for the lighting of the passage, as over each of them the rock, naturally of a light-brown colour, is quite black as if it had been burned. At last we reached a place which was evidently the bottom of a shaft. On piercing upwards with boring-irons between the large stones which closed the shaft, we came to the surface, but where we could not tell. I told Jenkins to hammer against the stones of the roof while I went to listen for the sound about the place where I thought the shaft must be. After some time I heard it near an old Turk's house, where I at once set some men to dig. The knocking continued, but dig where we would we could not find the shaft. At last the old Turk, with a look of consternation which I shall never forget, came and asked me into his house. On entering I at once saw the cause of his alarm, which was no other than Jenkins's boring-iron jumping up and down right in the middle of the floor. The man had been from home and knew nothing of our mining operations, so that his fear and surprise were indeed great when, after frequent premonitory noises from below, an iron rod suddenly shot up, upsetting some articles close beside him. The passage continued a considerable way

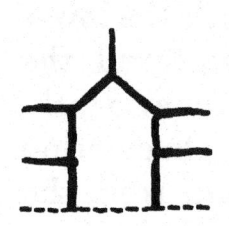

past this shaft, but we did not pursue it much farther as it got rather blocked up.

At the first turning past the well, where the passage turned to the left, we afterwards found another or rather a continuation of the same turning to the right. A little way along this one another shaft similar to the former was found. Taking its position above ground, we bored downwards with a crowbar, and I was certainly surprised at the second or third blow of the crowbar to see it slip from the man's hand and disappear. I expected to find the mouth of the shaft covered as in the other case with large stones supporting the superincumbent earth. But, strange to say, there was nothing but ordinary black mould, with not even clay or gravel. The thickness was not more than 4 or 5 feet, and it is certainly remarkable that this should have stood so for ages without giving way when a few strokes of a crowbar might at any time have sent it in. In the course of our excavations we accidentally came to another shaft, on clearing out which we found that it led to another passage 10 or 12 feet below the former. This lower one is exactly similar to the one I have already described, and zigzags about in different directions, with shafts here and there just like the other. In the course of our digging we have found that what we took to be the original entrance of the first gallery was a point in the middle of it, and that it continued in the opposite direction. Another crossing the first at right angles below it was discovered the other day, so that the whole place is in fact a great subterranean labyrinth. When in one of the passages

I noticed that the floor was soft and not of rock like the sides and roof. Getting a pickaxe, I dug down, and at a depth of 6 or 8 inches came to something that had the appearance of rock. The pickaxe went through it, however, and below there was another layer of earth similar to the upper one and of about the same thickness lying on the rock. The intermediate stratum, about an inch in thickness, was apparently a kind of incipient rock formed by the deposit of a stream of water. Most probably, perhaps, it was formed by some sudden inlet of water which, afterwards becoming stagnant, deposited the particles of which the stratum is composed on the surface of the loose mould, as had the water been in motion it would have carried away the soil and laid the deposits on the surface of the rock. The three layers of which the stratum is composed are very regular, and the composition seems similar to that of the rock out of which the passages are cut. Jenkins has been busy for the last fortnight clearing out and exploring, and we seem even now about as near an end as ever. I have not yet had time to make a plan of them, but I shall take the first opportunity of doing so. It is now necessary to advance with caution, as when Jenkins was in a new one yesterday his light went out, and when he came up he was much exhausted. He is not quite recovered to-day, but I hope he will be quite well again in a day or two. He has shown great zeal and perseverance in his underground labours.

We followed the face of the rock cutting down to the pavement until it turned to left, forming another wall running east and west and facing the north. A little to the north of this corner we found a colossal equestrian statue very finely executed in Parian marble. It lay at a depth from the surface of the ground of about 10 feet. It is a man on horseback, the upper part of the man's body and the horse's legs being away. . . . It will be of great value, as I believe it is the first equestrian statue of Greek origin that has been found. It is very large, its weight I should think being about 4 tons. Another piece of a statue was also found near the same place. It is one of a female figure standing on one leg with the other folded over it in front. It is broken off about the middle of the body and below the knee. The other pieces of sculpture which we have discovered are chiefly different parts of lions, resembling those in the castle walls brought there from the Mausoleum by the Knights of St John. Everything architectural as well as sculptural is of the finest style and execution. . . .

Yesterday we opened ground for the first time on Ross's platform, marked "Temple of Mars" in the Admiralty chart. There are some pieces of marble columns similar to those I have already mentioned, but not so large. They are lying on the surface, which beside them is scattered over with fragments of marble. The rock appears at a depth of not more than 1 or 2 feet, so that our chance of ever finding anything is very small. The position is certainly very commanding, and the platform is enclosed by a Greek wall. As yet we have discovered nothing, but it is necessary to explore a place said by a great archæologist to be the site of the Mausoleum.

Such is the present state of our operations. We hope to get the Mosaic field finished this week, after which our time will be wholly devoted to the Mausoleum. When it is finished Mr Newton intends leaving this for Cnidus.

Last Thursday we were surprised by the arrival of an English war steamer, the *Harpy*, commanded by Lieut. Brine, brother of Captain Brine, R.E. She came from Constantinople for witnesses to attend the court-martial of a former assistant surgeon of the *Gorgon*. As she was going to Rhodes for coal I took the advantage of a passage kindly given by Lieut. Brine. I wanted money for the pay of the sappers, &c., as it is impossible to discount bills here, and it is unsafe to trust money with the masters of the caiques coming here from Rhodes. We left this on Friday night and got back on Monday morning. I don't know whether you have seen Rhodes, but it is now quite unlike its former self, from the effects of the explosion last October. The magazine which exploded was filled with powder which had been left by the Knights when the city fell into the hands of the Turks. The Church of St John is so completely destroyed that it is difficult to tell where it stood, and for a great distance all round the desolation of the scene is perfect. I saw a small house about a mile off which had been knocked down by a large stone thrown all the way by the explosion. As the powder was partly or wholly underground an immense crater marks the position of the former magazine. . . .

We left about 5 P.M., and after rather a rough night got back here by sunrise.

Ever since about Christmas the weather has been very variable, with frequent storms. As long as the wind is from the north the weather is remarkably fine, but a south wind at this time of year seems to be invariably accompanied by very severe storms. It is rather strange that they almost always occur during the night, when there is a great deal of thunder, lightning, and rain, and they seldom last more than twelve hours, usually coming and going with the sun. The spring has fairly commenced, the almond-trees being, though still leafless, covered with blossom, and even the fig-trees are beginning to show their buds. The corn is well advanced, being in many places about a foot high.

The habits of the Turks here are quite of the age of the Patriarchs. I have not seen a single beggar since I came here, although there is no opulence. Every man has his own house and piece of land, which generally is planted with fig-trees, with corn sown in patches here and there. The more wealthy convert their land into lemon-groves, the produce of which they send in caiques to Smyrna. This is the extent of their commerce, as there seem to be even no Turkish tradesmen. The time of those actively employed seems to be taken up in the cultivation of the fields and in cutting and bringing home firewood. I have not seen a piece of coal except on board the *Gorgon* since I came here, and such articles as metals or timber are very scarce. The people, though very hospitable, are averse to selling anything, since from the want of communication the articles of common use are more valuable to them than money. There is abundance of mutton, such as it is, and goat's flesh, but beef does not seem to be much used. The brown bread if carefully prepared is very good, but usually gritty from the nature of the grindstones. Milk and honey are plentiful, and various preparations of these are used as articles of food. The principal concoctions are "yaourt," a kind of curd made of new milk, and "halva," a preparation of honey-and-flour used in place of butter. There are a good many olive-trees, and as each house seems provided with a place for pressing the olives, I have no doubt that the oil is in very general use. I have never seen any butter. Oxen are the only animals used in agriculture, being employed to draw the single-handed plough, which is the only agricultural implement I have seen. Asses, camels, and mules are the beasts of burden, horses belonging only to the more wealthy.

The supply of water since we came here has been abundant, although in summer I should think it rather scanty from the want of springs. The wells are very numerous, but are supplied only by water drained from the surface. All along the roads at distances from each other of about 2 miles are large tanks for the use of travellers. These are all built in the same manner. They are large circular holes about 30 feet diameter and 7 or 8 feet deep, lined on the sides with masonry. These side walls are carried to a height of about 6 feet above the surface, and are surmounted by hemispherical domes, also of masonry. A single door with steps leading to the bottom is the only entrance. The whole is whitewashed, for the sake of coolness, I suppose. They are placed in hollows, and all the surrounding water is collected by surface drains. The attention of the Turks to the laws of their religion is seen by their erecting beside every tank a little square platform for the purpose of prayer, an upright stone at one end showing the traveller the direction of Mecca. The roads are quite unfit for carriages of any description, and they are in such condition that the distance of what is called an *hour* on horseback is only about 4 miles.

I may here mention an instance of the feeling of the people towards us. There has been lying in the harbour ever since we came here a small Turkish man-of-war. When we were in great want of planks the captain of the schooner offered us some very good ones. On Mr Newton's speaking about the cost he refused payment, saying, "What is Turkish is English; there is now no difference." They often say to us, "Osmanli eyi, Inglesi pek eyi"—"Turk good; English very good."

BUDRUM, *March* 3, 1857.

. . . During the last month we have continued the same operations we were engaged in when I wrote. Our excavations are just beginning to let us form some idea of the probable form of the building. It seems, contrary to all expectation, to have been built on a *sunken* rectangular portion of the rock. We have not nearly explored the place, so that it is impossible to give a detailed description of it. The rock has been cut away on four sides to the depth of from 10 to 20 feet, thereby forming four perpendicular faces enclosing a sunken surface nearly level and about 100 feet square. Within this space the building itself must have stood. In Pliny's description of the Mausoleum he says that the building had its longest side —63 feet in length—facing the north, and that *toto circuitu* it was 411 feet. Since 63 feet is said to be the greatest length, this 411 feet must refer to some enclosing wall or peribolus. The perpendicular faces of rock which I have mentioned seem to correspond to this *totus circuitus*, as each of them is about 100 feet long. At first sight it would seem an objection then to place the building in a hollow, but I think a little consideration will show that the appearance did not suffer in consequence. According to Pliny's description, the building had a basement 37 feet in height, so that supposing it stood in the hollow, the greater part of this basement would appear above the surrounding rock, so that the proportions of the building would not suffer from part of it being hid. It would also, I imagine, answer better to Pliny's account, in which he says that it seemed suspended in the air, than if the foundations of the walls were visible from every point of view. Although the building was thus actually in a hollow, the site is very commanding, being considerably higher than the rest of the town lying to the east, south, and west.

We have continued exploring the subterranean passages I mentioned in my last. We have not been able to do much with the lower one, as the heavy rains at the beginning of last month half filled it with water. While taking the bearings of the upper one, I one day found a square opening in the side resembling a door, leading into a large chamber. The opening was just large enough to let me through, and I found that the chamber inside was almost full of loose earth and stones that seemed to have fallen in through a hole in the roof. Taking its position above ground, we commenced digging downwards till we found the opening in the roof. When a sufficient opening was made some workmen got into the chamber and commenced clearing it out, the earth being taken to the surface through the opening by means of baskets lowered over a pulley. It is now nearly a month since this began and it is still unfinished. The chamber is about 15 feet square and 12 feet high, and has all the appearance of a tomb. The opening in the roof is accidental, not being a regular shaft like several of those leading into the galleries. Besides the door by which we entered from the gallery there is another on the opposite side, but as yet we don't know exactly what it leads to. In one of the other sides of the tomb there are two openings, each about 2 feet square (near the roof), leading into what is probably another chamber. These chambers show that the galleries were made for sepulchral purposes.

As the proprietor of the field next the one

we were digging in would not allow us to continue our excavations beyond the boundary, we drove a gallery under the wall to see what his field contained. From the great depth below the surface the earth was so compact and firm that we formed the gallery without the use of frames. A few feet in we found the rock forming one of the four faces I have already mentioned. Turning to the left, we continued the gallery along the face of the rock, and a little way along got what has since proved to be the lowest of a flight of steps, about thirteen in number, cut in the rock. In order to find the width of this stair we commenced another gallery 15 feet to the left of the other and parallel to it. We found the same lowest step, and as we had done in the other, we continued the gallery till we came to the top of the stair. Just as we had begun cross-galleries along the steps to connect the two already made the proprietor came to terms and let us have his field. We at once began clearing away the earth from the surface, and have just reached the top step. We will uncover and photograph the whole flight. This stair is on the west side of the sunken rectangle, and leads from the upper level of the rock to the lower one on which the building stood. It probably led to the entrance, which I believe in Greek temples is always in the west side. We were stopped for some time by a house standing in the very middle of our excavating, which the proprietor, an old Turk, would part with on no account. We cut round about him to a great depth, till the house had quite the appearance of a fortress surrounded on all sides by a large ditch. As we were about to cut off his last means of retreat he gave way and sold the house. Before surrendering, the old body's wife made a spirited resistance, sometimes firing from the windows solid shot in the shape of large stones, at others red-hot in the form of burning charcoal. By a well-directed shot she succeeded in hitting Corporal Jenkins on the back of the head and sending him very speedily to the bottom of the ditch. When we took down the house we found in the foundations a large number of scorpions, centipedes, and asps. I have preserved a few in spirits as specimens.

In the course of these excavations we have found a great many fragments of the same kind as those I mentioned in my last. We have come on a great many pieces of columns, all in a good state of preservation. The other pieces are generally small, being probably the chips and fragments left by the Knights of St John when they broke up the marble to make lime.

The equestrian statue is now safely deposited on board, and all the mosaic packed and ready for removal. We filled in our excavations in the mosaic field on Wednesday last. . . .

Besides the Mausoleum, we are still digging at Ross's Platform (see chart, Temple of Mars). We have there found the foundations of a building about 70 feet long by 45 broad. There is, however, almost a total absence of architectural fragments of any description. This is accounted for by the story of the old man to whom the field belongs, who says that his grandfather remembered a marble temple with columns standing there, but being in a ruinous state some people came and carried it off as building material to Rhodes. The foundations are in the middle of a large platform surrounded on three sides by a wall of Greek construction, the fourth side merging in the slope of the theatre hill. . . . The foundations run parallel to these walls, which very nearly face the north, east, and south. Mr Newton agrees with Captain Spratt in the opinion that they are the remains of the Temple of Mars. On the west side of the platform, where the slope of the hill begins, we found some rock tombs, the entrances to which were below the surface of the ground. In form these rock sepulchres greatly resemble each other, almost all consisting of a large chamber nearly square, surrounded by a number of deep recesses. It would almost seem that they were family vaults, the recesses being intended for the different members. Sometimes the tomb is only a single small chamber. In every case, however, the entrance is so cut as to be closed by a single stone, which is often a marble slab. Generally there are small recesses between the larger ones for the reception of the votive offering. As the Mausoleum is so far from being finished, Mr Newton has given up all hope of getting to Cnidus before the *Gorgon* leaves.

She is only provisioned till the beginning of May.

On the 14th of February we were visited by H.M.S. *Swallow*, which called here on her way to Constantinople. . . . She brought us a number of newspapers, which of course were very acceptable.

Last Sunday week with Mr Stanhope I rode over to Myndus, the modern Gumishlu. It stands on the western extremity of the peninsula on which Budrum is situated, and faces the island of Kalymnos. Its distance from here is said by the Turks to be about four hours, but we found it considerably more, as we frequently lost our way. From the almost total disappearance of the ancient city, we were standing on the site a considerable time before we knew where we were. We found the remains of a temple, consisting of a number of marble fragments of cornices and pilasters, which lay scattered on the ground. The marble was Parian, but the execution and style of the architecture were greatly inferior to that of the pieces we are finding at the Mausoleum. We saw other foundations in different places, but nothing worthy of note. The positions of the ancient cities on the coast here are very like each other. At Cnidus, Myndus, and here at Halicarnassus there are fine natural harbours, and the cities occupied the sides of the hills rising from the water. Here, besides the inner harbour for small vessels, there is a large anchorage completely sheltered by the island of Orak, the ancient Arconesus. At Cnidus there are two harbours, one on each side of the isthmus connecting the mainland with the peninsula which protects both harbours. As in the case of the inner harbour of Halicarnassus, they are further sheltered by artificial moles. At Myndus the harbour is formed by the bend of a peninsula, and the entrance is nearly filled by a small island connected with the mainland by an ancient mole. These smaller harbours are not large enough for the shipping of the present day, but must have been admirably adapted to the galleys, &c., of the ancients. The scenery between this and Myndus is exceedingly beautiful, and the valleys very rich and fertile. There are, however, very few inhabitants, and these all live in villages, for the purpose, I suppose, of mutual protection.

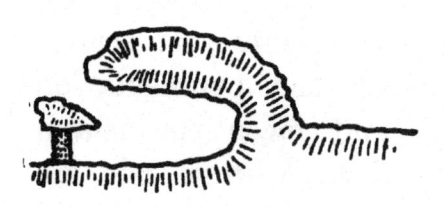

On the 28th of last month I was present at a very interesting scene called by the Turks *palivan*. It was on the last day of the ceremonies connected with the marriage of Salea Bey's daughter, and we were invited to be present. About 7 o'clock in the evening they sent us word that all was ready, and Captain Towsey, some of the officers of the *Gorgon*, Mr Newton, and myself set out for the scene of the evening's amusement. Before we had gone far from the *konak* we were met by a band of young fellows sent to escort us. Some played Turkish pipes and others beat the tom-toms, the only instruments used here with the exception of the Greek fiddle. The remainder of the party carried pine torches. When we arrived at the place we found an immense crowd collecting in a large open space surrounded by walls and houses. Two large fires of torch-wood were lighted, the space between them being kept clear by the master of the ceremonies. We were led by our escort through the crowd across the open space to the other side, where carpets and cushions were spread on the grass for seats. After we were seated and served with coffee we had leisure to survey the scene. The crowd consisted entirely of men, who throughout conducted themselves with the greatest quietness. The walls and house-tops were crowded with women, whose faces of course were hid under their white yashmaks. For some time after we arrived the only amusement was dancing. The music was discoursed, certainly not sweetly, by a Greek fiddle and tambourine, and the voices of the performers, while the dancing was kept up by one man after another stepping out from the crowd and going through an extraordinary set of evolutions, waving his head and arms about the whole time. During the intervals of dancing the music was taken up by the Turkish orchestra of pipes and drums. The great amusement of the evening, the *palivan* or wrestling, at last commenced, the master of the ceremonies clearing the centre space and bespeaking the attention of the spectators. Two men presently came forth to engage each other. They were both stripped with the exception of a slight covering, made of leather, round the loins. Having put themselves into an attitude with their arms on each other's shoulders, the master of the ceremonies made a speech, and the combatants, having first oiled themselves all over, commenced the struggle. In the *palivan* the victory is gained if one succeeds in throwing the other on his back, and as it is almost all done with the arms, great strength and activity are required. There is a great display of skill before the combatants actually close, in endeavouring at once to get a hold of the adversary and prevent his laying hold at the same time. There were frequently severe struggles on the ground after both had fallen. When one was declared victor after throwing the other, they put their arms round each other's necks in token of friendship and walked round the ring. The defeated then retired and the victor remained, while the master of the ceremonies challenged any one to come and wrestle with him. This continued till near midnight, when the crowd quietly dispersed. The *palivan*, which is a favourite amusement with the Turks on festive occasions, is very interesting from its great resemblance to the ideas one has formed of the Olympic Games. . . .

BUDRUM, *March* 18, 1857.

. . . The *Swallow*, Commander Waddilove, has just arrived from Constantinople. She has brought a firman from the Porte authorising us to remove the lions in the castle which formerly belonged to the Mausoleum. It would appear from the accounts brought us, that when the firman was asked for by Lord Stratford the request was granted by the Porte, and as the lions were in the walls of a fortress, the firman was placed in the hands of Fethi Pasha, the War Minister. When the affair was still under consideration at Constantinople he sent a scientific man, Arakil Bey, to Budrum, nominally to inspect some mines in this neighbourhood, but in fact to make a report on the lions. Consequently when the firman was placed in his hands he secretly sent an order to the commandant here to remove the three best of the lions and send them with the greatest despatch to Kos to wait a steamer for Constantinople. When at last he gave the firman to Lord Stratford he told him that some of the lions had been removed, but that the firman gave us authority to take the remaining ones.

Most fortunately, however, the *Swallow* arrived this morning just in time to intercept the three lions, which were all packed and on board a caique about to sail. The caique was at once towed alongside the *Gorgon* and the lions hoisted in. There are four others in the castle, two of which will probably be given as duplicates to the Turkish Government. They are all of the best style, and in the opinion of Mr Newton and Mr Watts the finest pieces of sculpture in Europe.

The excavations are going on very well. Ross's Platform is finished, so that all our force is concentrated on the Mausoleum. Last night we found half a lion there, the same as those in the castle. It will probably occupy six weeks to finish the digging there. . . .

BUDRUM, *April* 2, 1857.

... We are still engaged with the excavation of the Mausoleum, latterly with considerable success. In my letter of the 3rd ult. I mentioned that we had just uncovered the top step of the flight of stairs discovered by driving the galleries in the N.W. corner. ... We have not yet been able to define the exact position of the foundations of the tomb itself, but we have nearly finished uncovering the four sides of the enclosure, having found three of the returns of the surrounding rock. These four sides form a rectangle measuring 126 by 105 feet, the longer side being that running east and west. It is a remarkable coincidence that this dimension, 126 feet, should be exactly double of the length, 63 feet, given by Pliny as that of the longest side of the building. It further agrees with his statement that this side faced the north. Regarding the total circumference, a probable explanation of which term I gave in a former letter, there are two readings, one of which is 411 and the other 440 feet. The circumference we have found—2 (126 + 105) or 462 feet—thus differs only 22 feet from the second reading. Since we have found one side 126, double of one of the dimensions of the building given by Pliny, probably the 105 feet is double the other. According to this, the building must have measured $63 \times 52\frac{1}{2}$, and have stood inside an enclosure 126 × 105, with a flight of steps leading to an entrance on the west side. From the present appearance of the ground I imagine that there is a similar flight on the north side, but that part has not yet been excavated.

We have lately found several fine pieces of sculpture, chiefly parts of lions and fragments of frieze. The pieces of lions have always, with one exception, been the hind-quarters, the heads and fore-parts having probably been taken away by the Knights, as in the case of those that were in the castle wall. Last Tuesday we found the fore-part of one without the head, and it, as well as the hind-quarters we had found before, is of exactly the same style as those in the castle; but the surface is in better condition from its having been protected by the earth from the action of the weather. This morning we discovered a colossal statue of a female figure sitting in a chair. The head, feet, and one arm are wanting. A few days ago we found the body of another large female figure. They are both remarkably fine. As I hope to send photographs of them next time I write, I need not describe them more minutely. One of them is probably Artemisia, the wife of Mausolus, and the builder of the Mausoleum.

Every day we find pieces of the order of the building. Upwards of 30 pieces of column, all nearly entire, have turned up, and every day we find new pieces of moulding. We have a capital, not much broken, ready to be embarked.

The mosaic cases have all been got on board, and the carpenters are at work every day packing the marbles that are to go home. There will be upwards of 100 cases of one kind and another when everything is on board.

The lions in the castle were all taken out without accident. The walls were afterwards repaired by Lance-Corporal Francis Nelles, much to the satisfaction of the Turkish authorities. The commandant of the castle, who is also commandant of the castle of Kos, was extremely civil and obliging. He procured workmen, and himself superintended the extraction of the lions. I noticed that one of the workmen had a very heavy chain attached to his ankles, and on inquiry I found that he was a thief, hard labour in irons being the general punishment for convicts. This man, strange to say, acts as the musician of the garrison. . . .

We are now having a repetition of the *palivan*, which I gave some account of in my former letter. Six professional wrestlers, previously sent for by Mr Newton, came yesterday from Mughla, the capital of this district. His intention in getting them was to furnish Mr Watts with the subject of a picture. . . .

BUDRUM, *May* 2, 1857.

. . . Our excavations have been continued last month at the Mausoleum with even more than our former success. They have been carried on principally on the north side, where we found the foundations of a marble wall, that seems from its appearance and dimensions to have been one of the walls of the *peribolus*. It is about 2 feet thick, and consequently too small for one of the walls of the building itself. Its construction is somewhat remarkable. The lowest course consists of stones laid flat, and the next two of stones laid on edge with the outer side of each dressed. These three courses are all that are left standing, but from the appearance of some of the displaced stones which we have found, I infer that the bond has been formed by laying the fourth course in the same way as the first, as shown in the margin. Mr Newton has just succeeded in getting possession of the houses which stand on the N.E. corner, so that we shall be able to follow out this wall, and then the accurate position and bearings of the *peribolus* at least. While we were uncovering this wall, our attention was diverted from the question of position and bearings by finding a very beautiful head of a statue lying almost on the foundations. It is in a very good state of preservation, and affords another proof of the identity of the scene of our excavations with the site of the Mausoleum. The headdress is peculiar, and Mr Newton says that it is of the same date as the time of Mausolus, being the dress shown on all the coins of that period. Other proofs are given by the pieces of sculpture which we have since discovered in nearly the same position. The first of them was a lion, almost perfect, part of his legs only being wanting. It corresponds exactly with those formerly found, and with the others from the castle wall. Not being exposed to the weather, the surface is in very good condition. Traces of the colouring of the inside of the mouth are still left. Since this discovery we have found three other statues, one of a female figure about 10 feet in height from the neck to below the knees. We afterwards found a piece which will probably complete it. The other two are more mutilated. All of them, however, are

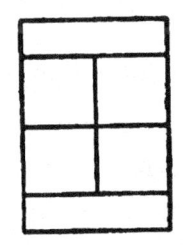

of the highest style. In the same place as these statues we have just found the hinder half of a very large horse. It is cut off nearly by the middle, and is very little damaged, so that we are in hopes of finding the other half. The joint is smoothly cut, and the centre is hollowed out to allow the other half to fit like a tenon and mortise. The length from this joint to the tail is upwards of 6 feet, so that the original length of the horse cannot have been less than 12 feet. The legs of the part we have found are broken above the knee. The weight I have estimated at about 6 tons. Mr Newton says it is the largest piece of Greek sculpture that has ever been discovered. Pliny, in describing the Mausoleum, says that the pyramid, which consisted of 24 steps, was surmounted by a chariot with four horses sculptured in marble by Pythis. As the height of the top of the pyramid was 140 feet, any piece of sculpture on it must have been of colossal size to be seen to effect from the ground. As the horse we have found has no rider, it must evidently be one of the four of the *quadriga*. The ground in which we found it is full of very large blocks of marble, which seem to have been those used on the pyramid. As all the stones as well as the horse have been found close to the marble wall and on the north side of it, and as the wall itself has evidently fallen outwards, it is probable that the pyramid fell in that direction, carrying the wall, statues, &c., along with it. When we get the horse on board we shall go on digging along the north side of this wall, when we hope to find some more remains of the building.

THE CHARIOT GROUP OF THE MAUSOLEUM.

A great many houses are in the way, and it requires a great deal of diplomacy and patience on Mr Newton's part to get possession of them. The firman does not authorise us to dig without the consent of the proprietors, and they are almost always very long in coming to terms, and they take care that the bargain is advantageous to themselves. Our digging is exceedingly popular among the Turks, on account of the amount of money thereby put in circulation among them. A large proportion of the able-bodied men of the town are employed as workmen, and receive much higher wages than they could otherwise obtain.

Mr Newton, in answer to a letter to Lord Stratford, was advised to push on the operations as long as the firman gave authority—viz., till November next—as there would probably be some difficulty in getting another. The *Gorgon* is now quite full, nearly 200 cases being on board, and her provision being nearly expended, she will probably leave in about a fortnight and go straight to Woolwich, where she will disembark her cargo. Mr Newton and our party will remain here and continue the operations with the Turks. As the statues I have mentioned have opened up a new field for excavation, we will probably be detained here two or three months more, by which time Mr Newton hopes to have another ship of war sent out. If one does not come he intends chartering caiques to take us with the tools, &c., to Cnidus, which is only about 20 miles distant. As there are no inhabitants near Cnidus we intend taking a party of Turks with us from Budrum. Mr Newton was over there lately for a few days with Capt. Towsey, and he says there is a good deal to be done.

H.M.S. *Weser*, Commander Wyse, came here on the 11th ult. for two of the castle lions to be given as duplicates to the Turkish Government. . . .

The Turkish fast Ramazan commenced on the 25th and lasts thirty days. During this time no Turk is allowed to eat, drink, or smoke from one o'clock in the morning, when a gun fires, till next sunset. On this account we are obliged to leave off work some hours sooner than formerly, as the men naturally get fatigued working in a hot sun without food and drink or, what to a Turk is even more necessary, his chibouque.

Just before sunset every man may be seen sitting with his pipe filled and ready for lighting whenever the gun fires. They are not allowed to go to bed till the next gun at one in the morning, a man with a drum going from house to house till that time to see that no one is asleep. Ramazan is succeeded by the Bairam, a time of festivity and open houses, which lasts five or six days. . . .

CHAPTER III.

FURTHER WORK AT HALICARNASSUS.

EXPEDITION TO MUGHLA — MELASSA — TRAVELLING IN RAMAZAN — A HOSPITABLE PASHA—A KHAN AT NIGHT—THE BRITISH UNIFORM IN TURKEY—REPORT ON THE MAUSOLEUM—MURDOCH SMITH'S RESTORATION OF THE BUILDING—VISIT OF THE VICEROY OF EGYPT AND OF THE FRENCH FLEET—TEMPLE OF HECATE AT LAGINA—LABRANDA—LETTER FROM LORD CLARENDON—FURTHER EXCAVATION OF MAUSOLEUM—KERAMO—EXCURSIONS ROUND BUDRUM—VISIT OF THE PASHA—THE TURKS AND THE INDIAN MUTINY—CHRISTMAS AT BUDRUM.

To Sir John Burgoyne.

BUDRUM, *June* 1, 1857.

. . . The *Gorgon* is still here, the *Desperate* having come a short time ago with another month's provisions and orders for the *Gorgon* to remain if her services were required. Lord Lyons wrote to the effect that when the excavations were finished here, the *Gorgon*, if Mr Newton wished, should go to Malta to refit, returning to carry on the operations at Cnidus, or else that she should return to England. This letter was written when it was thought that we should have finished here this month, and gone to work at Cnidus during summer.

It is now, however, quite certain that we shall not be able to leave Budrum before autumn, as much still remains to be done. Mr Newton's idea is that the *Gorgon* should go home before the equinoctial gales set in. By that time the grant of £2000 with which we began here will be too nearly expended to think of commencing Cnidus with the remainder. His opinion is that the operations there will require a new grant, and that if this and another ship of war are given by the Government, we could commence digging there after the Mausoleum is finished. . . .

I should have answered your letter some time ago, but immediately after its receipt I had to start on a short expedition which occupied ten days. Since my return I have been busy drawing out a report on the Mausoleum, and I deferred writing until I should be able to send you a copy.

The object of my excursion was to make arrangements with the Pasha of this province, who resides at Mughla, regarding future supplies of money on bills. Mr Newton would have gone, but the orders for the *Gorgon*, &c., were expected daily, so that he could not leave Budrum. Mr Newton also wished me to go to certain places which he had visited last year.

I left this on the evening of Sunday the 10th, accompanied by two Turks, who acted respectively as my dragoman and cavass. We rode all night, passing about daybreak Göwerjinlik, near the site of the ancient Bargylia. As the ruins of the ancient city are some distance off the road, I did not visit them, being anxious to get to Mughla

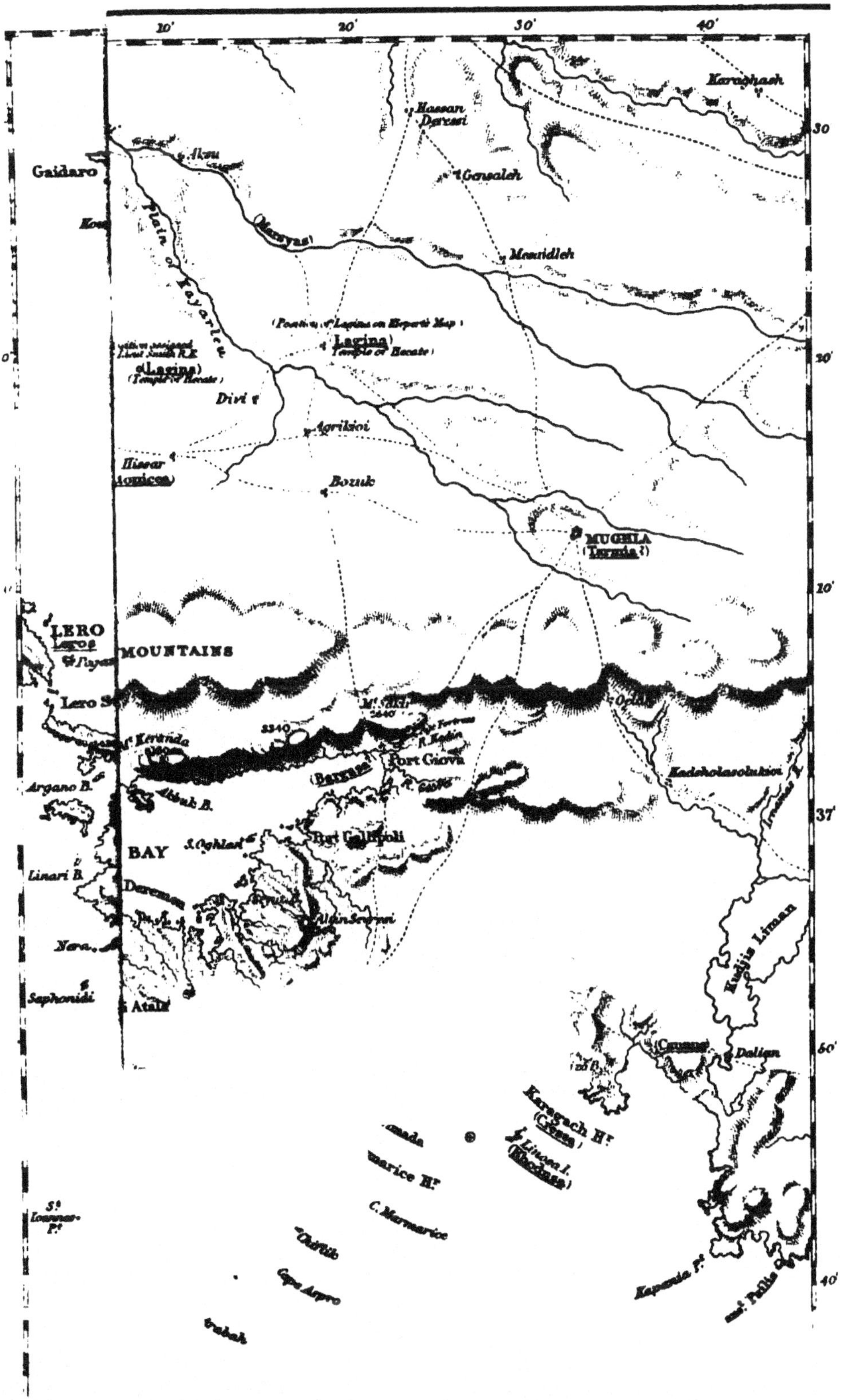
10'
20'
30'
40'
Karaghash
Hassan Dervesi
Aksu
Gaidaro
Gereleh
Plain of Yayarleu
Marsyas
Mesaidleh
(Position of Lagina on Kiepert's Map)
Lagina
(Temple of Hecate)
(Lagina)
(Temple of Hecate)
Divi
Agrilsioi
Hissar
Bozuk
MUGHLA
10'
LERO
Leros
MOUNTAINS
Lero S
Port Giova
Barzaza
Kadeholasoluksoi
37'
Argano B.
BAY
Port Gallipoli
Linari B.
Altin Scurvei
Nera
Saphonidi
Ataia
Kudjis Liman
Dalian
50'
Karagach Hr
Linosa I.
marice Hr
C. Marmarice
Cape Aspro
Kapania Pt
40'

without delay. Göwerjinlik consists of only a few houses by the side of a beautiful bay which forms a very good harbour. There were a number of caiques and small vessels lying there when I passed. Although the village is surrounded by high mountains, it lies·in a swampy hollow, and is, according to the account of the inhabitants, very unhealthy at certain seasons. It lies nearly N.E. of Budrum on the shore of the Gulf of Mendeliah, which is the second from the south of the large gulfs on the west coast of Asia Minor, the Gulf of Kos being the first. Ascending the hills to the north of the village, I had a magnificent view of the surrounding country. The principal feature in the landscape was the large valley of Tekerinbarek, which lay at our feet. This valley, containing, I should imagine, from 20 to 30 square miles, is perfectly level and very fertile. Here for the first time in this country I saw the peasants making use of harrows after sowing the seed. The crops of corn were luxuriant, having this year escaped the ravages of the locusts. In crossing the valley we saw swarms of these insects, but as they did not come till the corn was too strong for them, it has suffered little in consequence. Wherever they had been, however, not a blade of grass was visible. This valley, like Göwerjinlik, is subject to malaria.

Continuing our journey to the northward, we crossed the range of hills separating this valley from that of Melassa, at which town we arrived at night. Here I spent my first night in a khan, a place which it would be needless to describe. I had the misfortune to travel in Ramazan, so that from necessity and not from choice I had to perform the part of a devout Mussulman in fasting all day. After five days' travelling in Ramazan a khan is certainly not the most desirable place to pass the night in, as one has the trouble of looking for and cooking one's only meal. I took nothing with me, preferring to do everything as the people did, thus perhaps getting better acquainted with them. I rarely saw meat of any kind, the people living almost entirely on bread and different preparations of milk.

Melassa is the site of the ancient Mylasa, the capital of Caria until Mausolus changed the seat of government to Halicarnassus. It lies at the northern extremity of an extensive and very fruitful plain. Remains of the ancient city are to be seen throughout the town and in the neighbourhood. The principal object of interest is an ancient tomb, still in a good state of preservation. The tomb is square, consisting of a high basement, on which rest the columns supporting a pyramid. The architecture is of the Corinthian order.

The modern town, like most Turkish ones, is filthy and wretched in every way. Lying as it does in a valley, the drainage is bad, pools of stagnant water appearing in all directions. The supply of water is scanty, all that exists being brought from the neighbouring hills in wooden pipes. These pipes are simply long, thin, straight pine-branches hollowed out, and having their ends fitted into each other. These pipes lead the water to tanks and cisterns throughout the town.

Next morning we commenced our ascent of the range of mountains to the east of the town. In many places the road was only a narrow path along the edge of a precipitous face with room for only one horse at a time. Everywhere the scenery was magnificent. Here and there in this range we passed the tents of the Turcomans, who were tending their flocks and herds. I saw a great many sheep and goats and a considerable number of cattle. Camels are the beasts of burden. We frequently met a string of them numbering at least twenty or thirty. In the course of traversing this range we frequently crossed the small stream which supplies Melassa with water, as I have already mentioned. Towards evening I reached Eski Hissar, a village on the eastern slope of this range of mountains. It is beautifully situated on a small plateau at a considerable elevation above the plain below. It is the site of the ancient Stratonicea. Its present name, Eski Hissar, signifies Old Castle. A great many of the towns of Asia Minor are called Hissar; for instance, Kara Hissar or Black Castle, Güzel Hissar or Beautiful Castle. All towns with such names are the sites of former cities, the name Hissar being given from the ruins they contain.

Eski Hissar has many remains of Stratonicea. Everywhere columns, inscriptions, blocks of marble, &c., are to be seen. Many of them are very fine, but appear to great disadvantage immediately after seeing the exquisite workmanship of the Mausoleum. The wall of the city can be easily traced. I bought some coins here; but the people were quite aware of their value, from the circumstance of the place being frequently visited by Franks from Smyrna and other places on the coast, on their way to Mughla. As there was no khan I spent the night in a café. This café was simply four mud-and-stone walls containing a hearth and some old mats spread round it. The evening, however, was very interesting here and at all the other places where I passed the night in a café. When sunset was announced by the firing of a musket, a great many old Turks came to chat and smoke and drink coffee. They gave me a good deal of information regarding the country and its inhabitants, and were, as you may imagine, not a little surprised by my accounts of the wonders of England — such as railways, gas, telegraphs, &c. They are very simple in their manners, but by no means unintellectual. Their behaviour is always dignified and gentlemanlike, forming a remarkable contrast to that of the Greeks. In these inland places there are very few Greeks, they being essentially a maritime and commercial race, as the Turks are an agricultural and pastoral one. The women throughout the interior seem to be less secluded than they are in towns along the coast.

At daybreak I again started, descending into the valley at the foot of the mountains. It is known by the name of the valley of Ahurköi, from a village of that name. The termination *köi* signifies a village. This valley is very large, and is watered by one of the branches of the Tschinar, which is the ancient Harpasus, a tributary of the Mæander. In Kiepert's map of Asia Minor, which is the best and most recent, the course of the two branches of the

Tschinar is only dotted in from conjecture. I was fortunately able to trace the course of both branches from the town of Tschinar, where they unite, upwards to their sources. It agrees with the course dotted in in Kiepert. The two branches rise near each other in the mountains immediately to the west of Mughla. They then separate, both, however, flowing in a north-western direction until they unite at Tschinar, forming the Tschinar Tschai or River. From inquiries among the people I found that the northern branch was called the Aktschai, and the southern one, which flows through the valley of Ahurköi, the Guktschai.

We ascended the latter valley, frequently crossing the Guktschai, and crossed the mountains at its south-eastern extremity, arriving at Mughla in the afternoon. After taking up my quarters at the new khan I sent to the Pasha to inform him of my arrival and to request an interview. He sent one of his cavasses to escort me to the *konak*. I was very well received, the Pasha doing me the great honour of coming out to the head of the stair to meet me. I succeeded in transacting my business, although of course with some difficulty from my imperfect knowledge of Turkish. The Pasha then told me that, being Ramazan, he could not join me in pipes and coffee, but asked me to come and dine with him in the evening, which I did. There were several of his friends at dinner, but he insisted on my sitting at the head of the table. The dinner was what the Turks call *à la Franca*—that is, we sat upon chairs—but otherwise it was quite *à la Turca*, knives, forks, and plates being dispensed with. I admired the way in which their attention was divided between the dinner and their devotions, things being so arranged that neither suffered from over-attention to the other. Whenever the gun fired at sunset we partook of a slight repast of fruits and preserves just sufficient to take the sharp edge off an appetite of twenty-four hours' growth. This was succeeded by pipes and coffee, after which the Pasha and his friends retired to their prayers. By this arrangement the attention was not distracted from thoughts of the Prophet by the gnawings of hunger, nor was the body in a state of repletion ill adapted to the requisite obeisances and genuflexions. After prayers dinner commenced. Only one dish at a time is brought in and set in the middle of the table, each guest eating from it with his fingers. After a very short time this dish is succeeded by another and another, and so on until dinner is over. The Turks quite deserve their reputation for the cookery of sweetmeats. The place of wine was well supplied by iced sherbet. When I took my leave the Pasha invited me to come again and visit him after he goes to his summer residence at Karabagh.

The appearance of the khan at night was very animated. A large pine-fire was lighted in the middle of the square, and all round close to the houses were spread mats, on which the Turks were sitting enjoying their coffee and narghilies after the day's abstinence. A number of musicians sat in the middle, singing, playing, and making jokes, much to the amusement of the assembly. This was kept up till the gun fired at one in the morning, when every one retired. This, I found, is the way in which they spend every evening during the Ramazan.

Next morning being the bazaar or market day I had a good opportunity of seeing the town and people, as all the men and women from the surrounding country come on that day to buy and sell in the bazaars. The town is, on the whole, very clean and comfortable-looking, being well supplied with excellent water. There are fountains here and there all through the streets. I think I never saw a finer or more manly race than the men here, all of whom are tall and well built. Wherever I went my uniform was at once recognised, and I was warmly greeted on every side. A great many of the men had served in the Turkish Contingent, and they seemed to take great pleasure in showing me their medals, of which they are very proud. They all spoke to me of the kind manner in which they were treated by the English, contrasting it with their former treatment as Turkish soldiers. They said they had been paid well, fed well, and clothed well, and never defrauded. Many of them expressed their willingness to fight again with the English when another war comes, and many of them even asked me to take them with me that they might become English soldiers. They call us *gardeshlar* or brothers. It is the report of these men who served under the English in the late war, and who are now to be found in almost every town, that accounts for the universal feeling of friendship with which the people of this country regard the English.

The town is very beautifully situated, on the steep side of a hill which rises abruptly at the western extremity of the plain of Mughla. It is upwards of 2000 feet above the level of the sea. The plain, which is very large and fertile, is shut in on all sides by lofty mountains, some of them being even now capped with snow. From its great elevation the climate is very different from that of Budrum, more nearly resembling that of England. The harvest had been nearly finished when I left Budrum, and at Mughla I found the corn only a few inches above ground. Towards the end of this month all the inhabitants of Mughla leave the town and reside during summer in a wood about two miles distant along the plain. This wood is called Karabagh, or *black vine*, from the number of vines it contains.

When at Mughla I met a merchant from Smyrna, who had come to procure cargoes of valonia for the English market. His vessels were at Dschova, a port at the eastern end of the Gulf of Kos. I went with him to his store, where I saw a number of Turkish women and girls employed in picking the kernels out of the husks of the valonia. This certainly formed a great contrast with their formerly secluded reserved lives.

I left about midday, returning by the same way to Eski Hissar, which I reached at night. Next morning at daylight I went to Laina, the ancient Lagina. I could not understand the road that my guide was leading me at all, as it seemed quite in a contrary direction to the one in the map. I found, however, that he was right and the map wrong. In Kiepert it is placed between the two rivers I have already mentioned, the Aktschai and the Guktschai, whereas it lies south of both. Instead of being two hours to the N.E. of Eski Hissar, it is about an hour and a half to the N.N.W. I took the bearings of different places whose positions were certain and corrected its place in the map.

Although it was known from the accounts of ancient writers that Lagina contained a famous Temple of Hecate, it is remarkable that no one should ever have found its ruins till Mr Newton discovered them last year. It is the more strange, since the temple is still above ground, lying just as it fell. It is of the Corinthian order, and seems to have been wholly built of marble. The ruins are lying in two heaps, together covering a rectangular space of about 78 by 35 yards. The wall of the *peribolus* can be easily traced on three sides, the shortest of which is about 100 yards long. This wall has had small marble columns about 2 feet in diameter, the upper halves of which are fluted. Among the ruins I saw several pieces of frieze, and a great many inscriptions which Mr Newton copied last year. The principal reason of its lying so long undiscovered is, I think, its position, lying as it does among the mountains and at a distance from any of the common tracks or roads. Should a removal of any of the remains be thought of, from what I saw of the country I think that the best way from Laina to the sea would be along the valley of the Tschinar to Aidin, where it joins the Mæander, which at this point is deep enough for boats and rafts.

I left Laina the same afternoon, arriving at night at a café on the road between Eski Hissar and Melassa. Next day I got to Melassa, and after visiting the tomb I have already mentioned, I went to Paitschin, a small village at the other end of the valley. On the way I saw the remains of an ancient aqueduct which seems to have conveyed water to the city across the valley from the mountains near the present Paitschin. This village has been supposed by some to be the site of the ancient Pedasus, but although I made a minute inspection I found nothing that indicated a Greek city. The present village is built on the summit of an almost perpendicular rock surrounded by the ruins of a Genoese fort. This rock is separated by a natural ravine from an extensive plateau behind it. The part of this opposite the rock has been enclosed by fortifications, and farther out there are the remains of isolated towers and outworks. The people told me that the fort was taken by Sheh Ahmet, who afterwards built a splendid *konak* and a mosque. The mosque is still standing, but it is certainly not of Turkish construction. It has a beautiful Gothic doorway, and was probably a Christian church before it fell into the hands of Sheh Ahmet. The people also told me, and appeared to believe it, that Sheh Ahmet never died, but was miraculously transported to the arms of Mahomet. Here I had not even the comforts of a café for the night, but was obliged to content myself with an unoccupied cow-shed. I should have preferred the open air for many reasons, but we had to shelter ourselves from a thunderstorm which came on just after sunset. The want of comfort, however, was amply repaid by the grandeur and extent of the scenery.

The following morning I left for Karowa (Black Valley), which I reached in the evening. I was very well received by the Aga, Omar Effendi. Mr Newton had been told that this valley contained *eski tasch*, or old stones, a phrase by which the Turks understand ruins and remains of any kind, but there are none. The whole valley, which is covered with a dark brushwood, swarmed with locusts, parts of the ground being literally black with them. I left Karowa the next morning, arriving at Budrum the same evening.

During the past month our excavations have continued to be very successful at the Mausoleum. Two very fine pieces of frieze—one of them 6 and the other about 5 feet long—have been found. They represent the universal subject of the frieze—viz., a contest between Amazons and Greeks. We have also found the fore-quarters of the large horse I mentioned in my last letter. The other day the fore-part of the head was found with the bridle, which is made of copper, still in the mouth. Beside it was found a head, very perfect, on a scale corresponding to that of the horse, so that it doubtless belonged to the figure in the chariot. This head and a naked foot found a short time ago are perhaps the finest things of all. A lion which we found this month is the best that has yet been discovered, being more perfect and better finished than any of the others. A number of fragments have also turned up, some belonging to the horse, some to lions, &c. Now that all these things are being found, the people are beginning to ask the most extravagant prices for their houses. One of them belonging to a woman was got the other day by a new system. As she would not sell it we drove a gallery under the foundations to show her and the other proprietors that they could not stop us. When she saw that we would take the statues out by mining without buying the house at all, she at once changed her mind and sold it. They like very well to sell their houses, as Mr Newton gives them many times their real value, but they imagine that by refusing they can command their own terms. The mining, however, tells wonderfully, especially when combined with putting the devoted house in a state of siege.

When I returned from Mughla I began examining and measuring the large blocks of marble on the north side of the Mausoleum, which I mentioned in my last letter as probably forming the steps of the pyramid. This brought out some very interesting and important facts regarding the building, and Mr Newton desired me to embody my observations and calculations in a report which he would send to the Foreign Office. I have done so, and now send you a copy with the drawings.[1] Being very different from the various modern theories regarding the Mausoleum, I am doubtful of its being received. I should be exceedingly obliged to you for your opinion regarding the stability of the building I have suggested. As wood was never used in the construction of such buildings, and as in this instance the number of columns is limited to thirty-six, I could devise no other means than that of the horizontal arch for the support of the pyramid between the columns and the *cella*. This difficulty does not occur in the other restorations of the building, as they all assume the longest side of the building is 63 feet, thus getting a double row of columns. . . .

BUDRUM, *June* 22, 1857.

The *Supply*, a Government store-ship, has just arrived to take the place of the *Gorgon*. The latter will consequently leave for England within the next two or three days. . . .

On the 11th we were again visited by the *Desperate*, with Mr Campbell, the Consul at Rhodes, on board. He was paying his annual visit to the different vice-consulates in the islands of the Archipelago. . . .

The day before the arrival of the *Desperate*, Said Pasha, Viceroy of Egypt, called in for an hour or two in his yacht. He was on his way to Smyrna or Constantinople. On Saturday the 13th the French admiral, Count Willaumez, with a squadron of three vessels, came into the harbour on his way

[1] See Appendix, p. 353.

back to Smyrna from a cruise along the coast of Syria. He remained till Monday morning. On Sunday Mr Newton and I showed him the excavations and what marbles were lying unpacked. . . .

We have found no sculpture at the Mausoleum worth mentioning since I wrote last. We have finished the whole of the interior, but it will be necessary to dig a considerable space all round the building in order to make sure of finding everything, and also to determine if possible the position of the walls, boundaries, &c. In addition to this, the different galleries and chambers must be explored, and some wells cleared out, as they might contain remains of the building. These operations, I should think, will occupy three or four months more, so that there is little prospect of doing anything at Cnidus this year.

The Turks work admirably under Corporal Jenkins. He has, unfortunately, been on board for the last eight days under medical treatment on account of a bad leg, caused by the fall of a stone on his ankle. It is now, I am happy to say, quite well, and he will be on shore again to-morrow. I was much pleased by an instance of the good feeling of the Turkish workmen to him. For some time he has had a tame pigeon, and the other day some of the workmen got another one and took it off to the ship to give to him as a mate for his pet. . . .

BUDRUM, *July* 31, 1857.

. . . Since the departure of the *Gorgon* the operations have been continued as formerly at the Mausoleum. Now that the whole of the interior of the building has been excavated I think it improbable that we shall find much more sculpture. At present we are digging outside the building on the south and east sides where the rock runs to a great depth, thus making our progress rather slow. Some large pieces of marble —such as pieces of the architrave, steps of the pyramid, &c.—have been sent on board the *Supply*, the *Gorgon* being too full to receive them. We are also mining westward along the marble wall on the north side. Some of the workmen are now expert miners; I yesterday measured this mine, and found that upwards of 4000 cubic feet of earth had been excavated.

On the 11th of this month I started on an excursion to the Temple of Hecate at Lagina. I mentioned this place formerly in the letter giving an account of my journey to Mughla. The object of my visit on this occasion was to photograph if possible some of the pieces of frieze lying among the ruins, and also any remarkable views of the ruins of the temple, and make a plan of the place. If any chemicals remained, I also wished to take several views in Melassa (Mylasa) and Eski Hissar (Stratonicea). Another object was to try to find the site of the ancient Labranda, about which there has been a good deal of conjecture.

For these purposes I was accompanied by Lance-Corporal Spackman. I also took two Turks with me. In three days we arrived at Lagina, called by the Turks Laina. Having a tent with us we were enabled to encamp anywhere that was most convenient, and were thus independent of khans and cafés. At Laina we pitched our tent close to the ruins of the temple, which is upwards of a mile from the village.

As the pieces of frieze were lying in every kind of position, and sometimes hid altogether from view by other blocks of marble, it was necessary to clear a space in front of each piece, and also place it in an upright position, before it could be photographed. I accordingly went to the *kiayah*, or chief man of the village, and told him I would give eight piastres a-day to every man who would come and work among the ruins. The result was that eight men made their appearance next morning. They brought two or three rough handspikes with them, but as many of the blocks to be turned over weighed several tons they could not move them. On asking them if they had nothing better to bring, one of them said he knew where to get a *direk*. He brought the *direk*, which was nothing but a large spar used as a lever. It was of course a very clumsy affair, requiring several men to put it into position for every new application. They set to work, however, and before night we got two of the easiest pieces I could find properly placed. I had brought some rope with me, but they had a great antipathy to making use of it. The following day twelve men came, and the day after sixteen. They worked away with the *direk*, and in these three days placed six pieces of frieze in position, and turned up a number of inscriptions.

Meantime Corporal Spackman had commenced

operations. He had a great many difficulties to encounter, principally those arising from the very rapid evaporation of his different baths, caused by the great heat of the weather. In five days, however, he succeeded in getting good photographs of all the subjects I wished. . . .

I took impressions of all the new inscriptions found in the course of turning over the different blocks. I also made measurements and drawings of the different parts of the order of the building, which is Corinthian. When Corporal Spackman had finished photographing, I got him to assist me in taking measurements for the plan. By the time I had this completed, we had been altogether eight days at Laina. The latter part of our stay we were obliged to keep watch at night, as a band of eight robbers were prowling about the mountains in the neighbourhood.

This temple, which is mentioned by Strabo and other ancient authors, is spoken of as ἐπιφανέστατον, most famous. It was built by the Stratoniceans, whose city was only a few miles distant.

On Wednesday the 22nd we went to Eski Hissar, where we pitched our tent in a field just outside the village. I went by Gibeah, a small village between Laina and Eski Hissar, for the purpose of copying an inscription on a cippus there. We arrived early, so that we had time to get the photographs done there the same day. The bath had evaporated so much that there was not enough left to cover a plate. Collodion consequently could not be used, and Corporal Spackman had to take the views by the wax-paper process. He was quite successful.

Three views were taken, two of an ancient arched gateway with a monumental column near it, and one of a large Roman building which contains a number of inscriptions.

The Aga was very civil, taking me into his harem to show me some inscriptions there. As this was, of course, sacred ground, no travellers had ever seen these inscriptions. I copied them, three in number. Unfortunately I could not take impressions of them, as I had used up all my paper at Laina.

We were obliged to remain the whole of the next day at Eski Hissar for want of horses to take us to Melassa. During the day the Aga paid us a visit in our tent, which was the wonder of the whole population. In fact, wherever we went the people came in crowds to see it, saying, "Mashallah! Mashallah!" It was with great difficulty that we could keep them from crowding in; in fact, if I enjoyed any rank lower than *bimbashi* or colonel, it would have been impossible. This rank, which the Turks seem by general consent to have conferred upon me, was of great service throughout our excursion.

The following day, the 24th, we found horses and got to Melassa. Here we encamped by the ancient tomb mentioned in my report on the Mausoleum. It is nearly a mile from the town, at the village of Gümischlu, so named from the fact of silver being formerly found in the vicinity, *gümisch* being the Turkish word for silver. The following day Spackman took five wax-paper views—viz., two of the tomb, two of an ancient gateway which has on the keystone of the arch a battle-axe, the symbol of Jupiter Labrandenus and of the kings of Caria, and one of the Goorshoonli Jahmeh, or *mosque with the domes*, a very beautiful building of marble. It is the finest Turkish structure I have seen. . . .

On the 26th, while at Melassa, I went with Chiaoux, one of the Turks, to look for Labranda. This place was famous for a temple of Jupiter, from which he received the name of Jupiter Labrandenus. Some account of Labranda is given in Strabo. He says that it was 68 stades or $8\frac{1}{2}$ miles from Mylasa, to which city it belonged, that it was on a mountain, and was in the same direction from Mylasa as Alabanda. There are the ruins of a Corinthian temple at Jakli, a village to the N.W. of Mylasa, and these ruins have generally been taken as those of the Temple of Jupiter at Labranda. Colonel Leake, however, supposes them to be the remains of Euromus. After giving several reasons for supposing Alabanda to have been at Arab Hissar, a place on the Tschinar to the northward of Mylasa, he adds: "Upon the whole, therefore, I am inclined to think that Alabanda was at Arab-Hissar and Euromus at Jakli; and that the vestiges of Labranda will hereafter be found on the mountain to the north-eastward of Mylasa." I left Mylasa at daybreak and rode to Gargejek, a small village on the slope of the range of mountains to the north of Mylasa. I was in hopes of finding some peasant here who might give us some information regarding any *eski tasch* or old stones in the neighbourhood. I found the village deserted by all but two children, the inhabitants being all at work in the valley. These children told us that if we went two hours farther up the mountain we would find some people at a village called Kodja Jallöe. We went there, and I had the satisfaction of finding the ruins I was in quest of at Kodja Jallöe itself.

I found a great many massive walls beautifully built of squared stones without lime, and a number of broken pieces of marble columns lying about. Some of these walls are still standing to a height of upwards of 20 feet. I found a large tomb that was in a wonderful state of preservation, being almost as perfect as when it was built. It consisted of two chambers, one principal inner one containing three sarcophagi, and a smaller outer one, through which I had to pass in going to the inner one. There is a door leading into the outer chamber from the outside, and opposite to it another door connecting it with the inner. A rough plan of tomb is shown in the margin. The sides and roof are one continuous arch, which is, as nearly as I could judge by the eye, semicircular. It is constructed on the horizontal principle which I spoke of in the report on the Mausoleum. The figure in the margin is a section of the arch. Not one of the stones is displaced in the least, and, as in all Greek constructions, no mortar has been used.

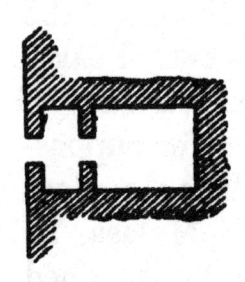

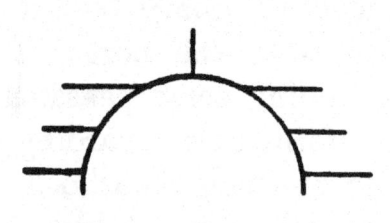

There is an upper storey, consisting of one room the whole size of the tomb, and roofed over with immense slabs. These stretch across from side to side, laid close beside each other. They all measured nearly the same, 16' 2" × 2' 9" × 1' 7". The tomb is built of blocks of stone of the surrounding rock.

Kodja Jallöe consists of only a few Turkish huts. It is situated very near the ridge of the Kodja Jallöe Mountains, the ancient Mount Latmos. These mountains are very picturesque, being rugged and precipitous, with olives on the lower slope and pines toward the summit growing in great luxuriance. Here and there the mountain is of white marble. The view from the ruins is very extensive, embracing all the south-western part of Caria and even the islands of Leros, Kalymnos, and Kos. A finer position could hardly be chosen. From the whole appearance of the remains I have no doubt of their being those of Labranda. Although about four hours from Mylasa, the actual distance cannot be more than eight or nine miles, thus quite agreeing with Strabo's account. From Mylasa its bearing is about $24\frac{1}{2}°$ east, or 13°, allowing for the variation of the compass. This also is almost exactly the bearing of Arab Hissar from Mylasa, so that if Colonel Leake's supposition regarding Alabanda is correct, this also corresponds to Strabo's description. There is no road to it but the path by which we went, the Aidin road crossing the mountains some miles to the eastward.

After returning to Mylasa we started for Budrum, coming by Jakli, where I saw the temple above mentioned. This building seems not to have been finished, as some of the columns still standing are unfluted while the rest are fluted. Some columns lying at the east end of the temple seemed half finished. In two days we reached Budrum after an absence of nineteen days. . . .

To-morrow the Korban Bairam, the great feast of the Turks, commences. As there will be no work for three days I have given Corporal Jenkins leave to go for two days to the island of Kos. It is the first intermission of continued hard work he has had since we came here. . . .

A detailed report on the excursion described in the preceding letter was made to Mr Newton, and, along with a set of illustrative photographs, was forwarded by him to Lord Clarendon, from whom the following reply was received:—

FOREIGN OFFICE, *October* 28, 1857.

SIR,—I am directed by the Earl of Clarendon to acknowledge the receipt of your despatch, No. 29, of the 16th ult., enclosing Lieutenant Smith's report on Lagina and Labranda, accompanied by photographs; and I am to instruct you to acquaint Lieutenant Smith that Lord Clarendon approves of his having made the expedition which forms the subject of his report, and that his Lordship has read this report with much interest.—I am, &c., SHELBURNE.

C. T. NEWTON, Esq.

To Sir John Burgoyne.

BUDRUM, *September* 10, 1857.

... Since I wrote last we have been engaged chiefly in clearing out the subterranean galleries at the Mausoleum. We don't know yet how far they extend. The whole length we are aware of is about 1500 feet. They are in two sets, a higher and lower, both cut out of the solid rock. In the higher set one can walk upright throughout nearly the whole length, but in the lower one is obliged to stoop, and in some places to crawl along like a serpent. When the clearing out of this set was first commenced about three weeks ago, there was only one shaft from the surface, and the air contained so much carbonic acid gas that no light could burn. By continually changing the men, who remained down only a short time, we cleared it out as far as another shaft, by opening which the ventilation became very good. There are now several shafts for both sets of galleries, with a windlass at each, so that the work goes on faster every day.

Besides the galleries, there has always been a party continuing the excavations round the building. In my report on the Mausoleum of June 1 I showed that the building itself occupied the space formerly supposed to be that of the *peribolus*, and I mentioned that it was probable that the *peribolus* was of much greater extent, corresponding with the circumference of 1340 feet, given by Hyginus. We have dug the whole space covered by the building and part of this *peribolus* — in all, about one-third of the whole supposed enclosure. The firman Mr Newton now has expires in November, by which time also the original grant of £2000 will be expended, and he now waits the decision of the Government as to which one of three courses of procedure he is to adopt. These are — 1st, to remain here digging until the £2000 are expended and then finish the operations; 2nd, to get a further grant of money and a renewal of the firman to enable him to excavate the whole of the *peribolus* of the Mausoleum; and, 3rd, to receive a grant and firman such as to allow of the originally contemplated operations at Cnidus being carried out after finishing the Mausoleum. He expects instructions in the course of next month. If the Government decide upon the third course the expedition would probably have to continue another year.

We have lately had a very important addition to our establishment by the arrival of an architect, Mr Pullan, who is to continue with the expedition.'

I have just returned from a short excursion up the Gulf of Kos, having gone for the purpose of visiting Keramo, the ancient Keramus.[1] . . . Before going to Keramo I sailed to the southern side of the gulf for the purpose of getting some planks that were on the shore there.

---

[1] Murdoch Smith's official report on this excursion is printed in *Further Papers respecting the Excavations at Budrum and Cnidus*, 1858, pp. 22-24.

I was detained here by stress of weather for ten days before we could get the planks on board the caique. Most of this time I spent with the Aga of the neighbouring villages. He treated me very hospitably, every day furnishing me with a horse and a guide, so that I was enabled to explore all the part of the Dorian Peninsula opposite the island of Symi. I found Greek remains at only one place, probably the ancient Acanthus. Here there was a wall of Greek construction, apparently a wharf one, on the sea-shore, and a number of ruins of much more recent date.

At this place there are four Turkish villages —Ellaköi, Haraköi, Baturköi, and Datscha—near each other. The peninsula here is only seven or eight miles broad from the Gulf of Symi on the south to the Gulf of Kos on the north. A ridge of not very high mountains extends east and west nearly parallel to the shore. On these the villages are situated, and from them two very beautiful and fertile valleys stretch away, one on each side, to the sea. These valleys produce a large quantity of figs, olives, and valonia. It was fig-harvest when I was there. All the villages were consequently nearly deserted by their inhabitants, who for the time were living in the valleys in bowers made of branches of trees.

Having at last succeeded in getting the planks on board, I took my leave of the Aga, and found on again embarking that he had sent down to the caique a large supply of fruit and poultry for my use during the cruise. I sailed straight to Keramo, and proceeded to examine the locality. The ancient town is situated on the northern shore of the Gulf of Kos, about half-way from the mouth to the head of the gulf. All along this shore there are high mountains sloping down to the water's edge, but at Keramo they recede from the shore, leaving a large plain between them and the sea. The greater part of this plain is covered by an impenetrable thicket or jungle, which is the cause of its great unhealthiness. Keramus is situated in this plain at the foot of the mountains, and is about two miles from the sea-shore.

The wall of the city is still standing to a considerable height throughout its whole circuit. It is of the construction termed *Cyclopean*, and is built of blocks of limestone, of which the mountains seem chiefly to be formed. Here and there are square flanking towers, the corners of which are not Cyclopean, but built of squared blocks of what I think is called by geologists conglomerate or pudding-stone. I counted eight small arched gateways throughout the course of the wall. At one place the wall curves inward so ⁀‿⁀ —evidently for the purpose of giving flank defence to what was probably the principal gateway of the city. This gateway is not standing, but there is every appearance of such a gateway having existed. From this gateway a road has extended towards the shore, as I noticed that the sarcophagi, which in other places are lying irregularly on the ground, are here arranged in two lines, leaving a road or street between them of a uniform breadth of about 36 feet.

Along the north side the mountains at many places are nearly perpendicular. At such places the wall does not occur.

Outside the city, at the foot of the mountains, I found the basement of a temple still standing. It is built isodomously of blocks of conglomerate, some of which are very large. One which I measured was 15′ 3″ × 3′ 4″ × 1′ 7½″. The superstructure has been of white marble. Pieces of the columns, architrave, &c., were lying about. The order is Corinthian and of the Roman period.

Inside the walls of the city are a number of large buildings of rubble-work, apparently of Christian date, probably churches and monasteries.

After remaining here two days I sailed back to Budrum.

Mr Newton and I intend going to-morrow to Myndus to examine that site. I visited it once last winter, but as I went and returned the same day, I had almost no time for examination.

Last week Mr Newton and Mr Pullan went to Kos for two days, and took notes of the antiquities there.

With the means Mr Newton has now at his disposal he intends, if we remain another year, to have a great many such excursions, so as to comprehend the whole of Caria in the final account of the proceedings of the expedition. . . .

BUDRUM, *October* 2, 1857.

... The work at the Mausoleum has been going on as usual last month. Of the two sets of subterranean galleries that I mentioned in my former letter, the lower have been finished, but we have not yet found the limit of the upper. The lower gallery passes all round the site of the building and close to it, and has ten shafts throughout its course. It seems to have been used for draining and the upper for sepulchral purposes. The outlet for the water in the lower one is on the east side, from which a branch goes in a S.E. direction toward the sea.

The upper gallery approaches the Mausoleum only on the west and south sides. We have cleared it out to a considerable distance from the building to the northward, where it runs toward the theatre on the hill. There is a shaft behind the theatre similar to those in the galleries, so that I should not be surprised if the gallery reaches it. Near the theatre there are several rock tombs, and I think it probable that the galleries are in connection with the ancient cemetery in which the Mausoleum appears to have been built.

On the south side we have come to a thin wall of Greek construction. Several months ago we found a similar one on the east side. In both cases the wall is only a foot or two in front of the perpendicular face of the rock. The Mausoleum was built on the projecting corner of a platform of rock cut in the side of the hill. This platform terminated close to the building in per-

THE RESTORED ORDER OF THE MAUSOLEUM.

pendicular faces on the east and south sides. The slope of the hill bounded it on the north, while to the west it extended an indefinite length. The thin wall I have mentioned as being only a foot or two in front of the perpendicular faces on the south and east seems, therefore, to have been simply for the sake of giving a better effect to the building by presenting to the eye a beautiful even wall instead of the rough and uneven face of the rock. These perpendicular faces are artificial, being the boundaries of the terraces into which the rock was cut below the building. These two walls are both within the *peribolus*.

We have made another important discovery this month by mining. By this means we have found the wall of the *peribolus* on the east side. The marble wall which I mentioned in former letters is the north wall of the *peribolus*, so that we have now two of the four boundaries of the whole enclosure. The wall we have found on the east is the same as the marble wall, both in construction and appearance. We are now mining right and left along this eastern wall from the point where we discovered it. By this means we hope to trace it to its return at the S.E. corner. This would of course give one dimension of the *peribolus*, and, combined with Hyginus's account, the other also.

The position of the building must have been remarkably fine, placed as it was on the corner of an elevated platform, its front, or eastern side, looking toward the city, and its southern open from the sea.

The building itself stood on, or rather covered, a rectangular space hollowed out of this elevated platform. This hollowing was probably to get a harder stratum of rock for the foundations. The level space to the west of the building and within the *peribolus* may have contained a sacred grove or something of that kind.

Mr Newton has not yet received a reply from Lord Clarendon regarding our future operations here and at Cnidus. He expects one, however, this month.

Mr Newton and I have made excursions to ancient sites in the neighbourhood every week since my return from Keramo and the shores of the Gulf of Kos.

On Saturday the 12th we went to Gumishlu, the site of the ancient Myndus. Next day we went from this place to Kadi Kalessi, where we passed the night. This, like Gumishlu, is a small village on the shore of the western side of the peninsula, of which the isthmus is at Budrum. It is at one end of an extensive and fertile plain, from which there is a considerable annual export of figs. The figs of this part of the country are rather small and of inferior quality. They go to Smyrna and Constantinople, and thence chiefly to Odessa. The finer figs destined for the English market come from the neighbourhood of Aidin.

From Kadi Kalessi we rode southward along the shore to Kara Toprak (Black Earth), so named from a black sand that lies on the shore, and which is used by the Turkish *hodjas* instead of blotting-paper. Kara Toprak is about an hour from Kadi Kalessi, and is at the other end of the plain already mentioned.

From Kara Toprak we turned westward toward Budrum, riding along the plain at the foot of the mountains bounding it on the south. After passing a village or two we came to the hills at the western end of the valley. Here at a place called Assarlik we found some remarkable tombs. They were destroyed, but enough remained to show their former construction. They consisted of a chamber arched over on the *horizontal* principle, surrounded at some distance by a circular wall. This wall, which is only two or three feet high, acted, I believe, as a revetment to the earthen mound or tumulus with which the interior chamber was covered. A covered passage led through this tumulus from a door in the outside wall to the chamber within.

One tomb of another kind was of very remarkable construction. It was a kind of dome built *horizontally*. The remarkable part of it, however, was that the base was rectangular, but the courses as they left the base became more and more circular, till, near the summit, they became quite or nearly so.

Here also we came to a very steep conical mountain, with traces of a Greek fortress on the top. Lower down, on the side of the hill, we saw an immense wall and gateway of Cyclopean masonry.

After passing the night at Assarlik we returned next day to Budrum, going along the southern shore of the peninsula. We visited on the way

Chifoot Kalessi (Jew's Castle), a remarkable rock on the sea-shore. It has been supposed to be the site of the ancient Termera.

The following week we explored in a similar way the northern shore of the peninsula. The principal place we went to see was Pacha Liman, said by some to be the ancient Caryanda, but we found nothing that could warrant such a belief.

This week we went to examine the remains of Bargylia. They consist chiefly of a theatre, an Odeum, a temple, and a Doric colonnade. With the exception of the Odeum they are all completely destroyed. The city stands on an eminence at the side of a creek. The sea seems to have receded here, leaving a large sandy tract in which there are a number of salt-pans. The place on this account is extremely unhealthy. We returned to Budrum by an inland route. . . .

BUDRUM, *October* 16, 1857.

I have just received your kind note of the 16th September. Along with it came a despatch to Mr Newton from the Foreign Office announcing the decision of Lord Clarendon regarding the continuation of our operations. The excavations here are to be completed and Cnidus undertaken.

An additional supply of stores being necessary for this, Lord Clarendon has given instructions that they be furnished by the Rear-Admiral Superintendent at Malta. The *Supply* will leave us next week for Malta to embark them and lay in a new stock of provisions. The stores we require are chiefly pickaxes, shovels, wheelbarrows, rope, spars, planks, iron, and steel. The *Supply* will also bring us six Crimea huts and some new tents, as we must provide accommodation not only for our own party but also for the Turkish workmen. Mr Newton is also going to ask Lord Lyons for a small detachment of marines as a guard. Such a guard would be desirable, as the place is sometimes the resort of robbers and pirates. Besides, the ship must lie at Budrum, there being no proper anchorage at Cnidus.

I enclose this with the plans made from time to time of the different fields in which we dug before concentrating our forces on the Mausoleum. . . .

As the plans are necessary for the illustration of Mr Newton's report, and also for the final account of our proceedings, you will perhaps be kind enough to see that they are forwarded to the Foreign Office after you have seen them. They might have been sent there direct, but I thought it right that you should see them previously.

BUDRUM, *November* 3, 1857.

. . . The *Supply* left this on the 20th ulto. I expect her back next week.

Mr Newton went with her as far as Kalymnos, from which with Corporal Spackman he intended crossing to Branchidæ, a famous site near the mouth of the Mæander. This place, which was a dependency of the neighbouring city Miletus, contained the celebrated temple of Apollo Didymeus. This shrine was one of the three oracles of the ancient Greeks. The ruins are chiefly above ground, and the *sacra via* connected with the temple can easily be traced. On each side of it is a row of marble statues of very early date. . . . The *Supply* will call for Mr Newton on her way back from Malta.

Nothing worth mentioning has turned up at the Mausoleum since I wrote last. We lost the trace of the eastern *peribolus* wall, so that to find the southern wall we were obliged to sink shafts to the rock in other places and drive galleries toward the supposed line of wall. We have not yet discovered it; but if any of it is still in existence, I have no doubt we will find it soon.

On Sunday the 1st inst. Budrum was in a state of great commotion on account of the arrival of the pasha from Mughla. It seems that the Turkish Government contemplate establishing European colonies on the Crown lands in Asia Minor. Preparatory to further steps being taken, a commissioner from the Porte, Abdullah Bey, has for several months been employed in this pashalik in going over the country examining the titles of the present possessors of the soil, so as to discover and survey what lands really belong to the Crown. Some similar object has now brought the Pasha to Budrum.

His entry was very imposing in its way. He was attended by a great crowd of well-mounted cavasses, all armed to the teeth with swords, pistols, yataghans, &c., and clad in all the colours of the rainbow. He is the same Pasha who received me so well when I went to Mughla last May. Soon after his arrival I paid him a visit, dressed of course in tunic, cocked hat, &c. Your recommendation in that respect was certainly well founded, as the dress had evidently a considerable effect. I had scarcely sat down when he told me with evident signs of joy that he had just heard that Reschid Pasha was again in office, and consequently that the English interest was in the ascendant at Constantinople.

The following day (yesterday) he returned the visit, which is considered, I believe, a high honour. He was accompanied by the Mudir of Melassa, and attended by all his train of pipe-bearers, bodyguard, &c. I was highly amused at the idea of his apologising to me, as he did, for the dress of the Mudir, who was not in uniform. I took him up to the Mausoleum and showed him what was to be seen. He was much pleased, but did not seem greatly captivated with the temporary plank bridges and ramps for the wheelbarrows. He intends leaving for Mughla to-morrow. . . .

BUDRUM, *December* 1, 1857.

At the Mausoleum our work has gone on as usual, but without any remarkable result. We are brought almost to a standstill by the obstinacy of the proprietors of the surrounding houses and fields. On this account we are reduced to the necessity of searching their property by mining, which from the nature of the ground is both tedious and difficult. Along the east and south sides, where we are now at work, the mines have to be driven through a mass of stones and rubble that in most places requires propping and framing, and the heavy rains with which we are now frequently visited add to the difficulties. The south wall of the *peribolus*, the immediate object of our search, has not yet made its appearance.

Mr Newton was away four weeks with Corporal

Spackman at Branchidæ, and is much satisfied with the results of his visit. The seated figures which I mentioned in my last as lining the *sacra via* were found nearly buried in the ground. After digging round them, Corporal Spackman succeeded very well in taking photographs of them, although the views are, of course, not so distinct as if the figures had been fairly exposed to the light. Besides taking the photographs, he made accurate drawings to a scale of all of them, and took two or three very nice water-colour sketches of the surrounding landscape. Towards the end of their stay there Mr Newton had a slight attack of fever, but recovered before their return to Budrum.

The *Supply*, with Mr Newton on board, left again on the 26th ult. for Smyrna to embark a statue which Mr Newton had obtained there for the British Museum. I expect her back in about a week. Mr Pullan, architect, and Corporal Spackman went with her to Kos, Mr Pullan to make drawings of some architectural remains there, and Corporal Spackman to take photographic views, chiefly of the landscape. The *Supply* will call for them on her way back from Smyrna.

When they have all returned Mr Newton intends commencing operations at Cnidus at once, by going there with Mr Pullan and a party of Turks. Corporal Spackman will probably go with them. I shall remain here with the rest of the sappers until the Mausoleum is completed. I think it probable that the proprietors here will give in when they see that we commence work in another place and are not confined to their own spot in Budrum. They have an idea, and a very natural one, that when such an expedition comes all the way from England and keeps working at one place a whole year, that we would give them any amount of money sooner than give up. The works at Cnidus will, I trust, tend to dispossess them of such an opinion. When the *Supply* comes back I shall get two of the huts on shore and erect them in the courtyard for the sappers and myself. They will be more comfortable than the tents during winter.

The news of the Indian Mutiny has gradually at last found its way to the ears of the people of this part of Turkey, and I have learned from various sources that many of the men, especially those who served in the Turkish Contingent, would be very glad to take service under the English in India. The annual conscription for the army took place here lately. The clerk who accompanied the colonel was clerk to the 8th Regt. T. C., under Major Mercer. I had several conversations with him, and he said that all the Contingent men, of whom there are large numbers in this pashalik, would be delighted to enlist under the English. It shows how widely spread is the good feeling the people entertain toward England, for they are quite well aware that the mutineers are partly Mahomedans. . . .

BUDRUM, *January* 4, 1858.

. . . At the time I last wrote, the *Supply*, with Mr Newton on board, had gone to Smyrna for the purpose of packing and embarking a statue bought there for the British Museum. They returned on the 6th December. Two days afterwards Mr Pullan and Corporal Spackman returned from Kos after having made a complete tour of the island. Almost all the time they were there the wind blew with such violence that it was impossible to get any photographs of the landscape.

On the 10th Mr Newton and Mr Pullan, with Corporal Spackman and F. Nelles, went in the *Supply* to Cnidus to commence operations there. The ship remained a night and landed the huts, tents, tools, &c., that were required. She also left with Mr Newton the carpenter and his mate, and a sergeant and six marines. I intended putting up one or two huts here for our accommodation in winter, but as Mr Newton wishes them all at Cnidus I have not insisted on it. . . .

I have kept from 120 to 130 men at work at the Mausoleum since Mr Newton left, but as the space is getting very limited I shall soon be obliged to reduce them. They are digging along the east side between the building and the eastern *peribolus* wall. A great many are employed mining on the south side, where the southern *peribolus* wall is yet undiscovered. We are obliged to mine there, as we cannot get possession of the ground to dig from the surface. I drove two galleries, about 100 feet apart, in a southerly direction from the southern limit of our own ground till they had passed the supposed line of wall a considerable way. In neither of these were any traces of the wall visible. I am now driving a gallery parallel to the wall and near its supposed position, and when it has advanced some distance I shall drive headings as close to each other as possible in the direction of the wall. By this means we ought to find the wall, if any of it remains. The branch of the upper gallery in the rock which I mentioned in a former letter as running up toward the theatre still goes on. We have cleared it out for a distance of about 300 feet from the Mausoleum. . . .

A letter to his sister gives an account of the expedition's Christmas festivities :—

BUDRUM, *January* 21, 1858.

. . . Christmas night I spent on board the *Supply*. Balliston the commander, Edgeworth the doctor, Spain the paymaster, and Layland the chief engineer formed with myself the party. Newton and Pullan the architect were at Cnidus. We got on very well, considering the place we are in. I knocked off the works that day, and the sappers spent their day on board with the warrant officers. In the evening the crew (such at least as could keep their legs) came aft and gave us a Christmas carol, after which we were favoured with a choice collection of patriotic and sentimental melodies. The choruses, at first uncertain whether they should belong to the former or the latter class, at last entirely subsided into the patriotic, the general burden being "Three cheers for the red, white, and blue," to which sailors, in order to fill up the pause at the end of the line, usually add, "all serene." In that popular song I suppose that you are aware that the chorus wishes the united services to endure for ever. Sailors are wont to sing, "The Navy and Army for ever," but on

Christmas night the voices of the sappers so prevailed that long before the end of the concert the Jacks were bawling out the proper version of "The Army and Navy for ever," much to the disgust of my friends at table. . . .

I was dreadfully put out for a while by my right-hand man, Corporal Jenkins, getting laid up with fever. I had consequently to do everything myself, as I could not trust any of the other sappers with his work. I had upwards of 130 Turks at work at the Mausoleum at the time, so what with them and other affairs to look after I had a precious time of it till he got better. . . .

We are now in the middle of our stormy weather again. I expect some night to have my tent about my ears. The days are like a Scotch summer, but the nights are so cold that water is frozen over in the morning. A tent is consequently not a very desirable abode; but it is "Hobson's choice," so I put up with it, and in fact, now after a fifteen months' residence in it, rather like it than otherwise. . . . I wish it were all over that I might see you all again. . . .

CHAPTER IV.

CNIDUS.

A SEVERE WINTER—WORK AT CNIDUS COMMENCED—EXCAVATION OF TOMBS — DAILY ROUTINE — SNAKE - CHARMING — QUARANTINE TROUBLES — DISCOVERY OF ODEUM — A SAILOR'S LETTER — THE SAPPERS' TRIUMPHAL ARCH — DISCOVERY OF THE LION TOMB—EMBARKATION OF THE LION—VISIT TO CONSTANTINOPLE—A RUN HOME — ATHENS — ANTIPAROS — CORPORAL JENKINS — A GREEK BRIDGE—VISIT OF PRINCE ALFRED.

THE winter of 1857-58 was one of unusual severity in Asia Minor. The hills above Budrum were covered with snow, a thing which had not happened within the memory of the oldest inhabitants. There were severe north-easterly gales; some of the tents at Budrum had to be struck to prevent their being carried away; and one of the huts at Cnidus was blown down.

Many of Murdoch Smith's letters to Sir John Burgoyne were accompanied by photographs illustrating the work of the expedition. On February 2, 1858, he sent home a selected series of sixty photographs, with a detailed description of each. These were sent by Sir John to Lord Panmure, who expressed himself highly pleased with them, and submitted them to the Prince Consort. His Royal

Highness and her late Majesty were both greatly interested in the expedition.

On February 5 Murdoch Smith shifted his quarters to Cnidus.

To Sir John Burgoyne.

RUINS OF CNIDUS, ASIA MINOR, *by* RHODES, *March* 5, 1858.

... On the 5th of February I came here in the *Supply*, and Mr Newton went to Budrum with her the following day. He came back to Cnidus a fortnight afterwards in a caique, by which I returned to Budrum.

In the course of excavating under a house recently purchased at the N.E. corner of the Mausoleum, several very interesting fragments were discovered. Among other things was a magnificent lion's head, which, in Mr Newton's opinion, is better than any of those previously found. It is very nearly in a perfect state. After the digging at this place was finished the proprietor of the houses still standing on the south side began to talk of selling them. Nothing, however, had been concluded when I left Budrum last Monday. Mr Newton is now there. He intended going to Mughla this month to see if he could not persuade the pasha to make these house-proprietors listen to reasonable terms. He will probably come here again when the *Supply* comes next month, till which time I shall remain here. Meantime a small force is kept mining in search of the southern *peribolus* wall, but chiefly in order to keep possession of the ground, a matter of some importance. The Mausoleum might have been finished long ere this but for the perpetual delays caused by the Turks not selling the houses which occupied its site. . . .

Our party at present here consists, besides the sappers and myself, of the ship's carpenter with three artificers, and a sergeant and six marines. We are very comfortably lodged in the huts brought up by the *Supply* from Malta. As the nearest village is upwards of two hours' distance, the Turkish workmen are obliged to live here. The numerous ancient tombs in the rocks form very good quarters for them. The number of men employed varies from 40 to 50. As workmen they are inferior to the Budrum men, a great many of whom are sailors.

The digging here has been chiefly carried on at the theatre, close to our encampment. The *vomitorium* or entrance has been cleared out, and now forms an excellent blacksmith's shop for Sapper Nelles. In the course of excavating some ancient tombs Mr Newton lately discovered a very beautiful little statue of Venus, nearly perfect. He also found the greater part of a female figure, life-size, and several inscriptions. This city was sacred to Venus, whose temple and statue were both famed among the Greeks for their excellence. A long and interesting description of them is given by Lucian.

The ancient city occupied the small peninsula called Triopium (now Cape Krio) and the adjoining part of the mainland. The latter part of the city rises in terraces from the shores of the two harbours to the Acropolis, which occupies the summit of a very steep hill, nearly 1000 feet high. The other side of this hill is almost perpendicular, so that the city is quite inaccessible from that direction. The only entrance is on the eastern side along the seashore, and this was defended by an immense wall with towers. The side of the peninsula Triopium facing the sea is a sheer precipice, and the mouths of the two harbours are so narrow that any entrance by them might easily be prevented.

In front of the theatre we have built a stone pier to facilitate the embarkation of any sculpture that may be found. While engaged in this work two days ago the ship's carpenter had his foot badly wounded by the fall of a large block of marble.

Our supply of water is rather limited, there being only one spring in the place, and that a very small one. The winter has been so remarkable for its drought that the Turks are getting alarmed on account of their crops. Expecting rain, we cleared out one of the ancient tanks, thinking that in a few days it would certainly be filled. Upwards of a month, however, has passed and still no rain. As the usual dry season is now rapidly approaching it is quite possible that the rain will not come at all. I have accordingly commenced building a large tank under the spring, to be filled by it, as the Turks say that if the drought continues the spring itself will dry up in summer. . . .

RUINS OF CNIDUS, *March* 31, 1858.

I wrote to you as usual with the returns and pay lists at the beginning of the month.

A few days afterwards Mr Newton returned to Cnidus, and the following day I went to Budrum. The object of my going was to overcome if possible our old difficulty—viz., the buying of the houses still standing at the Mausoleum. I spent a fortnight in talking, smoking chibouques, and drinking coffee with the Turks they belong to, but all to no purpose, as I had to come away on Monday last as far from a settlement as ever. The *Supply* will be here next week. Mr Newton intends going with her to Budrum, thence probably to Mughla to see the Pasha, and if there is no probability of getting hold of the houses, evacuating the place altogether.

The *Supply* goes to Malta in the beginning of May to reprovision, &c. . . .

The digging here for the last three weeks has been carried on among the tombs. Several very good things have been found. On the peninsula Triopium a very remarkable tomb was found containing a statue in its original position, a female head, and a number of inscriptions. The place where we are now at work is a little to the east of the ancient theatre, on the side of the hill half-way up to the Acropolis. Among some tombs there was found a female head quite perfect. It is Greek of the best period, and Mr Newton thinks it probable that it is the work of Praxiteles himself. A statue was also found there about ten days ago.

There has been no rain yet, so that the tank which I commenced at the beginning of the month will be of the greatest use in summer. It is now nearly finished. It will contain upwards of 1000 cubic feet of water. . . .

To Jeanie Smith.

RUINS OF CNIDUS, *April* 29, 1858.

. . . I am kept well occupied all day in looking after things, as I have no one here to help me, Corporal Jenkins, my good genius, being at Budrum. If one were not busy, the dreadful monotony of the life would soon kill one. You have no idea what a thing it is to be so completely out of the world with no one to speak to. I get up early in the morning, go about all day looking after the workmen, the diggings, &c., and in the cool of the evening before dinner take a ride for an hour or two. On Sundays I have a parade in the morning, after which church, at which, according to the rules of the service, I act as parson, by reading the Morning Service of the Church of England. I then generally ride away to some of the villages two or three hours from here, get some sort of lunch, a chat, and a smoke with the Turks, and ride back to our encampment in the evening. *Voilà ma vie!* Our camp looks very well now. The huts are all nicely whitewashed outside and in, and I am now having the square surrounded by a wall. I have just finished building a large closed tank for water in summer. It will be filled by the only fountain in the whole place, and which I believe dries up in summer. The pier is also completed, so that we are thoroughly established. We have been digging in several places, but for the last month nothing very remarkable has turned up. . . .

The weather is become very warm again, hotter than at midsummer at home. I have just had a large opening 2 or 3 feet square cut near the ridge of the roof of my hut. With this, the two windows and the door open, I think I shall be able to keep the place tolerably cool. Even now neckties and waistcoats are out of the question. All I wear is a pair of white drill trousers, a thin flannel shirt, and an almost transparent jacket. If David were here he could have quite as many snakes as he wished, if not a few more. They turn up wherever one goes, some of them 6 and 7 feet in length. The hot weather brings them out. In winter they are torpid. Even in our huts we have already killed two. I daresay you have heard of snake-charmers. I always thought it some trick till lately. One of our workmen, an Arab, I have seen catch the most poisonous snakes just as they turned up in the course of the diggings, and without doing anything to them whatever, put them round his neck, into his bosom, and even put their heads into his mouth. In fact he does anything with them, and they never offer to bite him. He says that if they did, it would not hurt him in the least.

To Sir John Burgoyne.

BUDRUM, *May* 16, 1858.

... Mr Newton went with the ship to Santorin with the intention of buying a statue belonging to the French vice-consul there. He did not do so, however, because on seeing the statue he found it much inferior to what the drawing of it had led him to expect. The owner, besides, asked the exorbitant price of 20,000 francs. Mr Newton offered him 2000, and was rather glad than otherwise that the offer was not accepted. He left the *Supply* at Syra, where he found a steamer going to Smyrna. From Smyrna he got the Austrian steamer to Rhodes, whence he took a caique to Cnidus, where he arrived on Thursday last, the 13th.

The following morning (Friday) I left Cnidus in the caique which brought Mr Newton. In the afternoon I got to Kos, where, fortunately, I found a caique just about to start with a fair wind for Budrum. I got here the same evening in time to get *pratique* at the quarantine before sunset. These quarantine establishments are a great nuisance here, as they allow free scope for the jack-in-office propensities of the Italians attached to them under the designation of doctors. The last time the *Supply* came from Malta the commander unwittingly broke quarantine by landing at the *konak* before sending for *pratique*. I afterwards went with him as his interpreter to soothe the feelings of the "doctor." He, however, thought fit to make a scene and talk in the most offensive manner. I told him that he was at perfect liberty to act as he pleased, but that such language could not be listened to by British officers. He of course could do nothing. Ever since that time he has annoyed us by the enforcement of such absurd regulations as not giving *pratique* a single minute after the flag is hauled down at sunset. The consequence is that one has to sit up all night in the caique, which at any season, especially in winter, is extremely unpleasant, and even dangerous in heavy dews. . . .

Corporal Spackman went with the *Supply* to Malta. His going is a decided loss to the expedition. Lance-Corporal M'Cartney is of great service as a photographer. . . . The difficulties of one kind and another to be encountered by a photographer out here are very great. . . .

Ever since the *Supply* left Budrum Corporal Jenkins has been here alone. Mr Newton while here was not successful in getting the houses at the Mausoleum. He went to Mughla and spoke to the Pasha on the subject. He promised to do all in his power, but said that in these days of the *Tanzimat*[1] even a Pasha could not do everything he wished. At present I am in hopes of getting the houses, after all, by means of our friend Salik Bey, who has lately returned from Constantinople. Another object I had in coming to Budrum was to make a plan of the part of the town surrounding the Mausoleum. Mean-

[1] Reform.

time Corporal Jenkins has not been idle. He has had a few workmen digging in different places. He is now at work at the Doric colonnade near the centre of the town, supposed to be the ancient Agora. He has found two or three small pieces of sculpture. While in the castle one day copying inscriptions, he saw the end of a marble slab in the ground that looked suspicious. He scraped away some of the earth and saw that it was a piece of frieze, no doubt from the Mausoleum. He covered it up again and very discreetly said nothing to any one about it. I trust the commandant, who lives at Kos, will let us take it. Were its existence made known, an intrigue would instantly be set afoot to prevent our getting it.

While at Cnidus during last month I dug at several places pointed out to me by Mr Newton before he left. At none of them, however, did I find any sculpture. The last place I examined was a sort of alcove near the end of the mole or breakwater on the northern side of the southern harbour. Near this alcove I came upon some steps or seats arranged like those of a theatre. I cleared it all out and had it photographed. Mr Newton says that it must have been a place for the recital of poetry. The lower seats, which were covered with earth to a greater depth than the upper ones, are nearly perfect. They are of marble. There is a narrow flight of steps up the middle, opposite the sort of pulpit in which the reciter stood. The radius of curvature of the seats increases with the distance from the front in such a manner that every one of the audience, looking straight before him, looked towards the pulpit. The place is small, not being capable of containing more than 160 or 180 people.

Ramazan is now over, and to-day is the last day of the Buyuk Bairam. During the Ramazan I had occasion to go to Ellaköi to see the Aga Mehemet Ali about fresh provisions for our party. Ellaköi is eight hours' distance from Cnidus. The scenery all the way is remarkably grand. At one place the road passes for a considerable distance along the side of a mountain, where on one hand is a precipice of several hundred feet, and on the other the mountain rising upwards like an immense wall to a height of some 3000 feet. This road is simply a path 3 or 4 feet wide, very stony and uneven. There was a perfect calm when I passed this place, so that the heat of the sun reflected from the rocks was excessive. Night came before I reached my destination, and as I had taken no guide with me I very soon lost all trace of my road. After several hours' riding about among the hills I had the satisfaction of seeing a light in the distance, which afterwards proved to be from the mosque of Ellaköi illuminated on account of the Ramazan. . . .

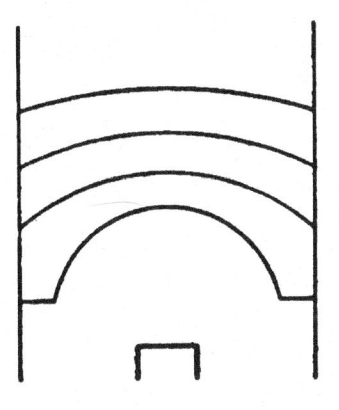

It was about this time that the following letter was picked up in the streets of Budrum and handed to Mr Newton, who afterwards printed it in *Travels and Discoveries in the Levant*. The writer was evidently one of the sailors of the *Supply*. Sir Robert used often to quote it as containing an excellent account of the excavations from Jack's point of view :—

Dear father and moter, with gods help i now take up my pen to right these few lines to you hopeing to find you in good health & sperits as thank god it leaves me at present. Dear father of all the drill that a seaman was put to i think the Supply's company have got the worst, for here we are at Boderumm a useing the peke madock & shovel. nevur was there such a change from a sea man to a navy; yes by George we are all turned naveys sumetimes a diging it up & sometimes a draging it down to the waters edge and then imbarking it. Dear father this is the finest mable that ever i saw; we get on so very slow that i fear we shall be hear a long time; the city of Ninevea as been sunk such a long time that we find nothing but mable; every thing els is compleatley roted away. what is most to be seen is the crockery ware that they used in those days; their is upwards of a hundred turks & Greeks mixt together; they have dug up to lions, but they are very much broken about from lying so long in the ground or by the shok of the earthquake when the place was destroyed. Dear father we have pleanty of frute one sorte and another, we have almons figs grapes pomegranets & melons, but i doant know whether melons are counted frute or vegetable, we eat them raw & so do every one els here. We have them in great plenty, they are by far the best frute that we can get here; i have one now on my right hand has big has a peck, or measure; the best of it is we cannot manage to eat more than half a dozen at the time but they are the best thing a man can eat when he is thirsty. Dear father we have had one male since we have bean here; i am a frade that the answers to my letters are lost, if so it was my fault —send me word of Eliza, the first chance i was sadley disopainted, i hoped to get intelegence of eliza. Dear father i will write every male from here, send me Georges and Charlotte adressis; give my kind love to her & tell her i have got a keepsake for her & saley; rember me to Jessy tell him i hope to have a turkish curieau for him. i think i shall bring him a gravestone they are very romantict and hanson; mind give my kind love to mother. god bless you direct to Boderumm malta or elswhere Mediteriaien.

To Sir John Burgoyne.

RUINS OF CNIDUS, *June* 1, 1858.

... The *Supply* returned to Budrum from Malta on Friday last, the 28th ulto. Having finished the plan of the environs of the site of the Mausoleum, and not being able to purchase the remaining houses, I got everything packed up and sent on board the *Supply*. On Sunday I came here in the ship, bringing Corporal Jenkins with me. Thus at last has terminated our long residence of nearly nineteen months at Budrum. I am very glad, indeed, to be able to say that our departure was regretted by all classes in the place, notwithstanding their Mussulman prejudices against the Giaour. Just before I left a good opportunity occurred of showing our goodwill to them. This was the marriage of the daughter of Ahmet Bey, one of the most respected inhabitants of Budrum. On the last day of the feast I erected a sort of triumphal arch of branches and flowers, and a tall flagstaff, on which were hoisted the English and Turkish flags. Under the arch the different processions passed. At night I got it illuminated, and fired off a number of rockets I got from the commandant of the Castle of Kos. When the last procession came, that of the bride going to her husband's house, I slacked off all the guys of the arch and flagstaff and placed a man at each. Whenever the bride had passed, these let go and down came the whole thing. As the Turks had never seen anything of the kind before, they were much surprised and delighted with the whole affair.

While I was at Budrum a magnificent discovery was made here. About a year ago a Kalymniote Greek told Mr Newton of a colossal lion in the neighbourhood of Cnidus. Although we had frequently looked for it we could never find it. At last Mr Pullan, in exploring a promontory about an hour to the east of Cnidus, had the satisfaction of finding it. It is in a crouching position, with the head turned toward the right. It is 10 feet long and 6 feet high, and almost perfect. The weight I have estimated at eight tons. It is cut out of a single block of Parian marble. The style is so similar to that of the best of the Mausoleum lions that Mr Newton has no doubt of its being the work of the same artist. It has evidently fallen from the top of a tomb close beside it. This tomb is close to the brink of a sheer precipice of 100 feet, and overlooks the sea. A road has been made down to the sea, and we are now busy with preparations for packing and embarking the lion.

Mr Newton, I am sorry to say, has suffered for the last eight or ten days from a rather severe attack of intermittent fever. He is better now, however, and intends going with the *Supply* to-day to Budrum to recruit his strength by a few days on board ship.

He has just received a despatch from the Earl of Malmesbury acquainting him that he was to consider himself limited to the sum of £4000 for disbursements here and £1000 for the payment of accounts in England. This £5000 is to be made the subject of a separate vote in the House of Commons. As the £4000 are now nearly expended, Mr Newton thinks that the work of the expedition will be over by the beginning of August, when we will return to England. . . .

Ruins of Cnidus, *July* 1, 1858.

The last time I wrote you was on the 1st of June, just after my arrival here on our evacuation of Budrum.

I then told you of the discovery of a colossal marble lion about an hour's distance from Cnidus. As I had not had time to examine it minutely I could not give you a very accurate description of it. Its weight is upwards of nine tons, and it lay in a spot from two to three hundred feet above the sea on a precipitous rock. Its value is estimated by Mr Newton at £10,000. As the task of removing this costly mass fell upon me, I think I cannot do better than give you an account of the whole operation. After a month spent in the greatest anxiety, I have now the satisfaction of having completed the undertaking with success. Yesterday the lion was safely deposited on a raft, and to-day it was taken on board the *Supply*.

The first thing I did was to make a road to the most convenient point on the sea-shore. I laid out a zigzag line on the face of the hill, and on this line made a road from 18 to 20 feet broad. At some places I was obliged to cut off pieces of the rock, and at others to raise the road 8 or 10 feet by embankment. These embankments I formed by first building a dry wall 6 or 7 feet thick as a revetment on the lower side. The hollow was then filled up with stones and loose pieces of the rock. The surface of the road was made by scattering on it small stones and earth.

While the road was in progress the ship's carpenters and Sapper Nelles the blacksmith were busy making a case in which to pack the lion and a sledge for transporting it. The case was made of 3-inch deals. At the four corners, and also at every alternate plank of the bottom and lid, a rod of half-inch iron was driven through the sides from the bottom. After the lion was in the case these bolts were all riveted on the lid. It was further strengthened with iron angle-plates. As far as I remember, the case is 12 feet long, 5′ 6″ high, 7′ 9″ broad at one end and 4′ 7″ at the other. The sledge was made of three elm beams about a foot square and rather longer than the case. Their front ends were slightly turned up. These were

THE LION OF CNIDUS.

bolted together with large iron rods in this way. In order to complete the case and sledge in time the carpenters and blacksmith more than once worked all night.

When the road, the case, and the sledge were finished, the next operation was placing the lion in the case.

For this purpose I erected large sheers. One of the legs of the sheers was a spar 52 feet long and about a foot in diameter. As I had not a sufficiently strong spar for the other leg, I fished the three largest spars we had. The guys were stream-cables, and were carefully made fast to masses of rock. As the strongest rope I had for a fall was only 4-inch, I rove it through two treble and two double blocks, thus giving ten parts of the rope to sustain the weight. The winch was lashed to the stump of a tree, and a leading block was attached to one of the legs of the sheers.

Before placing the lion in the case it was necessary to turn him completely round, as he was lying with his face on the ground. This I did by alternately raising and lowering him with the sheers, each time attaching the blocks to the slings a little on one side of the middle. The slings were padded with sheepskin to prevent their injuring the surface of the marble. Happily I succeeded in turning him without a scratch on the surface.

I then placed him in the case. After being solidly packed on all sides the lid was put on and the bolts riveted. The case was then placed on the sledge, and tackle being attached, we commenced hauling it down the road.

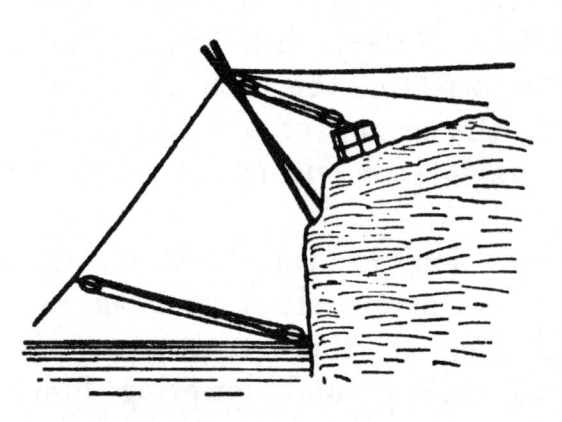

When well clear of the sheers I struck them and unlashed everything. I then took the spars to the shore, where the case had to be embarked, and erected sheers in the position shown. The only place I could find on which to rest the heels of the sheers was a narrow ledge in the rock only 15 inches in breadth. Under this ledge the rock descends like a wall into the sea. In order to place the sheers in their position I lashed them on the ground, the heels lying uphill and the throat towards the sea. I then built a scaffolding on a lighter in the water and launched the sheers until the heels came down to their position on the ledge, the throat meantime resting on the scaffolding. The head of the sheers was then lifted into its position in the usual way by means of tackle on the guys. The securing of these guys was rather difficult, as there was no place to which to make them fast. The way in which I did it was by cutting large grooves in projecting parts of the rock above, and passing the guys through these grooves and round the rock. The cutting of these grooves was a very tedious operation on account of the hardness of the rock. A number of men were employed at it every day for a fortnight.

When the sheers were thus erected I returned to the hauling down of the case. At some parts of the road I was obliged to put tackle upon tackle to enable the men (80 or 90 in number) to move it at all.

In three days they got it to the edge of the rocky escarp behind the sheers at the sea-shore. Here the real difficulty of the operation began. From the photographs and the above section you will see that it was impossible to get the case under the sheers by a considerable way. A pier or jetty was out of the question, as I had no means of making one. I was consequently obliged to attach the sheer-blocks to the case where it was on the edge of the escarp. To prevent the head of the sheers from flying up on account of the strain of the purchase being backward, I laid out an anchor and cable in the sea, making the cable fast to the throat of the sheers. I hauled this cable taut by applying to it a tackle made fast to the shore and nearly at right angles to the line of the cable [see sketch on next page]. To the case itself I attached a number of check-tackle made fast to the rock behind. I then built a platform, on which the winch was secured.

When all these arrangements were completed, I commenced heaving on the case with the winch-and-sheer purchase, a number of men being placed at each of the check-tackles behind. The case commenced to move, and was going out apparently all right when the portion of the rock to which the main check-tackle was attached gave way. The case and sledge instantly started forward and came with a tremendous smash on one of the legs of the sheers. This piece of rock was not detached, but a part

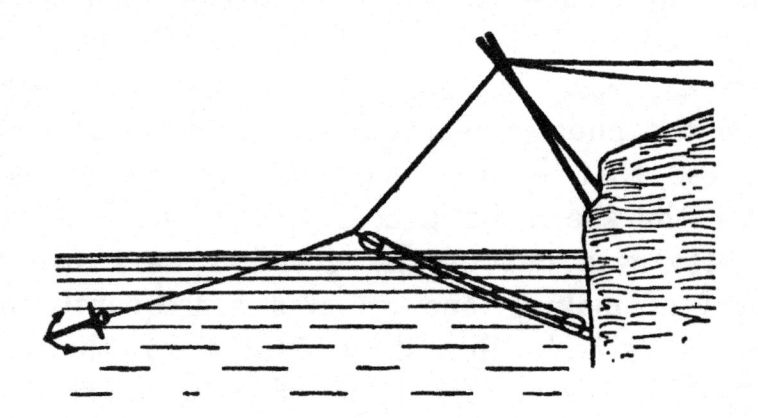

of the hill itself, so that there must have been a fissure in it beneath the surface, as, before we commenced heaving, it seemed capable of supporting almost any strain. When it gave way part of it rolled down the hill and knocked over one of the Turks, breaking two of his ribs. He is now, I am glad to say, fast recovering.

On examining the case and sledge I found them in a very critical position indeed. The case rested on the leg of the sheers by a single corner, while at the back it rested on the sledge at only one point, and the sledge itself was jammed between this point and a corner of the rock. The case, besides, had swerved away sidewards, so as to overhang not only the sea in front but also a sort of ravine in the rock on one side. The leg of the sheers kept it from falling forward, and the purchase tackle from falling into the ravine. It was so nicely balanced that the slightest touch made it rock from one side to the other.

The first means I tried to get it out of this most unpleasant fix was to renew and increase the check-tackles and haul sideways on the case to clear it of the sheers leg. As the ship was lying in the direction in which I wished it hauled, I got a rope from her windlass made fast to the front of the case. The sailors on board then set to work at the windlass, but the only effect produced was bringing the ship nearer shore. The case rocked but did not stir the eighth of an inch off the spar.

I examined the position of the case and sheers in every direction, but could think of no means whatever of getting out of the difficulty without a second pair of sheers behind to draw the case upward and backward. This second pair of sheers I knew I could not get, as the commander of the *Supply* was waiting till I had the case on the raft to get one of the spars of our sheers for his hoisting-sheers on board.

I went on board ship, however, and told Mr Balliston the commander that I could not move the case unless he could give me spars and chains for a second pair of sheers. He said he would willingly give me everything in the ship that I thought fitted for the purpose. I accordingly asked him for the derrick and the main-boom, which he gave me with all the cable he could spare.

With these and all the derrick tackle I went ashore and commenced getting up the sheers. As the main-boom was not strong enough of itself I fished it with two stout spars. The raising of the sheers was exceedingly troublesome, for several reasons. The unevenness and steepness of the ground, with the want of places for making tackle fast to, was one difficulty. But the peculiar difficulty was this, that in order to have the sheers in a position where they could be of any avail, it was necessary to have them striding across one of the guys of the lower sheers and most of the check-tackles of the case, and at the same time, that in the process of raising them they should not touch either the guy or the tackles. The danger in touching the guy or tackles was that the case immediately commenced rocking on its pivots in a manner that certainly endangered its position of equilibrium. I succeeded at last in raising them with safety by the following means.

On the high ground behind the upper sheers I made a platform of planks on the left of the guy of the lower sheers, and rather higher than the guy itself. On this I laid the heel of one leg, the other end of the spar being farther up the hill. I placed the other leg in a similar manner and lashed them, the head lying uphill and the heels pointing downwards towards the sea. It was consequently necessary to raise them by tackles from below until they had passed the perpendicular, and then lower their head into proper position by the guys behind. The difficulty of doing so was this, that as the heels were lying above their ultimate position, by hauling on the raising tackle below one would only have launched the heels down-hill. To prevent this I built two inclined planes to intercept them, and afterwards to guide them into their final position. I raised the head as far as I could with an artillery gyn, then made fast the raising tackle and hauled on it till the strain was taken off the gyn. I then removed the gyn and raised the sheers.

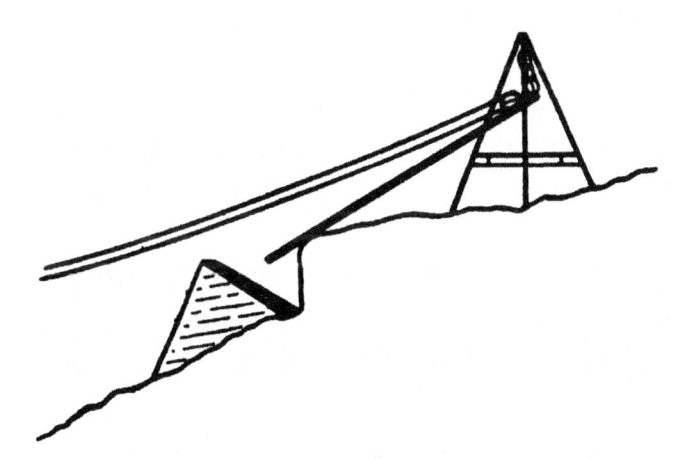

For blocks for these sheers I was obliged to take off the two double blocks from the lower pair of sheers, leaving on the two treble ones. This I did by *racking* the parts of the fall rove through the treble blocks, casting off the standing part, unreeving the two double blocks, and again making fast the standing part to the head of the sheers.

These two double blocks with the ship's derrick fall (a 6-inch rope) formed the purchase of the upper sheers.

The next thing to be done was to remove the winch to heave on the fall of the upper sheers. This was done by *stopping* the fall of the purchase of the lower sheers to one of the legs, and then unwinding it from the barrel of the winch. The winch was then removed and fixed for heaving on the case from the upper sheers, the purchase-tackle being attached to the back of the case. All these arrangements occupied three days.

On Friday the 25th they were completed, and in the afternoon I tried their effect. I commenced heaving, and continued until I saw that the 6-inch rope would not stand another turn of the winch. The guys of the upper sheers became as rigid as bars of iron with the immense strain to which they were subjected. Still the case did not stir. As I knew that a severe accident would occur, and probably a number of lives be lost, if anything gave way, I stopped and slacked up.

These means having failed, I could not at first see anything further to be done without stronger tackle. As the upper sheers were placed in such a position that the lead from their head to the case was exactly in line with the case itself, I could see no way in which to apply the material at my disposal in a stronger manner than I had already done. On telling Mr Newton this he said that if I gave him a written statement to that effect he would write a requisition to the commander to take the ship to Malta, where, it was to be presumed, I could find what materials I required. As I was very unwilling to go to Malta and incur the expense of the ship's going there except as a last resource, I deferred giving a decision till the following day. Meantime I restudied the position of everything to see if there was no expedient by which I could embark the case with the materials I had. The consequence of my study was to decide on another trial.

The general plan which I adopted was the following: As I had applied all the strength of my material to *moving* the case and had not succeeded in doing so, the only way left was to *fix* the case in its position, in such a manner as to make its support independent of the sheers on which it then rested, lower these sheers until they were clear of the case, and re-erect them in a position a little to one side of their former one.

The following day (Saturday) I accordingly commenced, the commander very kindly letting me have the assistance of the ship's carpenters. I am much indebted to them for the skilful manner in which they performed their difficult and somewhat dangerous work. I first placed four shores on the side overhanging the ravine. These rested on *shoes* screwed to the case. On the opposite side I placed three, and under the back of the case two, one at each corner. These nine shores I calculated would perform the duty of the purchase-tackle of the sheers—viz., keeping the case from falling sideways into the ravine. The remaining tendency to counteract was that of the case to fall downward and forward when no longer kept from doing so by the leg of the sheers on which it rested. This I did by packing solidly with planks the space under the case where it overhung the narrow ledge and the sea. I also placed a shore on the sea side against the front of the case, the other end of the shore resting on a piece of rock in the sea. As I had no spar large enough or strong enough for this, I got a spare jib-boom from the commander of the *Supply*. I then passed a 13-inch hemp cable round the case, making it fast to one of the places cut out in the rock for the reception of the guys.

The original check-tackles, the purchase-tackle of the upper sheers, and the 13-inch cable were then hauled taut and the shores wedged up. In case of any accident happening I took the precaution of filling up the small ravine at the side of the case with bundles of old hammocks, bags of oakum, &c., to keep the case from smashing on the rock if by any mishap it should fall. I also placed a raft of spars and planks in the water under it to break the fall, should it go in that direction.

Having thus taken every possible precaution against accident, I cut the racking of the purchase of the lower sheers and overhauled the blocks till the fall was quite slack. I then put tackles on the guys and commenced lowering away. To my great delight the sheers were lowered until they cleared the case, while the case remained perfectly steady.

I then hauled the heels of the sheers 2 or 3 feet to one side along the narrow ledge until the case was about midway between them, and then raised them to their proper elevation.

The purchase-tackle of the lower sheers was then hauled taut, the winch having been replaced in its former position. I then carefully removed all the shores one by one. This rather dangerous operation was done without the slightest accident.

After the removal of the shores the case was in its former position, only, instead of hanging balanced by a corner on the leg of the sheers, it had a solid bearing underneath, and was supported entirely by the different tackles. These were, the purchase-tackle of the lower sheers for weighing it and the 13-inch hemp cable, the purchase-tackle of the upper sheers and four check-tackles as checks for lowering it by behind. As of course everything depended on the steadiness of the men attending these tackles, I asked the commander for a party of English seamen to man them. He very kindly sent them. The careful and steady manner in which they obeyed every order contributed very much to the success of the operation. Everything being in readiness, I commenced by heaving with the winch until so much of the weight of the case was off the rock that the check-tackles got strained. These I then slowly slacked out, heaving with the winch at the same time. In slacking out I always kept the slacking of the large cable a little in advance of the tackles, so that the lowering was actually done by the tackles, while there was always the cable ready to check the case should any of the tackles carry away. In this way I continued until the case was hanging over the water right under the sheerhead. I then cast off all the check-tackles, brought the raft under, and lowered the case on to it by the winch.

The raft consisted of two lighters lashed together and planked over.

The difficulty of the operation was much increased by having to work for the most part with Turks, none of whom, with the exception of a few caiquemen I brought with me from Budrum, had probably ever seen or heard of a tackle in their lives.

The manner in which I was supported and assisted by Corporal Jenkins makes him worthy of the highest praise. His services, in fact, throughout the month I consider as invaluable.

After the lion was placed on the raft I lowered the two sheers and sent all the spars and heavy tackle on board, as the commander required most of them to complete his arrangements for hoisting in the case and lowering it into the hold. He also requested me to send the winch, and let Corporal Jenkins go on board to superintend its working with a party of the Budrum Turks of his own training. This was accordingly done, and Mr Balliston has since expressed to me his obligation to Corporal Jenkins for his valuable assistance.

Should no definite orders arrive in the meantime from the Foreign Office, our operations here will terminate about the beginning of August, when we will all proceed with the *Supply* to Malta. Tomorrow we commence excavating and examining the tomb on which the colossal lion was placed.

Mr Newton hopes to find some inscription that may give a clue to the history of this magnificent work of art. . . .

RUINS OF CNIDUS, *August* 20, 1858.

I wrote last on the 1st of July immediately after the embarkation of the colossal lion. . . .

At that time, in consequence of a despatch from Lord Malmesbury, we were making preparations for leaving for England about the beginning of this month. Shortly afterwards, however, Mr Newton received a despatch from Sir Henry Bulwer, the ambassador at Constantinople, ordering him not to break up the party at Cnidus, as the Government had determined to give a further grant of money to continue the excavations. As reference was made in Lord Malmesbury's despatch to the sculptures at Geronda, Mr Newton did not know whether this further grant was intended for their removal or for continued operations here. As the *Supply* must leave for Malta for provisions in the end of September, it was of great importance to get the firman for the removal of these sculptures at once, in order to complete their embarkation before her departure. This was the more necessary, as the operation would be one of great difficulty during the winter months. Mr Newton accordingly requested me to proceed to Constantinople to see the ambassador on the subject, and if possible get the required firman without delay. The *Supply* took me to Rhodes on Wednesday the 22nd July. There I remained till Friday the 31st, when I got a French steamer for Smyrna, which I reached the following day. On Tuesday the 4th August I left for Constantinople, arriving there on Thursday the 6th. I at once went to Therapia and called on Sir Henry. Having after a stay of eight days obtained the firman, I returned to Smyrna, where I presented it to the Pasha and received from him a letter to the local authorities of Geronda. The same day I left Smyrna by one of the Alexandria Turkish mail steamers calling at Rhodes. On passing Cape Krio, however, the captain very kindly stood close in to the shore and signalled to the *Supply* for a boat, by which I was landed at our encampment, thereby saving six or eight days at least. This was the day before yesterday, and to-morrow the *Supply*, with Mr Newton and Corporal Jenkins and a party of 50 Turks, leaves for Geronda. I think there will just be time to complete the shipment of the sculptures before the end of September, when, as I have already said, the *Supply* must leave for Malta.

While I was at Constantinople a despatch from Lord Malmesbury to Mr Newton arrived at the Embassy informing him that the Government had granted him a sum of £2000 wherewith to continue the operations at Cnidus. A renewal of the firman for another year has also been obtained from the Porte. The admiral commanding-in-chief in the Mediterranean has also been instructed either to order the *Supply* to return here from Malta or to send her to England and let another vessel come here in her place. The expedition will consequently go on for at least another year.

While Mr Newton is at Geronda I shall remain to carry on the excavations here. . . .

H.M.S. *Osprey*, with Mr Campbell, the consul of Rhodes, on board, is now cruising in these waters after pirates. She called here last Sunday.

The excavations at the lion tomb are now finished. The interior is a circular chamber some 18 or 20 feet in diameter with eleven niches in the wall, besides the entrance. They all radiate from the centre. This chamber was filled with earth and large stones, doubtless those of the pyramid which had fallen in. No inscription was found.

We are now digging in the Temenos of Demeter, where formerly we found some very fine pieces of sculpture. Lately, however, nothing has been discovered.

During the winter of 1858-59 Murdoch Smith was at home on leave, the work at Cnidus being continued under the personal direction of Mr Newton. He returned to the scene of operations in March 1859.

To Sir John Burgoyne.

Ruins of Cnidus, *March* 23, 1859.

... At Marseilles I took a passage direct for Smyrna, but on my arrival at Malta, where the steamer only remained three hours, I thought it barely possible that the admiral might be sending up a vessel to Cnidus. I accordingly went to his office, where I was fortunate enough to find his secretary. He told me that no ship was going from Malta, but that the admiral was just going to order the *Coquette* to go from Athens to provision our party. I hurried back to the French steamer, and there found that if I went to Messina I should meet the direct steamer from Marseilles to the Piræus and Constantinople. Two days afterwards I accordingly went to Messina. Having three days to wait for the other steamer, I had time enough to see that part of Sicily. After a very stormy passage I reached the Piræus on Saturday morning the 12th.

Not finding the *Coquette* in the harbour, I called on the consul, by whom I was told that she had gone on a short cruise but was expected back every day. She arrived on the Monday, but did not leave for Cnidus till Thursday. Meantime I remained at Athens, where the many great remains of antiquity were doubly interesting to me, after being so long engaged in searching for similar remains here. Besides examining the city of Athens itself, I had time for making short excursions in the neighbourhood. I ascended Mount Pentelicus, from the summit of which the valleys of Athens and Marathon, and in fact the whole of Attica, seemed spread out as on a map. Before leaving Athens I called on Sir Thomas Wyse, the English Minister, to give him an account of our operations here, as he has always taken the greatest interest in this and similar expeditions. I was also present at a Court ball given on the anniversary of the Queen's arrival in Greece. On being presented to the King and Queen, their Majesties both spoke to me about our works here. They were aware of our discovery of the Mausoleum, and also of the lion at Cnidus. All excavations and removals of sculpture by foreigners are, I know, looked on with a very jealous eye by the Greeks both of Greece and Turkey.

Leaving Athens early on the Thursday morning, we anchored the same night off Antiparos, where we remained over the following day to see the celebrated grotto. The mouth is near the top of a rocky hill, and the grotto itself slopes rapidly downwards for a distance of upwards of 400 feet. The descent was rather difficult, being effected by making a line fast to an alabaster column at the entrance and going down by it hand over hand. The difficulties were not lessened by our having to carry lights. The effect produced by the burning of the blue-lights we had with us was certainly very fine. The whole grotto is of alabaster. Some of the stalactites are of enormous size, hanging like huge columns from the roof. We got up to the entrance without accident, although our hands were in rather a lacerated state, the effect of the small hard lead-line we made use of in climbing. Travellers going to visit the grotto ought above all things to provide themselves with a light rope ladder or two for getting over the more perpendicular parts of the ascent.

The following day, Saturday, we reached Cnidus. Captain Foley did not anchor, as a southerly gale was springing up. Having landed me he went on to Kos, and returned three days afterwards when the storm was over.

I found Mr Newton well and Corporal Jenkins just recovering from a very severe attack of fever. I am glad to say he was soon quite well again.

During the past winter the excavations have been carried on chiefly at the Temple of the Muses, the Gymnasium, and some of the principal tombs in the cemetery, besides finishing the Temenos of Demeter and Persephone. Nothing important, however, in the way of sculpture has been found. Mr Newton and I have been exploring the country in the neighbourhood more minutely than had formerly been done. We have lately traced an ancient road for a distance of more than three miles from the city gates.

Mr Newton has just received a letter from Mr Hammond ordering him not to exceed the last grant of £2000, and that the expenses incurred in England are to be paid out of it. These, with what has been spent here during the last six months, finish the grant. The workmen were consequently paid off yesterday, and we shall now commence packing up stores, &c., and making preparations for departure. We must wait for the arrival of a ship of war, however, and also for positive orders to leave from the Foreign Office. Mr Newton writes by this opportunity to the Foreign Office, requesting them to communicate with him by telegraph through the Embassy at Constantinople. The probability is that we will leave about the end of April.

Enclosed I send an official letter regarding the services rendered to the expedition by Corporal Jenkins. . . . It is a matter of great satisfaction to me, and I am sure is so to you, that the reputation of the sappers has been throughout so effectually upheld by Corporal Jenkins in this expedition. . . .

The official letter may be given here, not only to indicate some of the difficulties which had beset the work of the expedition, but to record the service rendered by a first-rate non-commissioned officer, of whom Murdoch Smith always spoke in terms of the highest regard.

To Sir John Burgoyne.

RUINS OF CNIDUS, *March* 23, 1859.

SIR,—I have the honour to forward to you a letter from Mr Newton addressed to me regarding his opinion of the services rendered to the expedition by Corporal William Jenkins of the Royal Engineers. I am glad to be able to say that I quite coincide with them in every respect.

The work he has been engaged in has often been of such a nature as to require the greatest care and skill. He has frequently been required to excavate and remove massive objects of sculpture of great value. A glance at the sculptures themselves in the British Museum will show how successfully these operations have in every instance been performed. I may mention in particular the statues of Mausolus and Artemisia from the Mausoleum and the colossal lion from Cnidus. The statues were lying among and buried under large blocks of marble, formerly steps of the pyramid of the Mausoleum, and specimens of which are also in the Museum. The difficulty of extricating such delicate objects as these statues from such a mass, without injuring them in the slightest degree, was of course very great. The removal of the lion I described in a former letter.

But the merit of Corporal Jenkins will be more evident when you consider the means he had at his disposal. The operations have almost all been done by a body of Turkish workmen altogether of his own training. Until our arrival these men had probably never even seen, still less made use of, the simplest mechanical contrivances. In a very short time, however, Corporal Jenkins organised them into a most efficient body of workmen, more nearly resembling a company of well-trained sappers and miners than I could have thought possible. His discipline over them was complete, and they had perfect confidence in his upright dealing with them. Besides excavating and removing marbles, these men were employed in mining, erecting scaffolding, and blasting, and hardly a single accident of any consequence has ever occurred. The number of men amounted sometimes to 150.

I may also mention that not only by the workmen but by the Turkish population in general Corporal Jenkins was looked up to with the greatest respect. And in dealing with Turks I need not inform you that personal consideration is of the first importance.

I have therefore the greatest pleasure in complying with Mr Newton's request by bringing Corporal Jenkins's name under your favourable notice, and I shall be very glad to hear that you consider his merit worthy of promotion, or any other reward you may think proper to bestow on him.—I have, &c. R. M. SMITH, Lt. R.E.,
Commg. Det. of R.E. in Asia Minor.

Gen. Sir J. F. BURGOYNE, &c., &c.,
　Inspector-General of Fortifications.

CNIDUS, *May* 11, 1859.

. . . Last night a courier arrived from Smyrna with a telegraphic despatch to Mr Newton from the Foreign Office, ordering him to prepare to leave on the arrival of the *Supply*. We have all the antiquities and stores packed and ready for embarkation. As Mr Newton was previously informed that the *Supply* was to leave England about the 1st of April, we expect her here every day. The embarkation will not occupy more than five or six days, so that we will most probably leave for England within the next fortnight.

While the packing was going on Mr Newton and I have been exploring the country in the neighbourhood of Cnidus. Last week we discovered a very interesting bridge across a ravine. The span is made by means of a *horizontal* arch. This arch, if you remember, I suggested as having probably been used in the support of the pyramid of the Mausoleum. We had not time to examine the bridge thoroughly when we were there, but we are going to-morrow to do so. As it is perhaps the only Greek bridge in existence its discovery is rather an important one.

Last week, on the 3rd, we were visited by H.R.H. Prince Alfred in the *Euryalus*. The Prince, Major Cowell, and Captain Tarleton went over our excavations with Mr Newton and myself, and also went up to the Acropolis of the city. As it is about 1000 feet above the sea, and very rugged, the ascent in this season is not a very easy task. Before leaving Cnidus the Prince asked me to accompany them to Budrum, as they were going there to see the site of the Mausoleum. As Mr Newton had previously accepted Captain Tarleton's invitation to go, I was obliged to decline, as it would have been unsafe for both of us to be away for two nights together.

Captain Tarleton, however, very kindly relieved me of this difficulty by sending a marine officer on shore to take charge during my absence. We crossed over to Budrum the same afternoon, and the following day the Prince went ashore and visited the Mausoleum, the castle, our old quarters at the *konak*, &c. The Turks were extremely delighted with the visit, and especially with the Prince's partaking of their hospitality in the usual form of coffee and sherbet. I afterwards presented the captain of the castle in the Prince's name with a very handsome field-telescope, and the Mudir or civil governor of the town received a beautiful opera-glass by the hands of Mr Newton. The next morning we left Budrum and returned to Cnidus by Kos. The Prince having hurt his foot while bathing did not go on shore at Kos. Captain Tarleton and Major Cowell, however, called on the different authorities, and Major Cowell presented the Kaimakam with a silver revolver from the Prince. The Turks of all classes, both at Budrum and Kos, seemed to feel highly honoured by the Prince's visit, and to look on it as a reward for their civility to us throughout the expedition. The authorities who received presents from the Prince have been always particularly obliging. After landing Mr Newton and myself here the ship went on to Crete *en route* to Malta.

A few days later the *Supply* arrived and conveyed the explorers to Malta.

CHAPTER V.

THE CYRENE EXPEDITION.

GARRISON DUTY AT MALTA—DUMARESQ'S MONKEY—MURDOCH SMITH PROPOSES THE CYRENE EXPEDITION — LETTER FROM SIR JOHN BURGOYNE—START OF THE EXPEDITION—LANDING AT BENGHAZI—SUPPOSED BLOODTHIRSTY INTENTIONS — DESPATCH TO LORD JOHN RUSSELL — JOURNEY UP COUNTRY — COMMENCEMENT OF WORK AT CYRENE — TEMPLE OF DIONYSOS — RELATIONS WITH THE ARABS— MOHAMMED EL ADOULY—TEMPLE OF APOLLO—FINDS OF SCULPTURE —VISIT OF H.M.S. ASSURANCE — A NARROW ESCAPE — AMATEUR SORCERY — EXPLORATION OF THE CYRENAICA — A SCOTCH TURK— TEUCHIRA AND PTOLEMAIS—A SERIOUS DISTURBANCE—ATTACK ON THE CASTLE AT GHEGHEB — A FEAT OF ENDURANCE — UNRULY NEGROES—AN AWKWARD INCIDENT—EXCAVATION OF THE AUGUSTEUM — IMPERIAL PORTRAITS — FEVER — ARRIVAL OF H.M.S. MELPOMENE — TROUBLE WITH THE ARABS — A BLACKMAILER — FRIENDS IN NEED—EMBARKATION OF THE STATUES—SUCCESS OF THE EXPEDITION.

FROM June 1859 to November 1860 Murdoch Smith was employed on garrison duty at Malta, being attached to the 17th company of the Royal Engineers, commanded by Captain W. H. H. D. Dumaresq.

An interesting duty fell to his lot during this period. Early in 1860 a man-of-war was sent to Leghorn to salute the Sardinian flag. Murdoch Smith was sent on board her, and he had an opportunity of seeing Rome and Naples for the first time. At Malta, as at Chatham, the chief occupation of his spare time was boating, and he made many adventurous excursions round the island. He continued to cultivate assiduously his taste for music, and he occasionally played second violin at the opera.

Among his Malta reminiscences he used often to recall the doings of a well-known member of the R.E. establishment there in those days, Dumaresq's monkey, an animal of whose resourceful iniquities many stories were told. One of the weirdest of these describes how the monkey, having got hold of an unfortunate long-haired terrier, a special enemy of his, carried him up to the roof of the barracks, and then sitting down on the edge of the roof, where everybody could see him but nobody could get at him, deliberately proceeded to pull the terrier's hair out in handfuls. When the wretched victim had been plucked like a chicken, the monkey dropped him into the barrack square. Murdoch Smith himself was on one occasion the object of this brute's impish revenge. One evening the monkey was fooling about his feet and Murdoch Smith indiscreetly gave him a kick. Next moment the monkey had jumped on to his shoulder and had torn a strip out of his mess jacket from collar to waist, thus effectively ruining that somewhat expensive garment.

Murdoch Smith continued to correspond with Sir John Burgoyne. When, in September 1859, news came of the outbreak of the Chinese war, he at once wrote to Sir John asking to be sent to China, and suggesting that the company to which he was attached might be sent. The General replied that all the troops required for China were to be sent from India, otherwise his request would have been granted.

Disappointed in obtaining employment on active service, he turned his thoughts towards further archæological work, and it occurred to him that a rich and hitherto almost untouched field for exploration lay ready to hand at Cyrene. That city had for many centuries been the capital of a flourishing Greek colony, afterwards the Roman province of the Cyrenaica, and there was every reason to believe that interesting and valuable remains would be found on its site. Since the Arab conquest there had been no settled population in the Cyrenaica, which favoured the hope that such remains would be found in a comparatively perfect condition. In many places the great obstacle to the recovery of objects of classic art by means of excavation is the occupation of ancient sites by modern buildings. This is conspicuously the case at Athens and Rome themselves, and, as we have seen, this difficulty had seriously impeded the operations of the expedition to Halicarnassus. In the case of Cyrene, however, no such difficulty existed, as it was almost certain that the site of the city had been unoccupied for more than a thousand years.

On the other hand, there were circumstances peculiar to the position of Cyrene, and to the condition of the country, which made it very doubtful whether excavations could be carried on with much prospect of success. From its inland position in a mountainous country it was to be feared that heavy and fragile objects, such as marble statues, could not be conveyed to the coast for embarkation except at great cost of time, labour, and money. Another serious consideration was the character of the inhabitants, fanatical Bedouins, proverbial for their rapacity and violence. Further, Cyrene could only be reached by a long land journey from Benghazi or Derna, the only places on the coast at which the caravan required for such a journey could be procured, and also the only places where the authority of the Turkish Government was more than a name.

It appeared to Murdoch Smith that it would be worth while to make at all events a reconnoitring excursion to the Cyrenaica, and that this could be done with no great difficulty, the only absolute necessaries for its accomplishment being the use of a small vessel for two or three months, the sanction of the Foreign Office, and leave of absence from military duty. In the spring of 1860 there was a small sailing schooner lying in Malta harbour called the *Kertch*, which he thought would answer the purpose admirably. A few men from H.M.S. *Hibernia*, to which the *Kertch* was a tender, would be a large enough crew, and being a sailing vessel she would cost nothing in fuel. He talked over the project with his friend Lieutenant E. A. Porcher, R.N., then of the *Hibernia*, who expressed his willingness to join in the undertaking.

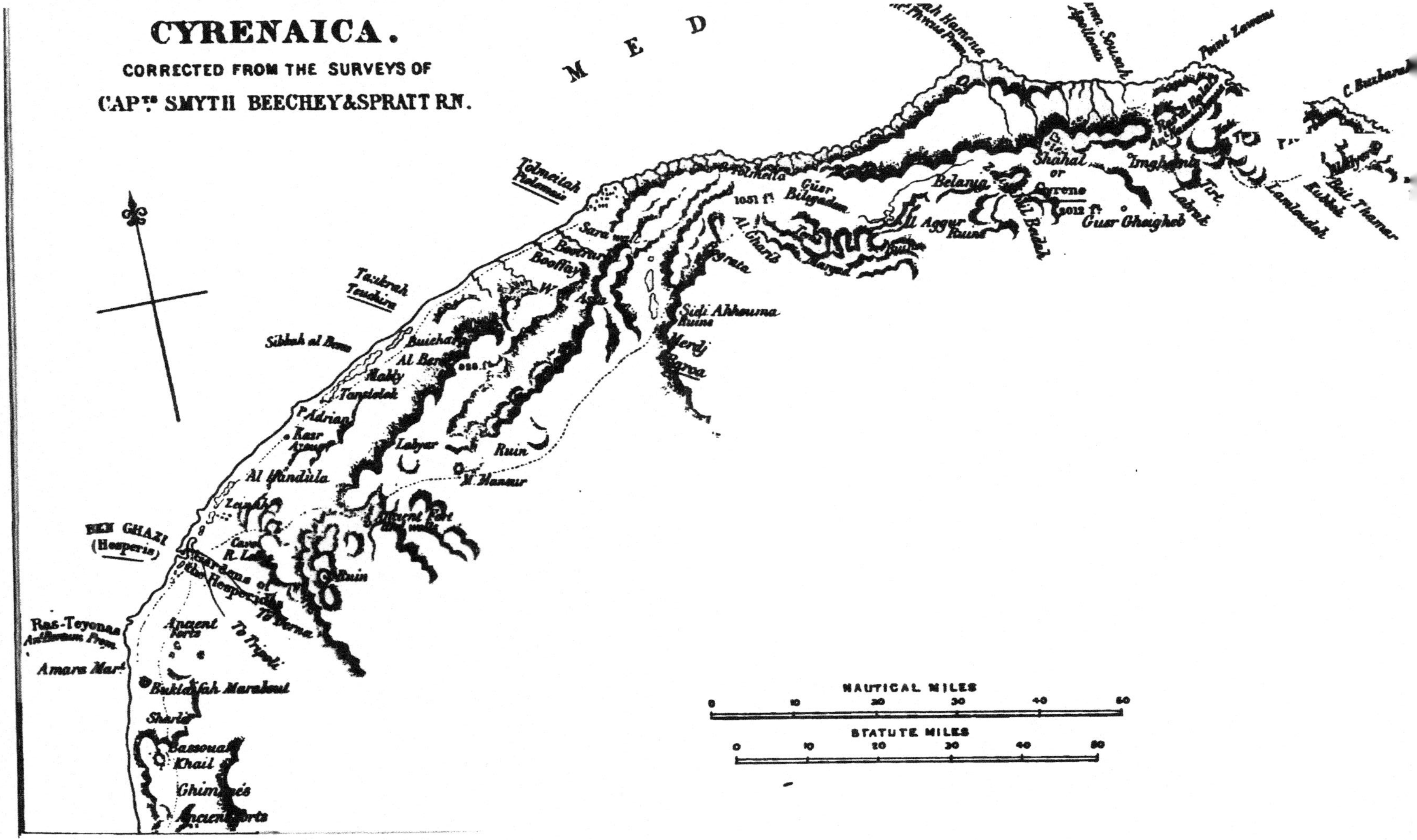
CYRENAICA.
CORRECTED FROM THE SURVEYS OF
CAPT^s. SMYTH BEECHEY & SPRATT R.N.
M E D
Tolmeitah
Ptolemais
Taukrah
Teuchira
Sibkah al Bom
BEN GHAZI
(Hesperis)
Ras-Teyonas
Amara Mar.
Buichar
Al Bern
Tansiolah
P. Adrian
Kasr
Al Yandula
Zeinab
R. Lathon
Gardens of the Hesperides
To Derna
To Tripoli
Ancient Forts
Bukla fah Marabout
Sharia
Bassouah
Khail
Ghiminés
Ancient Forts
Labyar
Ruin
W. Hansur
Ancient Fort
Ruin
Sara
Booffay
Aslan
Al Gharib
Sidi Ahhouma
Ruins
Merj
Barca
1051 ft.
Guar Bilgadem
Belanja
Shahal
or
Cyrene
2012 ft.
Guar Gheigheb
Imghernis
Tirt
Labrak
Lamloudah
Kubbah
Beit Thamar
C. Bushaeb
Point Zarrans
Marsah Sousah
Apollonia
Marsah Hamena
NAUTICAL MILES
0 10 20 30 40 50
STATUTE MILES
0 10 20 30 40 50

Their proposal was to visit the Cyrenaica at their own expense, for the purpose of examining the country with a view to a subsequent working expedition, provided the Foreign Office sanctioned the proceeding, and the Admiralty allowed the *Kertch* to be placed for a short time at their disposal. They thought it desirable to have some such vessel not only to take them to the coast of Barbary, but to remain there while they made their journeys inland. She would thereby serve as a base of operations, and would be of special use in the not unlikely event of their being obliged by the hostility of the Arabs to beat a hasty retreat. This proposal was submitted to Sir John Burgoyne and to Mr C. T. Newton, who gave it their cordial support. On their joint recommendation, Lord John Russell, then Foreign Secretary, sanctioned the project, and on July 16 Sir John Burgoyne wrote to Murdoch Smith as follows:—

WAR OFFICE, PALL MALL, 16*th July* 1860.

MY DEAR MR SMITH,—After much trouble and delay, the various authorities sanction your proposed excursion in Africa. I hope it is not too late in the season.

I have directed copies of my letter to the Foreign Office and the answer to be sent to you.

You will perceive the Admiralty cannot detach the *Kertch*, but propose some other arrangement.

In some note from the higher Powers it was

repeated that you were not on any account to make excavations or remove objects without full and distinct authority.—Yours faithfully,

J. F. BURGOYNE.

The Foreign Office will send out to you a photographic apparatus.

The travellers were furnished with letters of recommendation to her Majesty's agents in Barbary, and with a firman in their favour, which had been obtained from the Turkish Government. It was stated by the Admiralty that the *Kertch* was not available, being urgently required for other services, but that orders would be given to provide the explorers with a passage to the coast of the Cyrenaica. At the same time indefinite leave of absence was granted to both officers.

The want of a vessel like the *Kertch* to remain with them during the excursion caused a considerable modification of their plans. Instead of having their supplies and the means of retreat more or less at their own disposal, they were obliged by the new arrangement simply to take their chance among the Arabs, and get on in the best way they could, the expense, at the same time, being greatly increased. They were thankful, however, for what they had got, and began at once to make the necessary preparations for the expedition.

Their original intention had been to start in July, and to return to Malta before the winter.

Considerable delay, however, took place before a vessel could be had, and it was already winter before everything was ready for departure. They left Malta for Tripoli in H.M. gunboat *Boxer* on November 19, 1860.

The proceedings of the expedition and the results of its work have been described in detail in a fine folio volume, *History of the Recent Discoveries at Cyrene*, prepared by the explorers after their return to England, at the request of the Trustees of the British Museum, and published by Messrs Day & Son in 1864. The text was written by Murdoch Smith, and the book is lavishly illustrated from drawings by Porcher, and from photographs. It was brought out under Porcher's superintendence after Murdoch Smith's departure for Persia.

After a stormy passage the *Boxer* reached Tripoli on the evening of November 21. Benghazi was reached on the 30th. With the help of Mr Frederick Crowe, British vice-consul at Benghazi, the caravan necessary for the journey to Cyrene was got together, and by the 12th of December was ready to start. Cyrene was safely reached on December 23.

The object of the expedition was a great puzzle to the natives. At Benghazi the explorers wished to engage a few labourers for excavation work. Mr Crowe got them four negroes, whose liberation from slavery he had obtained from the Kaimakam. Three of them, having just been brought from the interior, could hardly speak a word of Arabic. They seemed very glad to join the party, and all went well until the caravan reached Merdj, about half-way to Cyrene, where their employers were told one morning, to their astonishment, that they had enlisted as soldiers. The Mudir of Merdj ordered them to be brought before him, but the only explanation that he could get from them was that they preferred becoming soldiers to being killed. They appeared to be highly indignant about something, and determined not to go on. No further explanation could be elicited. It afterwards came out that some of the black soldiers had assured them that Murdoch Smith and Porcher were taking them into the desert to cut their throats and look for treasure with their blood! The Mudir with great difficulty induced them to remain with the caravan, and it was some days before they were quite convinced that no harm was intended to them.

The explorers' journey up country and their operations during the first two months after their arrival at Cyrene are described by Murdoch Smith in a despatch to Lord John Russell.

AIN SHAHAT (CYRENE),
BARBARY, <i>February</i> 23, 1861.

My Lord,—In accordance with your Lordship's desire expressed in Lord Wodehouse's despatch of July 19, I take this opportunity of a courier's going to Benghazi to give your Lordship a short account of our proceedings up till the present time in the Cyrenaica.

Lieutenant Porcher, R.N., and myself left Malta

in H.M.'s gunboat *Boxer* on the 19th November last. As the vizieral letter which your Lordship was kind enough to obtain from the Porte was addressed to the Pasha of Tripoli, we went there in the first place to get the necessary orders from his Excellency to his subordinate the Kaimakam of Benghazi. Col. Herman, her Majesty's consul-general, had, however, already presented the firman and sent the Pasha's orders to Benghazi.

We left Tripoli on the 25th, and, proceeding under sail, reached Benghazi on the 30th. My original intention was to have gone to Derna and landed there after calling at Benghazi. Mr Crowe, her Majesty's vice-consul, advised us, however, to land at Benghazi and make it our starting-point, inasmuch as we should find considerable difficulty in procuring camels, horses, &c., at Derna in the absence of the English vice-consul, who, it seems, is nearly the only European there. Besides this there was the danger of taking a vessel to such an exposed anchorage in winter.

We accordingly landed at Benghazi, and the *Boxer* left for Malta the following day. We were detained twelve days getting horses and camels, during which time we were the guests of Mr Crowe, whose kind hospitality made our detention very pleasant.

Having procured the means of conveyance for ourselves, servants, and baggage, the next subject of consideration was that of escort. By order of the Pasha of Tripoli the Kaimakam was obliged to provide for our safety by furnishing us with a proper guard. Mr Crowe, however, advised us not to take soldiers with us, because their presence would only provoke the hostility of the Bedouins without being of any service in case of a real attack. He recommended us, on the contrary, to go as independently of the Turkish authorities as possible, and to rely rather on the protection afforded by the English name. Before we started he sent for a number of the principal sheikhs who happened to be at Benghazi at the time. When they came to the consulate he introduced us and told them the object of our visit, adding that he entrusted our safety to them. In reply they stated that they were glad of the opportunity of being of any service to the English consul, as he had always been their friend, and had often protected them from the unjust exactions and acts of oppression of the Turkish pashas. They gave us letters to the sheikhs of the tribes whose districts we should pass through, and also sent a man to remain with us at Cyrene for the purpose of getting everything we required which the country afforded.[1]

Everything being at last ready we left Benghazi on the 12th December, our small caravan consisting altogether of seventeen men, seven horses, and ten camels. We were accompanied by Mr G. Cesareo, the *cancelliere* of the consulate, who has remained with us ever since. From his knowledge of the language and the people his presence has been of the greatest service to us.

As the firman gave us authority to excavate and

[1] This man, Amor Bon Abdi Seyat, remained with the explorers till the end of the expedition, and was of the greatest service.

remove antiquities, we got four blacks at Benghazi and brought them with us to be employed digging. A few days ago we got a fifth. I brought a few tools from Malta, which, with the tents, his Excellency the Governor was kind enough to allow me to draw from the military stores.

The journey from Benghazi occupied twelve days, but we could not proceed very rapidly on account of the rain, which made the ground slippery for the soft feet of the camels.

The country is remarkably fine the whole way, and the scenery generally of a very pleasing description. It not infrequently resembles an extensive park in England. The population must be very small in proportion to the extent of country, as we did not see more than three or four Bedouin encampments the whole way, which, by the somewhat circuitous route we followed, could not be less than 180 miles. Almost all the soil seems well adapted for cultivation, although only a very small portion is ploughed by the Arabs. When there is the usual amount of rain in winter this portion yields a plentiful harvest of corn. No means whatever are used by the Arabs for storing the winter rains. In summer they are consequently obliged to drive their flocks long distances to obtain water, and many extensive and beautiful plains are then absolutely deserted. After a dry winter the Arabs are reduced almost to starvation by the failure of the crops and the death of the cattle, which form their sole property.

About half way from Benghazi we halted for two days at Merdj, one of the two Turkish military posts in the Cyrenaica. The other, Ghegheb, is about four hours' distance from Cyrene. At these two places there are small castles with garrisons of about 100 men each. They are the residences of the Mudirs, whose only duty seems to be to extort as much money as possible from the Arabs —first for themselves, secondly for the Kaimakam, and lastly for the *hasneh* or public chest. The Mudirs of Merdj and Ghegheb are always Arabs. They are changed very frequently, as the sale of the office is a profitable source of revenue to the Kaimakams.

At Merdj, the site of the ancient Barca, we were received most hospitably by the Mudir, Hadji Achmet Bin 'l Agha. Besides supplying all our wants during our stay, he gave us as much barley for the horses and camels as we could carry, besides a sheep, dates, figs, bread, &c., for ourselves.

We reached Cyrene on the 23rd December in the midst of a storm of wind and rain, from which we sought shelter in some tombs near the Fountain of Apollo. Finding them very convenient from their vicinity to the fountain, we fixed our residence in them.

Cyrene stands on the northern or seaward edge of an extensive plateau whose elevation is about 2000 feet above the level of the sea. The ground descends abruptly to another plateau about 1000 feet below. The latter extends nearly to the sea, where there is a rapid descent similar to the upper one. The face of the upper slope presents a succession of rounded hills separated by deep ravines or *wadys*, as they are termed by the Arabs. The city of Cyrene occupies two of those hills, so that it is naturally defended on three sides by steep declivities, and is divided by the wady into two nearly equal portions. Most of the buildings, however, are on the western one.

The principal cemeteries are on the face of the slope overlooking the lower plateau east and west of the city itself. All round the city, however, in a southern direction there are innumerable tombs.

From the position thus occupied by the city your Lordship will be able to imagine the magnificence of the view which it commands. There is an unbroken prospect east and west of a plateau beautifully diversified by woods and wadys as far as the eye can reach, while to the north the sea itself is seen beyond at a distance of seven or eight miles.

Having only four men, we thought the cemeteries would afford the best field for excavation, as the objects to be found there would probably be more portable than those in the city itself. We accordingly commenced work in the western cemetery. A short experience, however, convinced us that very little was to be found among the tombs. Being for the most part excavated in the rock, they could be easily rifled by the successive inhabitants of the country. One tomb in particular showed me how little was to be expected from further excavation. The door was buried four or five feet underground, and when I entered I found the tomb almost filled with long thin stalactites reaching nearly to the floor. I had, in fact, to break them off to get in at all. I found, nevertheless, that the tomb had been entered and completely robbed of its contents. The depth of the door below the surface and the great length of the stalactites, which must have formed since the tomb was entered, would seem to show that it had been pillaged very many years ago, probably in the time of the early Christians under the Byzantine Empire.

We accordingly gave up the cemeteries at the end of a fortnight and turned our attention to the remains of buildings within the walls. We chose a prominent site near the centre of the city, which seemed to be a small temple with a large *peribolus* enclosed with a wall and portico. We began digging all round the walls of the temple, which we found had no peristyle. The front has a *pronaos* with four columns, the outer ones of which were engaged in the lateral walls. It seemed to have been originally of the Doric order, but restored in later times in Corinthian. Its size was only 47 by 26 feet, while the colonnade of the portico enclosing the *peribolus* was nearly 300 by 200 feet. The colonnade could be easily traced on three sides, consisting altogether of 87 columns—viz., 33 on each side and 23 in the end. I could not make out exactly how the opposite end, which was the front, had been arranged. A gateway and part of the *peribolus* wall on the S.W. side is still standing nearly perfect. The rest is a heap of ruins, while the position of the temple itself was only shown by a swelling of the ground in the middle.

After clearing out the space outside the temple we commenced digging inside the *cella*, and were

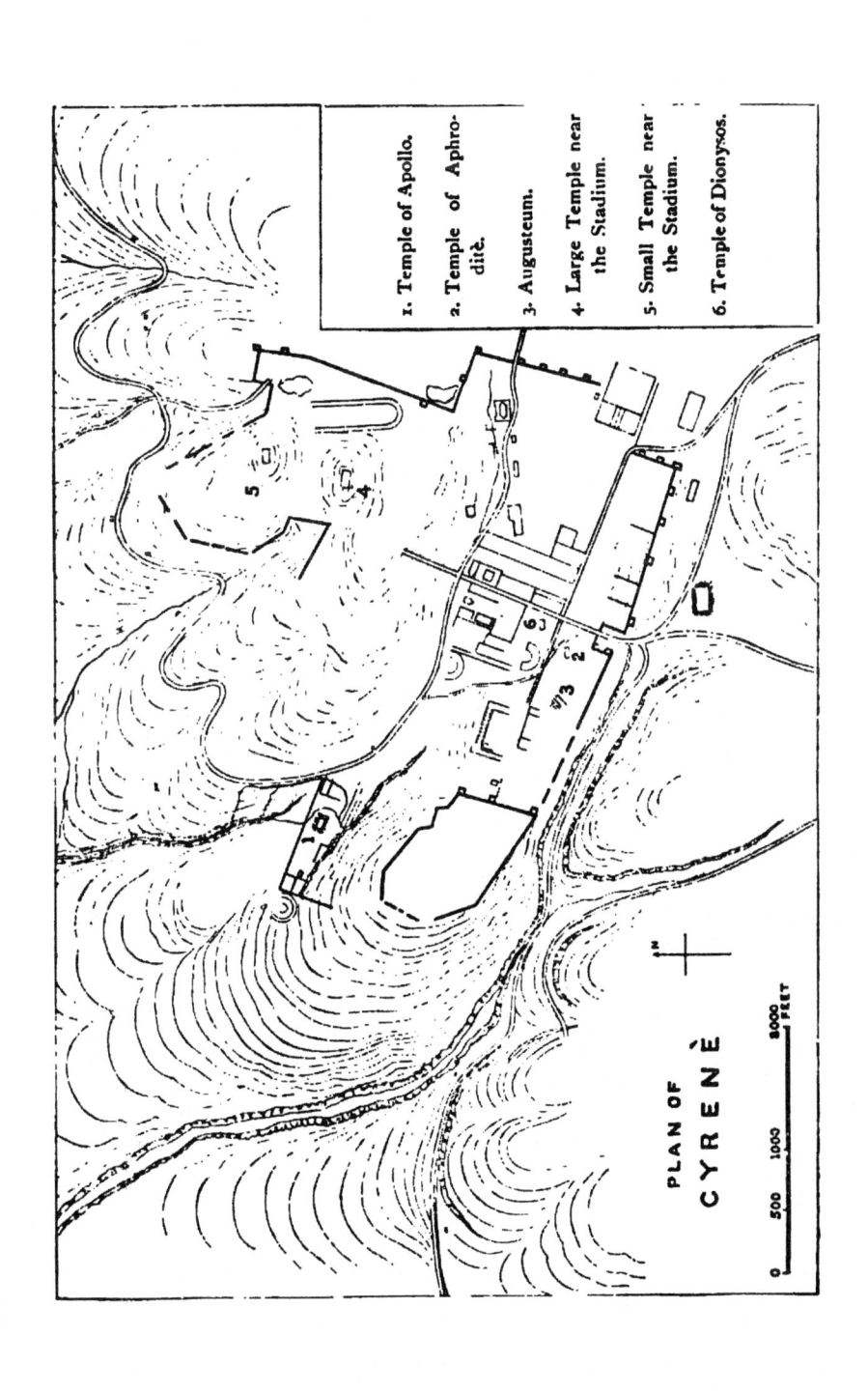

1. Temple of Apollo.
2. Temple of Aphrodite.
3. Augusteum.
4. Large Temple near the Stadium.
5. Small Temple near the Stadium.
6. Temple of Dionysos.

PLAN OF CYRENÈ

soon rewarded by finding a beautiful statue of Bacchus [Dionysos], which of course identified the whole building. It was about four or five feet underground, lying on the floor, which was paved with thin marble slabs. The whole of the interior, besides, bore evidence of having been veneered with marble.

The statue is as nearly as possible life-size. As found it was perfect, with the exception of the head, the right forearm, and the left hand. The head and left hand, however, we discovered afterwards. The whole statue, the head included, is in an excellent state of preservation, and the head and hand can be replaced without leaving any very perceptible trace of the fracture. The style, in my opinion, is very good. . . . The lower part of the statue is quite perfect. The drapery over the feet, as also on the rest of the body, is exceedingly graceful. It is all much undercut and highly finished.

We had considerable difficulty in removing it without injury to our tomb, owing to the total want of any means for raising and transporting weights. While making preparations we had a tent pitched close to it, in which the blacks lived, to protect it from the Arabs, whose fanaticism leads them to destroy every statue and inscription they see. We then made a sort of sledge of the trunk and lower branches of a tree. On this we got the statue placed by means of poles used as levers with slings attached. After packing and lashing it securely to the sledge, a camel was yoked in, which, with our assistance, got it down in safety.

It is now in our tomb covered with a tent and walled up.

After finishing the temple we made some excavations immediately above one of the theatres on the side of the street which leads up the central valley of the city. Here we found a number of marble bases of columns *in situ*. As the ground was ploughed and sown we were prevented following out the line and getting a plan of the building. In the course of the excavation we uncovered two draped statues about life-size. They were without heads, and one of them was broken off below the knee. Otherwise they were in a pretty good state of preservation. From the appearance of the marble I imagine that they were originally placed in the open air in the spaces between the columns. They are of later style than the Bacchus, and seem to belong rather to the Roman than the Greek period. They are not destitute of merit, however, and would repay, in my opinion, the trouble of removal. To protect them from injury we reburied them where they were found.

For the last two or three weeks we have employed the blacks at the ruins of a temple near the Fountain of Apollo. It is the one mentioned by Captain Beechey as the Temple of Diana, but from the inscriptions which we found on the site I am rather inclined to call it the Temple of Apollo. It stands in the middle of the platform in front of the fountain, in one of the finest positions in the city.

The fountain issues into the middle ravine from a channel about a quarter of a mile long cut into the heart of the western hill of the city. Below the fountain this ravine is bridged across by a lofty and massive retaining wall, still standing as the revetment of the platform thus formed. The water of the fountain, after traversing the platform, falls over the wall and finds its way down the wady to the plains below.

The Temple of Apollo stands on this platform, about half way between the fountain and this wall. It is of the prevailing order of architecture—viz., Doric. It is of considerable size, the columns being 4' 2" in diameter. . . .

Two days ago, while digging inside the walls of the *cella*, we found a small female draped statue in marble. [Photograph referred to.] It is about 3' 6" high. The surface is in perfect condition, and as we found it 9 feet below the surface we hope to find the head also. We have not yet reached the pavement at one corner at a depth of 9 or 10 feet, so that there is a probability of our finding some valuable sculpture or inscriptions before finishing the excavation.

The above gives your Lordship a short account of what we have done in the way of excavation and its results hitherto. Our means being limited to five men, a crowbar, and half-a-dozen pickaxes and shovels, we could not undertake anything of a more extensive nature.

As we are convinced that the statues, particularly the one of Bacchus, would form a very valuable addition to the department of antiquities of the British Museum, we have the honour to place them at the disposal of her Majesty's Government, and to request your Lordship to consider the propriety of furnishing us in summer with the means of removing them. The means I would suggest as best adapted to the purpose I have detailed to your Lordship in a separate despatch, No. 2.

With reference to the question of transport, Lieut. Porcher and myself went lately to Marsa Sousah, the ancient Apollonia, for the purpose of examining the road and the anchorage. There is no harbour for a vessel in winter, but in summer a steamer might remain with safety long enough to embark everything. The road, for the greater part of the way, is along the track of the ancient one. Although by no means good, and in some places, as in the descent of the lower plateau, difficult, there is no insuperable obstacle. Such a carriage as an artillery drag could with a little trouble be taken over any part of it. The distance is four hours, about fourteen miles.

Before removal the statues would require to be packed in strong cases, for which service a ship's carpenter supplied with the proper material would be sufficient.

Since our arrival Lieut. Porcher has made a large number of drawings of the different objects of interest here, particularly the tombs. I have also made plans of some of the more characteristic of them, so that we hope before leaving to be able to furnish such detail as will give a pretty accurate idea of this remarkable necropolis.

Our operations have been somewhat delayed during the two months we have been here by the uncertainty, and sometimes by the severity, of the weather. We intend commencing now a series of tours in the surrounding country.

Ten days ago we went to a place the Arabs told us of, called by them Imghernis. It contains a number of buildings still standing to a considerable height, besides tombs and cisterns cut in the rock. Not having any books of reference, I cannot identify the place, but I will shortly return to make a plan and take a few photographs of the ruins. Next week we propose going to Derna, visiting any remarkable places there may be on the road.

Our intercourse with the Arabs has generally been of the most friendly nature. We have had only one serious question with them, when one man threw stones at us and another threatened to shoot us. After a month's delay of the Mudir, the two men were at last apprehended by order of the Kaimakam and sent to Benghazi. This morning, however, I heard that the Mudir, having received 200 dollars for the purpose, allowed them to escape. The result, I have little doubt, will now be his own deprivation of office.

The Arabs are not controlled in any way by the Turkish Government except in the matter of the taxes, which are levied by the Pashas and Mudirs through their own sheikhs. They are almost always in a state of war among themselves. Murder is thought no crime, and is not taken notice of in any way by the Government. If a man of one tribe kills a man of another, the friend of the deceased shoots, not the murderer, but the first man of his tribe whom he sees. This is considered a point of honour by them. The men, even when ploughing, always go armed with one or two pistols, a knife, and a long gun, which is generally fitted with a bayonet. This is the case throughout the country, although the importation and sale of gunpowder are strictly prohibited. . . . I have the honour, &c.,

R. M. SMITH, Lieut. R.E.

This despatch was accompanied by a series of photographs, and by a second despatch detailing the stores required for the removal of the statues, and suggesting that a vessel should be sent for that purpose to Marsa Sousah about the month of May, when the summer weather had fairly commenced.

One of the letters given to the explorers by the sheikhs whom Mr Crowe had assembled at the consulate at Benghazi was addressed to a certain Mohammed El Adouly, an Arab of considerable influence in the Cyrenaica. He was a native of Benghazi, but having married the daughter of one of the sheikhs of the Haasa tribe, who occupied the country in the neighbourhood of Cyrene, he kept his flocks and spent the greater part of the year in that district. The day after the explorers arrived at Cyrene he paid them a long visit, bringing with him the welcome present of a camel-load of milk and butter. He proved their constant friend during the whole time of their residence, and on many occasions was of great service to them. Not being entangled in the perpetual feuds of the rival tribes around them, he was equally respected by all, so that they could hardly have had a safer friend. In commencing excavations they were largely indebted to his local knowledge.

The excavation of the Temple of Apollo was commenced on the 31st of January 1861. Although the form of the building could be easily traced, very little of it remained above ground. Operations were begun by clearing out, down to the level of the pavement, the space between the columns and the wall of the *cella* along the western and northern sides, on both of which were found parts of the columns *in situ*, and fragments of the entablature. The space for digging was very limited, all the surrounding ground and even part of the temple itself being covered with crops of grain. The explorers would willingly have bought these up, but found this impossible owing to the religious feeling of the Arabs, who regarded the fruits of the soil as the immediate gift of God, and would have resented their destruction as an act of sacrilege. However, notwithstanding these limitations, the explorers were before long rewarded by making one of their most important discoveries, a colossal statue of Apollo, lying on the floor of the Temple, about 10 feet below the surface of the ground. The head was broken off, and the body was in three pieces, the lyre and other adjuncts being broken into numerous small fragments. As the fractures were clean and sharp and their edges unchipped, it was hoped that the whole figure might afterwards be put together without difficulty. This was done with great success, the small fragments having been carefully collected and preserved. The statue as it now stands, without the slightest restoration, in the British Museum, is built up of no less than 121 separate pieces.

The removal of this statue to the tomb occupied by the explorers was a matter of no small difficulty, and their troubles were increased by the conduct of their negroes, who thought this a favourable opportunity for advancing the most extravagant claims for remuneration. At last they went off and left the explorers to get the Apollo to the tomb without them. This was impossible, and the statue had to be reburied to protect it from the Arabs. Luckily, however, three other negroes, sent by Mr Crowe, arrived from Benghazi about this time, and it became possible to resume work. After several days of very hard work the Apollo was safely housed. The sledge was used as before, and a camel yoked in to help to drag it. The road was rough and all uphill, and as the camel, although an excellent beast of burden, was quite unaccustomed to pulling, he would do nothing when he found he could not walk away with the load easily. He had consequently to be unyoked, and the explorers and their men had to drag the sledge foot by foot themselves.

Among other finds made in the Temple of Apollo were a marble head of Cnæus Cornelius Lentulus Marcellinus, the first Roman proprætor of Cyrene, and a statue of the Emperor Hadrian. The head of the latter was of a separate piece from the body, and could be removed from it at pleasure, being fitted into a socket—an economical expedient for making the statue of a deceased emperor do duty as his living successor's, after the simple change of the head and the name. Later on the same temple yielded one of the most valuable and interesting of all the works of art found by the explorers, a beautiful bronze portrait head, in fine preservation. It is believed to represent some king of Numidia or Mauritania. The eyes have been inlaid in vitreous pastes, portions of which still remain in the sockets. The lips seem to have been covered with a thin plate of silver or some artificial substance, which served to represent their difference of colour. The hair and beard are finished with great care and refinement of treatment. The head is one of the finest ancient iconic bronzes yet discovered. Among smaller finds may be noted a figure of Jupiter Ammon, a group representing the nymph Cyrene strangling a lion, and a Diana.

The new labourers remained until the 20th of April, when they had to leave for harvest work at Benghazi. The explorers then tried some Arabs, but were soon glad to get rid of them, as they gave a great deal of trouble and did very little work. At the end of April it was determined to stop the excavations for the present.

The explorers had in the meantime carefully examined the country between Cyrene and the sea, with a view to ascertaining the best method of transporting the statues to the coast, and of embarking them. The greatest difficulty to be overcome was the descent of the Augubah, the range of steep declivities near the sea, between the Cyrene plateau and the shore. The only practicable pass near Cyrene was on the track of the ancient road to Apollonia, now called Marsa Sousah. It was evident that the transport of the statues over such a road would be a difficult undertaking, still it appeared quite feasible. Lord John Russell had readily granted the means of transport applied for in Murdoch Smith's second despatch of February 23, and at his request a man-of-war with the necessary stores was ordered to proceed to Marsa Sousah. Owing to the want of communication with Europe, Murdoch Smith did not receive Lord John's reply to his despatch until after the actual arrival of the vessel in the month of May. About the same time a letter was received from Mr Panizzi, principal librarian of the British Museum, stating that the Trustees had voted a subsidy of £100 towards the expenses of the expedition.

H.M.S. *Assurance*, Commander C. M. Aynsley, arrived off Marsa Sousah on the 10th of May, and a letter was at once sent up country by an Arab informing the explorers of her arrival. They were delighted with the news, and hurried down to the coast to receive the vessel.

A party of thirty bluejackets and marines was immediately landed and encamped on the beach. The waggons and stores which had been sent were disembarked, and two ship's carpenters sent to Cyrene to make packing-cases for the marbles. Through the good offices of Mohammed El Adouly the camels necessary for transport were obtained, and on May 14 the party started for Cyrene. To get the waggons up the Augubah was a matter of no small difficulty. It was, however, successfully accomplished, and Cyrene was reached on the 24th. Meantime the carpenters had packed the statues, and the loads for the waggons were ready. On one waggon were placed the Bacchus and the largest of the small statues, and on the other the Apollo in three cases. The smaller objects were packed in boxes to be carried by camels. The statue of Hadrian and a few other marbles were for the present left behind.

During the transit to the sea a catastrophe was very narrowly escaped.

"We started from Cyrene," writes Murdoch Smith, "on the morning of the 29th, and, taking only one waggon at a time, reached the plain at the base of the hills the same night. The five following days were spent in crossing the lower plateau to the top of the Augubah, where we arrived on the 3rd of June. The wheels of the waggons were by this time considerably shaken by the heavy jolting over rocks and stones, but still remained unbroken.

"We had now to face our chief difficulty, the descent of the Augubah. After considering every possible way in which it could be done, we decided on lowering the waggons straight down the face of the hill by means of tackle. The least rugged part of the hill being selected, our first care was to provide the means of making fast the lowering tackle, which was done by placing heavy boat's anchors in holes cut for the purpose in the rock. The front axle of the waggon was then lashed to the body of the carriage to prevent the fore-wheels from getting locked against the sides of the waggon, and thereby upsetting it. A tackle, consisting of a $3\frac{1}{2}$-inch rope, rove through two double blocks, was then made fast to the anchors, and to the centre of the fore-axle, and the waggon lowered slowly, hind-wheels foremost. About one-third of the way down there was a nearly level ledge or terrace, forming part of the ancient road to Apollonia, which served as a convenient halting-place from which to make a fresh start. To reach this point, however, the waggons, as they were being lowered, had to be guided in a slanting direction across the face of the hill, which was safely done with the first waggon by means of handspikes. Not content to 'let well alone,' we unfortunately thought to improve upon this simple method in the lowering of the other one. In addition to the anchors already in position, another was placed some distance to the right, and directly above the part of the terrace to which the waggons had to be taken. After the waggon had been lowered to a convenient place, the standing part of the tackle was to be transferred from the first anchor to the second one, thereby causing the waggon, when the lowering was continued, to slant across to the right until it was directly under the second anchor, to which the whole tackle was then to be transferred, and the waggon lowered straight down to the halting-place on the terrace. It was, in fact, an application of the principle of the *whip* used for taking weights over a ship's side. Unfortunately, the second anchor was not properly placed in the hole made for it. The petty officer sent to look after it, instead of letting it remain as we had left it, thought he had improved its hold by placing it horizontally in a cleft of the rock, so as to act not as an *anchor*, but as what is called a *toggle*. The result was, that whenever it felt the indirect strain of the slanting motion of the waggon it at once tilted up and lost its hold. To our horror, away went the waggon at a tremendous pace, and the anchor after it almost flying. For a second or two the destruction of the waggon and the Apollo seemed inevitable, as it was heading straight for a precipice two or three hundred feet in height, when, to our relief, it gave a great bound, and landed itself in a large cavity in the rock. Strange to say, not even a spoke of a wheel was broken. With considerable difficulty we got it out of its lodgment and along the terrace to the part selected as the starting-point for the further lowering to the bottom of the hill. Here the face of the hill presented a continuous slope, about 400 yards in length, and so steep that it was impossible to climb it at some parts except on hands and feet. All the ropes the ship could afford were spliced to make a tackle of sufficient length. The anchors were again placed in holes cut in the rock, and the fore-axles of the waggons lashed as before. The great danger to be avoided was the *serging* of the waggon, caused by the elasticity of such a length of tackle. To prevent this a few men with hand-spikes went with the waggon to keep it moving as uniformly as the nature of the ground would admit. Both waggons reached the bottom without accident, and were saluted on their arrival there by three hearty cheers from the whole party."

The whole of the sculptures were safely embarked on board the *Assurance*, and on the 8th of June she sailed for Malta, and Murdoch Smith and Porcher returned to Cyrene.

In the despatch of February 23 reference is made

to the explorers' relations with the Arabs. Murdoch Smith was right in his conjecture that the conduct of the Mudir of Ghegheb, Lemin Ben Sitewi, would get him into serious trouble. On the application of Mr Crowe the Mudir was deprived of his office and sent as a prisoner to Tripoli, whence he was not allowed to return to Benghazi until all his money had found its way into the coffers of the Pasha. Thus after two months' delay the dignity of the British officers was publicly vindicated.

The chief source of trouble with the natives was the hostility of the Achwani, the devotees who inhabited the Zauyah, a sacred enclosure whose limits included a considerable portion of the site of Cyrene. Their sheikh, Sidi Mustapha, who in his youth had been a notorious thief, but who had suddenly become intensely religious and joined the fanatical sect of El Senoussi, professed great indignation at the presence of the hated Nazarene within the limits of the Zauyah, and caused them a great deal of trouble, chiefly by threatening and interfering with their native servants. However, the public disgrace of the Mudir had a very salutary effect, and after that there was much less trouble.

The explorers gained considerable influence by their reputed skill as doctors, although they disclaimed any pretensions to a knowledge of the healing art. "People came with diseases of every kind," says Murdoch Smith, "in the expectation that they were at once to be cured. Knowing nothing of the nature or causes of disease, they look upon it as a supernatural visitation, and therefore conclude that it is only to be abated or cured by supernatural means, of which medicine and written charms (*kiteeba*) are the most effectual. The latter, being altogether mysterious, are held in the highest esteem. Owing to the ignorance of the people, the few among them who can read and write are looked upon with a respect somewhat allied to fear; and if, in addition to the accomplishments of reading and writing, a man has the reputation of being a *marabut*, or saint, he is treated with the greatest reverence. Such men are called *fikkis*, and not unusually turn their reputation to good account by selling written charms to their credulous clients. As we were often seen reading and writing, the Arabs became fully convinced that we must be great *fikkis*, although, as Christians, we could not have derived our power from the proper quarter. Applications for *kiteebas* were therefore very frequent, not only in cases of sickness, but also for the remedy of all sorts of domestic troubles and grievances. A woman, for instance, came for a *kiteeba* to enable her to retain the undivided affections of her husband, and thereby restrain him from taking another wife. A man whose hopes of marrying the object of his affections had been frustrated by the enmity of her relations, wanted one to overcome their opposition and secure the success of his suit. One young lady begged for a *kiteeba* that would get her a husband, and another asked for one to prevent her being married to a man she disliked. In vain we tried to persuade the people that charms were valueless, and that the idea of their efficacy was kept up by the *fikkis* solely for their own advantage. The belief in their power was too deeply rooted to be shaken by anything we could say, and our unwillingness to write them was attributed to mere churlishness. This being the case, we were often obliged to act as sorcerers to get rid of importunate applicants. In giving a *kiteeba* we took care at the same time to recommend the use of such natural means as we thought most conducive to the desired result, and enforced our advice by saying that the *kiteeba* was so written that it could have no effect if the means recommended were not adopted. If the desired result was obtained, the success was of course ascribed to the virtue of the charm; and if not, the failure was attributed to a final cause,—it was *mektub*, written as the will of God in the Book of Fate."

One of the explorers' lady patients brought them as a fee a young gazelle, which became a great pet —to the disgust of their dog—and remained with them till their departure. It used to wander about the hills during the day, always returning at night.

During the year spent in the tomb at Cyrene Murdoch Smith had with him only three books of general literature — Shakespeare, Schiller, and Molière. To be exiled for a year, in such excellent company, from newspapers and circulating libraries, was by no means an intellectual misfortune.

Before the arrival of the *Assurance* the explorers had made several excursions to different places in the Cyrenaica, and in particular to the sites of the minor cities of the Pentapolis. Visits were paid to Imghernis and to the beautiful coast town of Derna, the ancient Darnis, where they were hospitably received by the Mudir and the military commandant. The latter insisted on parading the troops of the garrison for their inspection. The Arabs of the coast towns, being to some extent civilised, look down on their brethren the country Bedouins, and think them fair game for practical joking. An amusing instance of this occurred on the occasion of this visit in the case of the explorers' camel-driver. "While lounging about the bazaar," says Murdoch Smith, "an auctioneer showed him a pair of pistols he was selling at the time, and asked him what he thought of them. '*Wallah! zain!*' (By God! good!) was the reply. In a short time the auctioneer returned, bawling out a large price as the last bid, and handing the pistols to the camel-driver, again asked his opinion of their quality. '*Wallah! zain!*' repeated the camel-driver. 'Well, no one has bid higher than you, so here they are, and give me the money.' 'But I never bid for them at all! I have no money to buy such pistols as these!' 'No money! Never bid! Did you not say "*Wallah! zain!*" when I bid a price for you? *Wallahi!* if you do not pay you go to prison.' The other Arabs in the bazaar took up the chorus, '*Wallahi!* you shall go to prison. We'll have none of your Bedouin tricks here!' and to the castle prison he was hauled off accordingly. He was, of course, released when his companion, Abderrahim, came and told us of his misfortune."

On April 13 the explorers left Cyrene on an excursion to the Western Cyrenaica, with the object of visiting the sites of the cities of Teuchira and Ptolemais. April is the pleasantest month of the year for travelling in North Africa, and they had a very enjoyable journey. At Merdj they were hospitably entertained by their old friend the Mudir Hadji Achmet Bin 'l Agha. At his house they met the new Mudir of Ghegheb, who had been appointed in succession to the disgraced Lemin Ben Sitewi. The new Mudir was a somewhat weak individual, and the Pasha of Tripoli had appointed as his official adviser Bou Bakr Ben Hadood, head of the Birasa tribe—an appointment which, as we shall see, was to cause trouble later on. They also at this time came across a queer specimen of the Scot abroad, a certain Suliman Captan, grandson of a Scotch captain who had turned Mohammedan and settled in Tripoli, where he became a sort of admiral under the Beys of the Karamanli dynasty. Suliman Captan had been Mudir of Ghegheb immediately before Lemin Ben Sitewi, and the tribes about Cyrene still retained a lively recollection of his rule. On one occasion a tribe of Arabs having refused to pay their tribute, he went to their camps, attended by only eight soldiers, to insist upon payment. Thinking this a favourable opportunity for paying off many old scores, the tribe surrounded him in overpowering numbers, determined to take his life. Nothing daunted, he cut his way through the mob, and succeeded in gaining his castle, although with four bullets in his body and the mark of a bullet-graze on his forehead.

Continuing their journey, the explorers visited Tocra, the ancient Teuchira, named by the Ptolemies Arsinoë, and Tolmeitah, the site of

Ptolemais. Careful notes were taken of the existing remains, and numerous sketches were made by Porcher. A beautiful drawing of Ptolemais by moonlight is one of the finest of the many fine illustrations in the *History of Discoveries at Cyrene*.

On April 24 the explorers reached their quarters at Cyrene, having during their absence of twelve days travelled some 250 miles.

During the fortnight which intervened between their return to Cyrene and the arrival of the *Assurance* a serious disturbance took place in the country, which had a considerable influence on the subsequent history of the expedition. Reference has been made to the appointment of Bou Bakr Ben Hadood as the official adviser of the new Mudir of Ghegheb. This Bou Bakr was regarded as a tribal enemy by the Haasa, on whom he had at one time inflicted a signal defeat. The consequences of his appointment are thus described by Murdoch Smith :—

"According to custom, the sheikhs of the different tribes, and among others the ten sheikhs of the Haasa, among whom we lived, went to the castle to pay their respects to the newly appointed governor. Before this time, however, Bou Bakr had told the Mudir that the Haasa sheikhs were a rebellious turbulent set, whom he should seize and imprison on the first favourable opportunity. Their coming to the castle on a peaceful errand was accordingly taken advantage of for carrying this sage advice into execution. The men of the tribe, on learning that their sheikhs had fallen into the power of their old enemy, appealed to us for assistance, and requested us to write to the consul at Benghazi to obtain the liberation of their chiefs. We told them that as the matter in no way concerned ourselves or any one in our service, it was impossible for us to interfere. They thereupon called a *medjlis*, or assembly of the whole tribe, in which it was determined to release the sheikhs by force before further evil should befall them. They accordingly assembled, to the number of about 1000, in the neighbourhood of the castle, and attacked it at midnight. The gate soon yielded to their blows, and the garrison was at their mercy. Some firing had meantime taken place, in which six Arabs and two soldiers were killed or wounded. The prisoners were immediately released; but the castle was searched in vain for Bou Bakr, who had wisely retired the day before to the camps of his own tribe of Birasa.

"The sheikhs, however, were no sooner at liberty than they began to reflect on the unpleasant position they were placed in by the rash zeal of their followers. The Sultan's castle had been attacked, and the Sultan's soldiers killed; and although they themselves had been prisoners at the time, they knew that it would be vain to disavow their complicity in the act of their tribe. Such an open and violent insult to the Government must, they feared, be in some way avenged by the Pasha, who might possibly send hosts of soldiers to exterminate the tribe. At all events they would suffer severely by being excluded from their only markets, Benghazi and Derna, by the fear of their falling into the hands of the Pasha. A *medjlis* was called to deliberate on their difficulties, at which it was determined to make a second application to us for assistance. The sheikhs accordingly came to our quarters, and in the name of the whole tribe begged us to intercede in their behalf. They urged that they had been imprisoned simply to gratify Bou Bakr, and for no offence of their own; nevertheless, that, to preserve the peace, they had represented to the Mudir that they could not answer for the consequences if at least one of their number were not allowed out of prison to control the passions of the Arabs, while the remaining nine were retained as hostages. As this was refused, and they were all kept in close confinement, they knew nothing of what was going on until they heard the firing and battering at the gate of the castle during the assault. It would, therefore, be unjust to punish them for a crime of which they were perfectly innocent, and it would, even be hard to hold the tribe responsible for its actions when suddenly and treacherously deprived of the advice and guidance of their only chiefs. It was certainly wrong to attack the castle; but what was to be expected in the circumstances? and had they not warned the Mudir of the consequences of his own act? Besides, by appealing to us in the first instance, the tribe had taken the only peaceable means they had of obtaining the release of their sheikhs.

"We asked them why they did not tell or write all this to the Pasha, who was the proper judge of their conduct. Their answer was, 'You know yourselves well enough what the result would be; our remonstrances would never be listened to, and we or our messengers would only be seized and imprisoned with irons: our only hope in a case like this is in the consul.' We said that if the consul interfered the Pasha had a perfect right to say, 'Are the Haasa Arabs Englishmen? This is none of your business.' 'There is no chance,' replied they, 'of his saying anything of the kind; when the consul speaks, the Pasha must obey.'

"As we knew very well that the Pasha had not the power to punish the tribe, we thought it probable that he would be glad of any excuse for saving his dignity by pardoning the offence. We therefore believed that our intercession would be as welcome on the one side as on the other; and, if successful, that it would be most useful to ourselves, by establishing our influence over the tribe in whose country we resided.

"Mr Crowe having left for England, we wrote to the above effect to Mr Aquilina, then acting as vice-consul at Benghazi, and requested him to use his own discretion in bringing the matter before the Kaimakam. He immediately called at the castle and read a translation of our letter to the Kaimakam, who, as we had conjectured, readily promised to pardon the tribe. We soon after received a letter from the Kaimakam himself, informing us that in consequence of our intercession he had been pleased to forgive the Haasa the very serious crime of which they had been guilty, on condition of their good behaviour and prompt payment of the *miri* in future.

"This letter reached us soon after the arrival of

the *Assurance*, when Mr De Fremeaux was with us on a visit from Derna. Immediately after its receipt we summoned the sheikhs to a meeting, at which Mr De Fremeaux read and explained the letter of the Kaimakam. Highly delighted with the happy termination of their difficulties, they were profuse in their expressions of thanks, and said that they and their tribe were now our servants for ever."

During the visit of the *Assurance* seven more negroes had been sent up from Benghazi by the acting vice-consul, Mr Aquilina. With these men work was recommenced on the 9th of June, by beginning the excavation of a large temple in the eastern part of the city, near the Stadium. This was by far the largest temple in Cyrene, measuring 169½ feet in length by 58 feet in breadth, and being ornamented both internally and externally with fine marble colonnades. From the excavations the details of the structure were ascertained, and a plan of it was drawn, but no sculpture of any importance was found, the temple evidently having been wantonly wrecked by the hand of man.

On June 17 the explorers were agreeably surprised by the appearance of a large party of naval officers, who had landed from H.M.S. *Scourge*. They were the bearers of a telegram from the Admiralty stating that the explorers might shortly expect further assistance, and a letter from Mr Panizzi announcing that the Trustees of the British Museum had voted a further sum of £500, and had sent out a carpenter, Mr William Dennison, to assist in packing statues, &c. Mr Dennison, who arrived in the *Scourge*, remained with the explorers, and was of great service in superintending the excavations.

With the funds now available operations on a much more extensive scale could be undertaken, and on the 6th of July Murdoch Smith left for Benghazi for the purpose of getting money and men. Time being of the utmost importance, he started accompanied by a single Arab, and taking no camels, consequently he had neither water nor baggage. He pushed on with characteristic energy, and, it may be added, with characteristic disregard of his own health, and reached Benghazi shortly after sunset on the 9th. He thus accomplished the whole journey of 160 miles in three days, and without water after leaving Merdj on the evening of the 8th—an extraordinary feat of endurance, considering the season of the year, and one for which he afterwards paid dearly.

As it would have been unsafe to carry back a sum of money, Mr Aquilina gave him two orders, one on Mr De Fremeaux, consular agent at Derna, and the other on Mohammed El Adouly, from both of whom the money was to be drawn in instalments as required. This proved a most convenient arrangement, although a Bedouin camp seemed an odd place for negotiating bills and keeping a banker's account.

There was now no difficulty in obtaining as many workmen as were required. Twenty-eight negroes were engaged at the rate of five Turkish piastres (10d.) a-day and their food. These were high wages for the country, but it was impossible to keep men at Cyrene at such a distance from their wives and families except by paying them so highly that they did not like to give up the work, and it was always difficult to get workmen to supply the places of those who left, as the blacks were afraid to go to Cyrene by themselves on account of the danger of being seized and re-enslaved by the Arabs on the way. With the seven men already at Cyrene the number of workmen available for excavation work now amounted to thirty-five.

During his visit to Benghazi Murdoch Smith received a state visit from the Kaimakam, attended by the chief local officials. Suliman Captan and some of the principal Arab inhabitants also called. A day had accordingly to be devoted to returning these visits. It was found that the visit of the *Assurance* had become magnified by report into a formidable affair. The Kaimakam told Murdoch Smith that he had been officially informed that an English fleet had come to Marsa Sousah and disembarked several thousand soldiers, who were to be employed in occupying the country, and that the laying of the telegraph between Malta and Alexandria, by way of Tripoli and Benghazi, then in progress, was only part of a general scheme of conquest. According to the general belief, the explorers' statues and waggons were artillery, their road to the coast a military one for the use of the army of occupation, and their excavations forts and batteries.

Murdoch Smith started on his return journey to Cyrene on July 12 with his party of negroes. They were a somewhat troublesome flock to handle. It was with the greatest difficulty that they could be induced to husband the small supply of water which it was possible to carry, and long before they reached Merdj they had eaten all the food which had been provided for the whole journey. There was no bread to be had at Merdj, but fortunately he succeeded in procuring a supply of dates, which served for the remainder of the distance.

On the day on which the caravan left Merdj an awkward incident occurred. In the afternoon Murdoch Smith was riding on some distance ahead of the caravan, when his attention was attracted by about a dozen Arabs seated under a tree near the path, with their horses standing beside them. They looked rather suspicious, and commenced talking rapidly to each other as he came up; but as this was nothing unusual he rode on, thinking that they were probably a travelling body halting for a rest. In a few minutes, however, he heard a loud shouting and screaming in the rear, and on hastening back to see what was the matter, he saw the negroes running in all directions, and in such a state of terror that it was some time before he could make out what had happened. He finally learned that the Arabs whom he had passed in the wood had charged into the straggling caravan and seized one of the negroes; and while some of them were binding him on the back of a horse the others formed a circle round him with their bayonets at the "charge" and threatened to shoot any one that interfered. When their prisoner was secured they rode off with him into the wood, and before Murdoch Smith came up they had all disappeared. He succeeded in finding out who the perpetrators of the outrage were, but although the matter was at once reported to

Benghazi, nothing was ever done, the Kaimakam being unwilling, or more probably unable, to apprehend the offenders.

Two days later the caravan reached Cyrene.

By this time the excavation of the large temple near the Stadium was almost finished, and that of a smaller temple near it had just been commenced. This also, it was found, had been purposely destroyed. In it were found some fragments of sculpture, of very fine style, but small and few in number, the most perfect of these being two small marble statuettes, probably of Venus and the nymph Cyrene.

On July 31 the whole force returned to the Temple of Apollo and its immediate neighbourhood. The excavation of the building was completed and further finds of sculpture were made, including a statue of Archippe, of the family of the Ptolemaic dynasty, a colossal female figure, probably a portrait of one of the queens of Egypt, and a nude Bacchus.

On August 23 the explorers commenced the excavation of a building to the westward of the Temple of Dionysos (marked "Augusteum" on the map). Their attention had been attracted to this place by the torso of a Roman emperor in armour, which had been seen and noted by Captain Beechey, who visited Cyrene in 1821, and who was of opinion that it was the statue of one of the Ptolemies. Considering the number of years it must have lain exposed on the surface of the ground, the marble was in a wonderfully good state of preservation. After removing it to their tomb the explorers commenced digging in the immediate neighbourhood of the spot in which it was found. In the course of their excavations they found traces of a large building consisting of several rooms, some of which had their walls and floors veneered with thin slabs of marble. The construction and position of the building, and the nature of the sculpture which they discovered in it, led the explorers to believe that it had most probably been the palace of the Roman governor. Two exceedingly valuable pieces of sculpture were found here, a very fine and quite uninjured bust of the Emperor Antoninus Pius, and another of Marcus Aurelius.

Further excavations were also conducted at the Temple of Venus, a little to the south-west of the Temple of Bacchus. Here further finds of sculpture were made, including a remarkably graceful small nude figure of Venus Euploia, a Pan, which retained much of its original colouring, an Apollo, a marble head of Perseus, and a marble relief representing Libya crowning with laurel the nymph Cyrene, who is in the act of strangling a lion.

From September 3 onwards most of the workmen were employed in improving and repairing the road to Marsa Sousah, preparatory to the removal of the statues when a vessel should arrive. Special attention was devoted to the Augubah. The track of the ancient road winding round the faces of the hills at a comparatively easy slope had been discovered. By clearing away brushwood, restoring cuttings and embankments, and in some places making an entirely new section, a practicable road was constructed down the face of the mountain, and

BUST OF ANTONINUS PIUS.

the old road was cleared and improved all the way from Cyrene.

Owing to the want of means of communication with England, no answers had as yet been received to the letters sent home by the *Assurance* in June, so that the explorers were quite uncertain about the arrival of a ship. In writing to Lord John Russell and Mr Panizzi, they had recommended that a much larger vessel than the *Assurance* should be sent, so that a large working party might be landed to embark the statues. They had also recommended that the vessel should arrive at Marsa Sousah before the middle of September, so that the marbles could be embarked before the fine summer weather should break up. Day after day, however, passed without any word of the arrival of the vessel, and the explorers began to contemplate a continued stay in the country for another winter. Since the end of August Murdoch Smith had been confined to the tomb, and most of the time to bed, by a severe attack of fever, the result of fatigue and exposure at night during his journey to Benghazi in July. With one of their party thus on the sick-list, and a prospect, growing every day more certain, of a further residence of eight months in the country, the explorers looked with some anxiety for the expected ship.

At last, on September 26, a large frigate appeared standing in towards Marsa Sousah. She proved to be H.M.S. *Melpomene*, commanded by Captain Ewart, from whom the explorers soon after received a note announcing his arrival. Porcher went down to the ship early next morning to make the necessary arrangements, and to accompany the working party, while Murdoch Smith remained to look after the packing and other affairs in Cyrene.

Excellent arrangements had been made by Captain Ewart while on the passage from Malta, and everything was ready for beginning the work immediately after the arrival of the ship. The working party had already been told off and thoroughly equipped and organised. All the stores required for packing the statues were landed immediately, and sent up to Cyrene as rapidly as camels could be got to carry them. Two carpenters and a guard of ten marines came up to Cyrene the same day, and the work of making cases and packing was begun at once, under the superintendence of Mr Dennison. A working party of ninety men, fully equipped with tents, water-breakers, provisions, &c., was then disembarked under the command of Lieutenant Carter, R.N. Three artillery platform waggons were employed, to each of which a crew of thirty men was told off under the command of a midshipman. The ship was anchored about two miles to the westward of Marsa Sousah, directly opposite the new road which had been made over the Augubah. As communication with the shore was very liable to be interrupted by the heavy surf on the beach, a depot of provisions and fresh water was established on land under the protection of a guard. From this depot the working party could draw its supplies, and the cases of sculpture brought down from Cyrene could be safely left in charge of the guard.

The working party started from the depot with

the waggons on the morning of September 28. The road proved quite practicable, and the party arrived at Cyrene on the following day. By that time the carpenters had a sufficient number of statues packed to load all the waggons. The 30th was occupied in securing the cases on the waggons, and on the 1st of October the party started for the shore. The descent of the Augubah was accomplished without accident, and the cases were safely deposited at the depot on the evening of the 2nd. Two other trips were afterwards made with equal success. In the course of the third trip, however, a difficulty arose with the natives, which very nearly led to the most disastrous consequences. The incident is thus described by Murdoch Smith:—

"Ever since the arrival of the marines and carpenters at Cyrene scores of ugly-looking Arabs kept prowling about our tomb with the evident design of picking a quarrel with us. Occasion for doing so was likely to occur at any moment, and especially when we absolutely refused to comply with some extravagant demands on the part of the camel-drivers. An open quarrel, however, was fortunately avoided until the first arrival of the large waggon party.

"The sailors, who were then encamped on the hill opposite our tomb, were in the habit of washing and bathing at the Fountain of Apollo, a practice at which the Arabs became greatly enraged. One evening, a little before sunset, as we were sitting down to dinner, we suddenly heard a few shots fired, and immediately afterwards the loud screeching by which the Arabs were wont to call each other to an armed gathering. Numbers soon answered to the cry, and came pouring into the wady from all directions. On inquiring into the cause of the disturbance, we learned that some sailors and marines had been bathing as usual at the fountain, when a number of Arabs, annoyed at what they thought their indecency, began pelting them with stones. A marine had thereupon loaded his rifle with blank cartridge and fired in the direction of the Arabs, thinking thereby to frighten them away. His foolish act had, as might have been expected, a totally different result. In less than an hour the wady in front of our tomb was swarming with armed men. As we had in this instance been the aggressors, we at once sent Amor for the sheikhs of the collected force, and explained to them that we quite disclaimed the act of the marine, whose rashness, however, was somewhat excused by the previous conduct of the Arabs. The sheikhs, who seemed peaceably disposed, replied that the whole disturbance had been caused by our men occupying the fountain all day and preventing the Arab women from coming to fill their water-skins. As there was some truth in this, we promised that in future the men should be allowed to use the fountain only at particular times; and we requested the sheikhs to come to us if at any time they had cause of complaint, and not to speak to our men, who knew nothing of their language. The Arabs, only partly pacified by our assurances, remained where they were all night, and spent great part of the following morning in firing at marks close to our tomb, for the purpose of making an imposing show of their power to treat us as they pleased.

"This disturbance was hardly settled when a certain Sheikh Said 'M Rubbut made his appearance at the head of his tribe, and demanded a large sum of money under the pretence of harbour dues or something of the sort. On our refusing to pay it he went off in great wrath, vowing vengeance on our whole party. The following day he returned with a similar demand, but this time for the much smaller sum of 200 piastres (18s.) On our again refusing to acknowledge his right to any sum, however small, he lowered his tone considerably, and said that, having no wish to quarrel with us, he would forego his claim, but begged two or three bullock-skins which were of little or no value to us. To a request in this form we willingly acceded, as we were anxious at all hazards to keep the peace until the marbles were safely taken to the beach. By this time the waggons were on their way to the depot on the shore, after their second trip to Cyrene.

"The day after the departure of the waggon party Sheikh Said again paid a visit to our tomb, and told me that he was not satisfied with the skins, and that he would not allow the waggons to pass unless I paid him a large bakshish besides. Seeing that his object was simply to levy blackmail, and that yielding in any way to his demands would only encourage him to make further exactions, I refused to give him anything and ordered him to leave the tomb. With the threat that none of us should leave the country alive he went away and encamped in the lower plateau, near a steep ravine which the waggons had to cross. He there barricaded the road with trunks and branches of trees, and for two days prevented any communication between Cyrene and the working party or the ship. Some of our camels on their way from the depot, laden with planks, were seized and detained. Our retreat from Cyrene was effectually cut off, and we were altogether in rather a helpless state.

"In this dilemma I thought of the sheikhs of the Haasa, whom we had befriended after the attack of the Castle of Ghegheb, and who had then expressed their desire to repay us in any way in their power. I accordingly sent for Hussein and Hadji Hassan, the two head sheikhs of the tribe, and after reminding them of our interference with the Pasha on their behalf, told them that they could never have a better opportunity of proving the sincerity of their gratitude than now, by ridding us of the presence of Sheikh Said and his followers. I also assured them that as we were living in the territory of the Haasa, of which Sheikh Said's tribe was a subdivision, they themselves would be held responsible by the consul for our safety. They at once promised to request Sheikh Said to depart peaceably, and if he refused to do so, to drive him away by force. With some of their subordinate sheikhs they immediately went to carry their promise into effect, and returned after two or three hours with the intelligence that Sheikh Said had gone when they ordered him, and that the road was therefore quite clear.

"Although he had thus apparently obeyed the order of the sheikhs, he had by no means given up the game. Foiled at Cyrene, he merely shifted his ground, and lay in wait for the waggon party in a wood at the top of the Augubah, hoping, no doubt, to extract something from them by his threats. The waggons soon afterwards came up from the shore and halted for the night. The tents were no sooner pitched than Sheikh Said and some of his followers entered the camp and threatened Porcher and the whole party with utter destruction if he did not agree to give him a bakshish. Porcher had not yet heard of our two days' siege at Cyrene, but gave him the same answer I had done — viz., a point-blank refusal. The sheikh thereupon left the camp, and collecting all the men of his tribe, placed them in a large open space at the foot of the Cyrene range, while he himself came up to our tomb to offer me, as he said, a last chance. I told him I had already given him an answer, and that if he wanted to attack us we were quite ready to receive him. On his departure I again called upon the head sheikhs for assistance, and they again obliged him to move off; so that the waggon party reached Cyrene for the third time without an actual encounter.

"The friendly interference of the principal

sheikhs of the Haasa had thus been of great service to us hitherto, by preventing a collision which must have led to very serious consequences. Had it come to blows or bloodshed, even the Arabs who were most friendly to us would have been compelled to take side with their brethren against the Christians. With thirteen miles of bad road and close cover between Cyrene and the coast, we must have suffered great loss in fighting our way to the shore against overwhelming numbers. Such a result had fortunately been avoided; but we now began to have doubts of the good faith of the friendly sheikhs, and to suspect that, after all, they might be in secret league with our enemies. We were led to fear that this was the case by the pertinacity and confidence shown by Sheikh Said, and by the fact that Hussein and Hadji Hassan acted in concert with our old foe Sidi Mustapha, who was loud in his denunciation of Sheikh Said's acts. We naturally thought that if the heads of the Haasa and the chief of the Zauyah were sincere in their professions of friendship, Sheikh Said would not presume to threaten and annoy us.

"Affairs being in this state, we thought it advisable to apply to the Mudir of Ghegheb for protection, although we had little hope of his rendering us any really efficient assistance. Our object was rather to put ourselves in the right, by being able to say that we had appealed to the only representative of the Government in the country. I was still too weak to ride as far as Ghegheb, or I should have gone to see the Mudir before now; but Porcher went immediately after his arrival at Cyrene with the waggons. The Mudir himself, he found, was absent, and the *kolaghassi* or major who was acting in his place said that all he could do was to send two *koralié* with letters to Sidi Mustapha and the sheikhs Hussein and Hadji Hassan.

"Finding that no assistance was to be expected from the Mudir, and that we must rely solely on our own resources for protection, we were anxious to get everything on board as soon as possible, especially as every day's delay seemed only to add to the difficulties of our position. We therefore determined to make the third trip of the waggons the final one, although by doing so we were obliged to leave behind us the large statue of Archippe and some of the inscriptions. Future visitors to the ruins of Cyrene will probably find the statue where we left it, at the western end of our upper range of tombs, and the inscriptions in a subterranean chamber almost immediately beneath the same spot.

"The 10th and 11th were spent in loading the waggons, packing up our personal effects, and collecting the necessary number of camels. We made our preparations as quietly and secretly as possible, in the hope of giving the slip to Sheikh Said and his friends, by reaching the shore before he should hear of our departure from Cyrene. Meantime the road to the coast was clear, and everything promised a peaceful termination to our long sojourn among the Bedouins. On the night of the 11th, however, one of our Arab servants brought us word that Sheikh Said, having heard of our intended movement, was again in position on the road with a larger force than ever, determined to fight us if we did not satisfy his demands.

"Early next morning the marines were paraded under arms, and told off in two parties to act as advanced and rear guards to the main body with the waggons and camels. It was some time, however, before everything was ready for a start. Crowds of Arabs collected round our tomb, clamouring and struggling with each other for the empty bottles and other articles which we were to leave behind. At last the camels were loaded, and we were on the point of beginning our march when, somewhat to our astonishment, we saw a number of Arabs coming up the wady, among whom we recognised Sheikh Said and our former friends Sheikhs Hussein and Hadji Hassan. It seemed as if our suspicions of these Haasa sheikhs were, after all, but too well founded, and that they were now openly associated with our enemy in order to share with him the expected booty.

"Such, however, was not the case. Leaving the other Arabs who were with them, the two sheikhs came up to our tomb and told us that, having accidentally heard that Sheikh Said was again in arms against us, they had hurried off during the night to the position taken up by him in the lower plateau, and by threatening himself and all his followers with instant death, had compelled him to come to make his submission to us. As no blood had actually been shed, they had given him their word that we should not injure him. On being assured that we would respect the safe-conduct they had given, they brought up their prisoner, who forthwith, in the most abject terms, expressed sorrow for his past offences and begged to be forgiven. Thus, fortunately, ended an affair which, but for the gratitude of the powerful tribe we had formerly befriended, would in all probability have resulted in a great loss of life.

"To ensure us from further molestation Sheikhs Hussein and Hadji Hassan accompanied us to the beach, where we induced them with some difficulty to entrust themselves to leave *terra firma* and pay a visit to the ship. When they came on board Captain Ewart made them a liberal and most welcome present of powder, and at their own earnest request I gave each of them a certificate of good conduct addressed to the English vice-consuls at Benghazi and Derna.

"The waggon party reached the head of the Augubah the same night, and on the following morning descended to the plain, where they were met by the ship's band, who escorted them to the beach. Before evening everything was safely embarked."

The work of the explorers was thus brought to a successful conclusion. Liberal bakshish was distributed to their friends and attendants, in particular to their faithful henchman Amor Bon Abdi Seyat, who had stood by them well during the whole of their residence in the country, and who was now rewarded by the gift of their two horses and a large supply of powder. At daylight on the morning of the 14th the *Melpomene* weighed anchor, and reached Malta on the 17th, where it was found that a report had been sent from Benghazi by the new submarine telegraph to the effect that in an attack made upon the explorers by the Arabs at Cyrene, one of them had been killed and the other wounded. At Malta the sculptures were transferred to H.M.S. *Supply*, in which vessel they were safely conveyed to England.

The expedition had been a splendid success. In the foregoing narrative it has only been possible to refer to a few of the more important objects discovered during the excavations. Altogether the finds included a hundred and forty-eight pieces of sculpture and thirty-three inscriptions. Detailed descriptive lists of these, with photographs of all the more important sculptures and facsimiles of the inscriptions, are given in the *History of the Recent Discoveries at Cyrene*.

The whole of the objects found were placed by the discoverers at the disposal of the Government, and with a few exceptions are now exhibited in the British Museum. In writing to Murdoch Smith on December 17, 1861, on behalf of the Trustees of the Museum, Mr Panizzi said:—

"On Saturday last I had the pleasure of laying before the committee Mr Newton's report on the sculptures with which the Museum has been enriched through the successful exertions of yourself and Lieutenant Porcher at Cyrene, and I now take the earliest opportunity of communicating to you the high satisfaction of the Trustees in learning that the collections in the department of Greek and

Roman Antiquities have been so largely increased with objects both artistically and historically interesting. In returning you the best thanks of the Trustees for all that you have done to bring about this important result, I am to express the deep sense they entertain of the intelligence, zeal, and persevering labour which both you and Lieutenant Porcher have devoted to this expedition from beginning to end."

In 1886, after Murdoch Smith became Director of the Edinburgh Museum of Science and Art, the Trustees, on the recommendation of Dr A. S. Murray, Sir Charles Newton's successor, presented one of the Cyrene statues—the Dionysos—to the Edinburgh Museum as a further mark of appreciation of his services.

CHAPTER VI.

THE PERSIAN TELEGRAPH.

EMPLOYMENT AT THE WAR OFFICE—APPOINTED TO THE PERSIAN TELEGRAPH STAFF—TELEGRAPHIC COMMUNICATION WITH INDIA—COLONEL PATRICK STEWART—TELEGRAPH CONVENTION OF 1862, PERSIA—THE *CHAPAR*—PERSIAN CHARACTERISTICS—MAJOR BATEMAN CHAMPAIN—MAKING OF THE LINE—MURDOCH SMITH'S TROUBLES—*MUDAKHIL*—THE LINE COMPLETED—A POLITICAL HITCH—MURDOCH SMITH BECOMES DIRECTOR—A DIPLOMATIC TRIUMPH—THE RACECOURSE INCIDENT—THE CONVENTION OF 1865—VISIT TO BELUCHISTAN AND TO INDIA—LATER HISTORY OF THE TELEGRAPH—A TELEGRAPH MUDDLE—FORMATION OF THE INDO-EUROPEAN AND EASTERN COMPANIES—LATER CONVENTIONS — EFFICIENCY OF THE TELEGRAPH — LORD CURZON'S ESTIMATE OF ITS EFFECT ON PERSIA.

IN November 1861 Murdoch Smith came home on leave. While in England he was offered the adjutancy of the Royal Engineers at Aldershot. He was, however, anxious if possible to get out of the routine of garrison duty, and applied to the Adjutant-General for employment in London. His request was granted, and he obtained an appointment in the fortifications department at the War Office.

He entered on his duties in the office of the Inspector-General of Fortifications on January 17, 1862, and remained there till August 11, 1863.

He always looked back with pleasure to the months spent at the War Office. His work was interesting and responsible, and was diversified by a good deal of travel about the country, including a long visit to Weston-super-Mare in connection with the defences of the Bristol Channel, and another to Edinburgh in connection with those of the Forth. He established himself in pleasant rooms at Westminster, close to the Houses of Parliament. Although only six-and-twenty, he was already a man of mark, and some of the pleasantest and most interesting society in London was open to him. Music was still one of his chief pleasures, and he was a constant frequenter of the opera. His spare evenings were spent working at the Cyrene book. His great friend at this time was Captain (now Major-General) H. T. Siborne, R.E., then also employed in the War Office. Captain Siborne shared Murdoch Smith's enthusiasm for boating. The two friends kept a boat at Lambeth, and every summer morning they used to turn out at six for a pull on the Thames, returning to breakfast at the National Club in Whitehall Gardens. They made many Saturday-to-Monday excursions up the river together, which in after-days Sir Robert used to recall with great enjoyment.

One day in the summer of 1863 he had gone out to luncheon with some of his colleagues in the office. One of the party, who was looking over the day's *Times*, suddenly exclaimed, "Hallo, Smith! here's something in your line," and read out a paragraph stating that a convention had been concluded with the Shah of Persia providing for the construction, under English superintendence, of a telegraph line through Persia in connection with the Indo-European telegraph system, and that the work was to be carried out by officers of the Royal Engineers.

That newspaper paragraph was the starting-point of Murdoch Smith's whole subsequent career. He at once decided that the Persian enterprise offered the very opportunity for which he had been waiting. He applied for employment on it, and was appointed one of the section superintendents of the line. In the course of the autumn he was sent out to the Persian Gulf in charge of an R.E. detachment, and reached Busrah on November 15. Thus began that connection with Persia which was to last for almost a quarter of a century.

He has himself told the story of the early days of the Persian telegraph in a paper read to the Royal Scottish Geographical Society in 1888.[1]

"'The first idea,'" he writes, "of connecting England with India by telegraph began to take shape during the great crisis of the Mutiny thirty-one years ago, when the necessity for such means

[1] *Scottish Geographical Magazine*, January 1889. I am indebted to the courtesy of the Council of the Society for permission to make the extract in the text. A detailed history of the making of the telegraph is given by Major-General Sir Frederic Goldsmid in *Telegraph and Travel* (Macmillan & Co., 1874). A technical account of the line, by Mr J. R. Preece, will be found in the *Journal of the Society of Telegraph Engineers*, vol. viii. (1879), pp. 403-433.

of communication had become painfully manifest. By the most rapid means then in existence it took nearly three months to get answers to communications passing between London and Calcutta—a time more than sufficient for the loss of an empire.

"The line chosen for the projected telegraph was naturally that of the Overland Route. This involved the laying of long submarine cables in the Mediterranean, the Red Sea, and the Indian Ocean. The failure of the first Atlantic cable had, however, so disheartened the public that submarine cables were regarded as investments of too hazardous a nature to be undertaken by prudent people without special guarantees. Unaided private enterprise could consequently not be expected to undertake the great risk of a telegraph line to India, more especially of the portions in the Red Sea and the Indian Ocean. In the Mediterranean a beginning had already been made by a private company whose cable from Marseilles to Malta it was hoped would be extended to Alexandria. Following the system adopted in the case of the Indian railways, the Red Sea portion was constructed and laid in 1859, with a Government guarantee of 5 per cent, shared equally between the Imperial and the Indian Treasuries. The cable, however, had barely fulfilled the conditions required by the terms of the guarantee when it collapsed, leaving the British and Indian Exchequers burdened until the present day, and for some years yet to come, with an annual payment of £18,000 each. Shortly afterwards —

viz., in 1861 — the Mediterranean Company laid a short-lived cable from Malta *viâ* Tripoli and Benghazi to Alexandria.

"Warned by the costly failure of the Red Sea route, the Government of India turned their attention to the Persian Gulf. With the aid of the British detachment, who had charge of the telegraphs established in Turkey for military purposes during the Crimean war, the Turkish Government had shortly before this time erected a line from Constantinople across Asia Minor and down the valley of the Tigris to Baghdad. This line, it was thought, might by arrangement with the Turkish Government be extended to the head of the Persian Gulf, and a cable be laid thence to the most western point which could practically be reached from India by a land line along the coast of Beluchistan. Negotiations were accordingly opened at Constantinople with a view to the accomplishment of this project, and a careful survey of the bottom of the Persian Gulf was ordered to be made. The general direction of the scheme was placed in the hands of the late Colonel Patrick Stewart, R.E., C.B., a most distinguished officer, who had already given signal proof of remarkable energy and capacity while in charge of the field telegraphs during the Sepoy war. The negotiations at Constantinople resulted after some time in a convention which provided for the erection, with British assistance, of a line from Baghdad *viâ* Busrah to Fao, at the mouth of the Shat el Arab or united Tigris and Euphrates. Colonel (now Sir) Frederic Goldsmid, then Collector of Karachi, was instructed to proceed along the coast of Beluchistan to ascertain the exact political condition of each district, and to make arrangements, by subsidies or otherwise, with the local chiefs for the protection of the proposed land line. This task—thanks to tact and diplomatic skill—he successfully accomplished, and in accordance with his report it was decided to construct a line from Karachi along the Mekran coast (as this part of Beluchistan is generally called) as far west as Gwadur, a fishing village in the occupation of the Sultan of Muscat. The gap from that point to Fao it was decided to fill up by means of a submarine cable, to be manufactured and laid at the expense of the Indian Government, without the intervention of a guaranteed private company.

"The project therefore at this time (1862) stood as follows: 1st, The lines as they then existed between London and Constantinople; 2nd, a Turkish line already opened between Constantinople and Baghdad; 3rd, a line to be made with British help from Baghdad to Fao; 4th, a submarine cable to be laid from Fao to Gwadur; and 5th, a land line to be erected from Gwadur to Karachi. From London to Constantinople there was no special organisation for the transmission of international traffic. Each State had its own system adapted to suit its own internal requirements. From Constantinople to Fao the Turkish Government retained the entire charge and working of the line in their own hands. From London to the head of the Persian Gulf messages would consequently have to undergo most varied treatment, and be transmitted by clerks of many nationalities, all totally unacquainted with the language in which the telegrams were written. It was hoped that when through communication was once opened the different Governments concerned would be induced to give special facilities for the transit of Indian messages. One of the sections, however, above enumerated—that, namely, in Turkish Arabia, from Baghdad to Fao—was thought likely to prove very unsafe, and liable to constant interruption at the hands of the lawless Arab tribes of Mesopotamia. It was therefore deemed advisable to open negotiations at the Court of Teheran with a view to obtaining an alternative line between the Persian Gulf and Baghdad through Persia. The negotiations, however, seemed very unpromising, and not likely to lead to any practical result.

"Such were the projects and prospects (not very bright it must be confessed) of telegraphic communication with India when Colonel Patrick Stewart assumed general charge of the scheme in 1862. Accompanied by Major (afterwards Sir John) Bateman Champain, R.E., he went to Persia for the purpose of examining the country from a telegraphic point of view, and of ascertaining what prospect there was of a satisfactory arrangement being made with the Persian Government, without which all idea of a line through that country was, of course, out of the question. The situation of the principal cities in Persia, which it was presumed the Persian Government would naturally wish to connect with the capital, Teheran, by means of the proposed

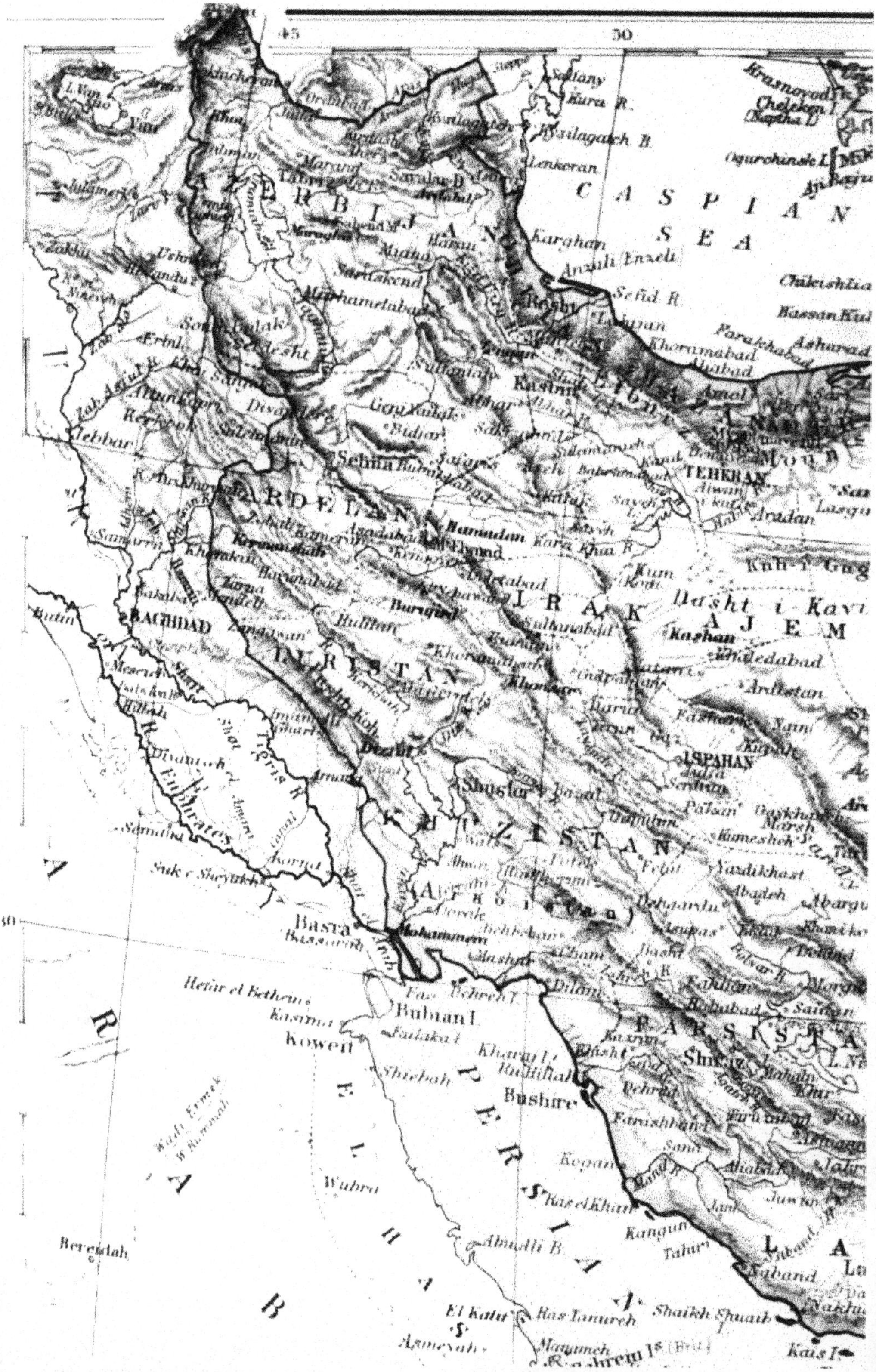

45
50
L. Van
Kura R.
Lenkoran
Krasnovodsk
Chelekan I.
A Z E R B I J A N
C A S P I A N
S E A
Kargban
Sefid R.
Resht
Kasvin
TEHERAN
Sehna
A R D E L A N
Hamadan
Kermanshah
Kum
I R A K   A J E M I
Kashan
Dasht i Kavir
BAGHDAD
L U R I S T A N
Dizful
Shuster
K H U Z I S T A N
ISPAHAN
Tigris R.
Euphrates
Suk e Sheyukh
Basra
Mohammera
Koweit
Bubian I.
Bushire
Shiraz
F A R S I S T A N
P E R S I A N   G U L F
A R A B I A
Berejdah
Wabra
El Katif
Ras Tanureh
Kais I.

Mergen
ok Tepe
Cheshme
Dasht-i-Khul
Sarakhs
Gumbazli
Astrabad
Shahrud
Zaguda
Tawran
Sang gird
Siah Kuh
Sultanabad
Turbat-i-Sheikh Jam
Great Salt Desert
Faizabad
K H O R A S A N
HERAT
Pushta Daran
Jowzar
Tabbas
Tun
Bushruyeh
Kain
Duluk
Birjand
Allahabad
Dasht-i-Lut
Yezd
Kuh Naiband
Naiband
Salimkuh
Gudinamek
Lash
Helmund or Halmand R.
Nasratabad
Koh Khwaja
Sehoka
Kerman
Khabis
Gok
K E R M A N
Bam
Nahimabad
Rigan
Bashkand
Sarhad
Bampur
Kasimabad
Faizabad
Khurasan
Baud i Murg
Bandar Abbas
Larak
Ras Musendom
Ras al Kheimel
Limah
lask
Bashkird
Sand Desert
Kej
Mekran
Ras Mundani
Gwadar
Kair
Dibba
A R A B I A N S E
East 55 of Greenwich

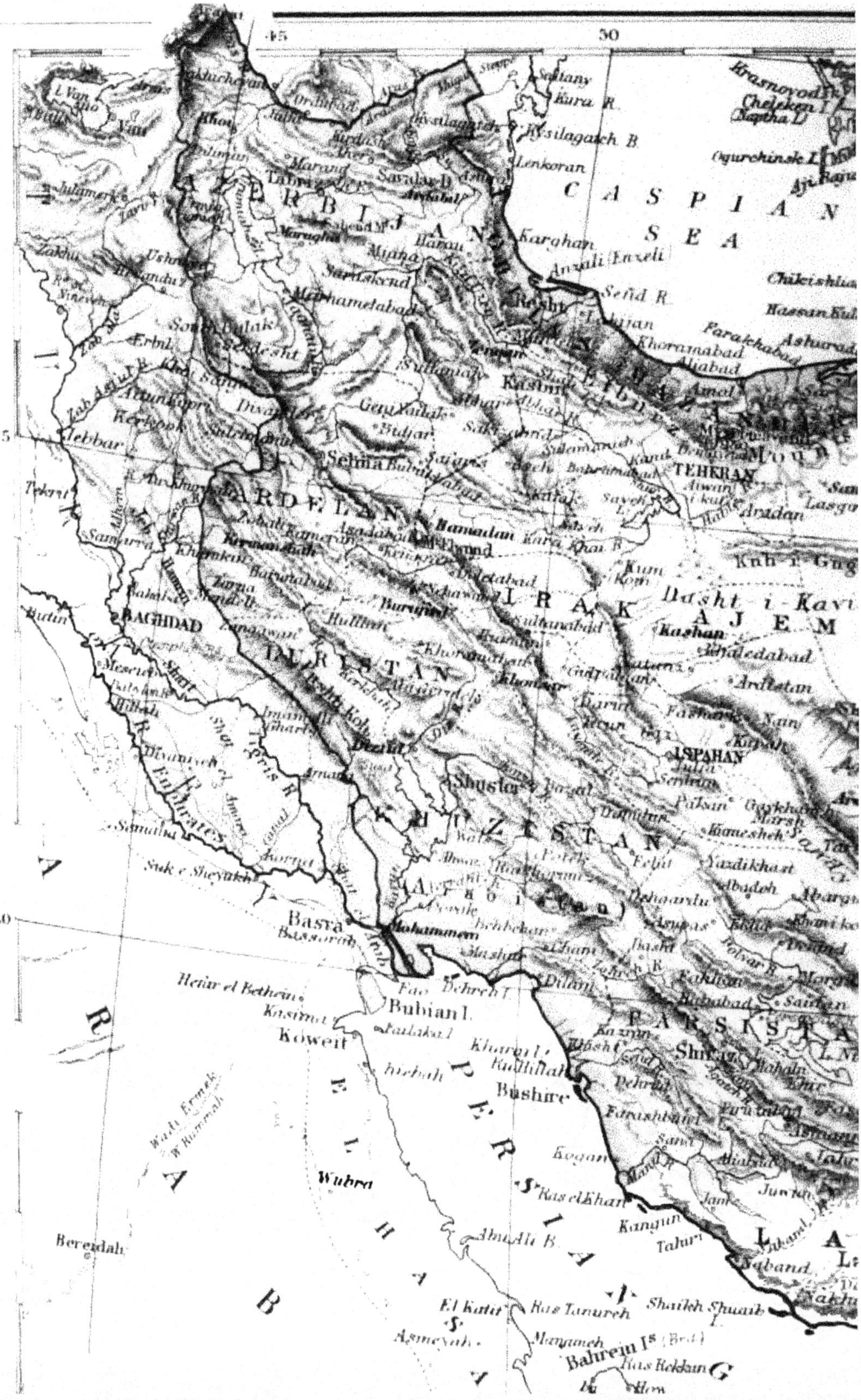
45
50
CASPIAN SEA
Krasnovodsk
Cheleken I.
Naptha I.
Salyany
Kura R.
Kysilagatch B.
Lenkoran
Ogurchinsk I.
Nakhichevan
Khoi
Marand
Tabriz
Savalan
Ardebil
Maragha
Miana
Sarujbulak
Zengan
Sultanieh
Kasbin
Karghan
Anzali (Enzeli)
Resht
Sefid R.
Lahijan
Kharamabad
Aliabad
Amol
Farakhabad
Ashurada
Tehran
Saveh
Kum
Kashan
Aradan
Dasht-i-Kavir
IRAK AJEMI
Natanz
Ardistan
Ispahan
Julfa
Yazdikhast
Abadeh
L. Van
Van
Julamerk
Zakhu
Nineveh
Erbil
Altun Kopri
Kerkook
Sulemanieh
Tekrit
Samarra
Baghdad
ARDELAN
Kermanshah
Hamadan
Burujird
Dizful
Shuster
Sultanabad
Kanawar
LURISTAN
KHUZISTAN
ARABISTAN
Hillah
Tigris R.
Euphrates
Samawa
Suk e Sheyukh
Basra
Bassorah
Mohammerah
Fao
Behbehan
Ram Hormuz
Bubian I.
Koweit
Hejr el Bethein
Feilaka I.
Kharak I.
Bushire
Shiraz
FARSISTAN
Firuzabad
Kazerun
Daliki
Kogan
Ras el Khan
Kangun
Tahiri
Naband
Shaikh Shuaib I.
LAR
PERSIA
GULF
Ras Tanureh
El Katif
Manameh
Bahrein Is.
Ras Rekkan
Wubra
Bereidah
ARABIA
EL HASA
Abu Ali B.
Wadi Ermek
W. Rummah
Asmevah

Tape
Chesme
Dash
i-Khul
Lutfabad
Saraklis
Mashhad
Kara Bel Plateau
Gumbaz
Zaguda
Sang ...
Siah Kuh
Tawran
Sulaimanabad
Great Salt Desert
Tahrud
Faizabad
K H O R A S A N
HERAT
Pushta Daran
Jowzar
Tun
Kakhk
Bushruyah
Kain
Biyaza
Duluk
Allahabad
Khusf
Tabbas
Nahand
Kuh Nahand
Yezd
Salimkan
Shewan
Farah
Lash
Kala-Bist
Kash
Godi namek
Darak
Dara
Nasratabad
Nadali
Kaleh-i-Fath
Lut
Khabis
Kerman
Gok
God-i-Zirreh
Gurg
K E R M A N
Bam
Nahmabad
Rigan
Washt
Khurain
Bampur
Sarbaz
Kasimabad
Bandar Abbas
Lingah
Ras Musendam
Ras al Kheimeh
Dibba
Bushkurd
Jask
Ras Mundani
Charbar
Gwadar
A R A B I A N
East 55 of Greenwich

telegraph, at once indicated the route which the line should follow—viz., Bushire, Shiraz, Ispahan, Teheran, Hamadan, Kermanshah, Baghdad, a distance of about 1300 miles. On reaching Teheran, however, Colonel Stewart found there was little prospect of a practicable telegraph convention being agreed to. The Persian Ministers were naturally somewhat suspicious of our motives and objects, and made all kinds of impracticable proposals in order, as was supposed, to delay or defeat the scheme we were pressing on their attention. Their policy appeared so clearly to be what in parliamentary language would now be called 'obstruction,' that Colonel Stewart determined to go straight to London to push on the main and original portions of the project—viz., the Baghdad-Fao land line, the Fao-Gwadur submarine cable, and the Gwadur-Karachi land line—leaving Major Champain to go over the Teheran-Baghdad route, and then follow him to London.

"The convention with Turkey having by this time been signed, steps were at once taken to get the manufacture of the Fao-Gwadur cable begun, and the materials prepared for the Baghdad-Fao and Gwadur-Karachi land lines. When these operations were approaching completion, news was unexpectedly received of the signature of a telegraph convention at Teheran, which revived the all-but-abandoned project of an alternative line through Persia. As the main line through Turkey ultimately fell into practical abeyance, and the Persian line became the main channel of communication, it is of some interest to recall the terms of this first

Persian Telegraph Convention. The idea of *our* erecting and working a line in Persia was by it entirely set aside. On the other hand, Persia undertook, on our providing the wire and insulators (the cost of which she was to repay by instalments), to make and work a line herself from Bushire *viâ* Teheran to Baghdad, and to allow us, at a tariff to be fixed afterwards, to have our Indian messages transmitted by its means. The only intervention on our part provided for by the convention was the presence of *one* English officer for a limited period in Persia to *advise* as to the best method of construction. Unpromising as such a convention was, it was decided to take action on it, in the hope that something more practical might therefrom be ultimately evolved.

"By the middle of 1863 the manufacture of the cable had been all but completed; the sailing vessels in which it was to be conveyed to the Persian Gulf had been chartered and fitted for its reception; the Mekran coast land line had been fairly begun; and the materials for the Mesopotamian and Persian land lines had been got ready for shipment. The staff of the various sections had also been appointed—some in England, some in India—and all started for their several destinations before the end of the year.

"The year 1864 was almost entirely spent in construction work on the different sections. The cable was successfully laid in the spring the whole way from Fao to Karachi, with intermediate stations at Bushire, Mussendom, and Gwadur, the portion east of Gwadur having been added to the original scheme as an alternative to the Mekran coast land line. The process of laying the cable was not so simple a matter as such operations have now become. The Suez Canal had not yet come into existence, and the cable had consequently to be conveyed round the Cape of Good Hope in sailing vessels, which, during the actual laying of the cable, were towed by steamers of the old Indian Navy; the Karachi-Gwadur land line was completed; and the necessary buildings for the accommodation of the staff were erected or adapted at the different stations in Beluchistan, at Mussendom, at Bushire, and at Fao. The Baghdad-Fao line was completed in the course of the year, so that the project of a telegraph from London to India had by the end of 1864 become an accomplished fact. But there are telegraphs and telegraphs, and a vast amount of work had yet to be done before anything like regularity or efficiency was attained in the parts of the system not under the direct control of the Indian Government. Strange as it may appear, it was in Europe that by far the greatest difficulties existed. The lines east of Constantinople—partly, no doubt, through the smallness of the local traffic—were far more satisfactory than those to the westward. To devise and urge on the most necessary ameliorations, Colonel Stewart hurried to Constantinople as soon as the Persian Gulf cable had been laid. There, owing to the general injury to his constitution caused by the unsparing manner in which he had for years overworked himself, he succumbed to an attack of fever in January 1865. Colonel Goldsmid, with whom was associated Major Champain, succeeded him as Director-in-Chief of what had now come to be designated the Indo-European Telegraph Department, and I succeeded Major Champain as Director of the Persian section. . . .

"It will probably, however, give a clearer idea of the subsequent history of the telegraph if I here break the chronological order of the narrative, and for a few minutes call your attention to the main physical features of Persia and the general condition of the country at the time of our arrival.

"Physically, Persia may be described as a great plateau, overlooking the Caspian Sea on the north, the plains of Mesopotamia on the west, and the Persian Gulf on the south. To the north-west and to the east the plateau extends into the Armenian provinces of Turkey and Russia on the one side and into Afghanistan on the other. To reach the plateau, the plains of which are at an average elevation of 4000 to 5000 feet above the level of the sea, great mountain barriers must be surmounted, no matter from what side the approach is made. On the side of the Caspian, this barrier consists of a range of mountains known in Europe as the chain of the Elburz—a name, however, which in Persia is applied only to one particular mass of it near Teheran. On the side of the valley of the Tigris and the Persian Gulf, range after range, running in a general N.W. and S.E. direction, has to be crossed before the main plateau is reached. The table-land itself is intersected by numerous ranges and detached masses of mountains except in Eastern Persia, where great plains are the main feature. With the single exception of the provinces which lie between Elburz and the Caspian, the climate is remarkably dry. Throughout the summer little or no rain falls, there are few rivers other than mere freshets in spring-time, and most of the agriculture is carried on by artificial irrigation, which depends chiefly for its supplies on the melting of the winter snows. The temperature of the plateau is what one would expect to find it under those conditions in the latitude of Persia —viz., very hot and dry in the summer, very cold and snowy in the winter, and temperate in spring and autumn. In the more elevated districts, and especially in the mountain passes, several of which our telegraph crosses at an elevation of 8000 feet above the level of the sea, the cold in winter is excessive, and the snow often such as to render all locomotion utterly impossible. The hardships, and even the dangers, attending a journey in the mountainous parts of Persia in winter can hardly be realised by those who have not undergone them; and winter is, unfortunately, the season when the telegraph lines are most liable to damage and interruption, and when consequently such journeys have most frequently to be undertaken by those who have charge of the maintenance of the lines.

"There were no carriageable roads, and wheeled vehicles were practically unknown. The roads were merely mule-tracks. Merchandise was carried on the backs of camels, mules, and donkeys, and the personal baggage of travellers almost exclusively on mules. Of those useful animals and of horses there was an abundant supply of excellent quality at very moderate prices. Accommodation for caravans was to be found on most of the main roads at caravanserais, from twenty-five to thirty miles apart, at most of which fodder for the animals was procurable. This, however, was by no means universally the case, and at many of the caravanserais nothing but the rude shelter of the bare walls and a meagre supply of brackish water was obtainable. For all his personal wants the traveller had to carry his own supplies with him. Owing to the want of means of communication, the local governors were all but uncontrolled by the Central Government at Teheran. Each governor, so long as he held office, was supreme, even in matters of life and death, within his own province, and practically did what seemed good in his own eyes. Leaving the towns out of account, the country population consisted of about equal numbers of sedentary cultivators or *rayats*, and nomadic pastoral tribes or *Eeliauts*. The latter are a very independent and somewhat turbulent set of people. They are well armed and well mounted, and their property, consisting as it does of tents, flocks, and herds, is altogether movable. During a great part of the year they frequent the most mountainous and inaccessible parts of the country. No wonder, therefore, that, like the Highland reivers of our own country in former days, they are apt to regard robbery as a fairly legitimate means of supplying their wants and improving their lot. Under such conditions it was not surprising that the roads should sometimes have been infested by armed bands of robbers, who had as little scruple in taking the lives as in helping themselves to the property of those who were unfortunate enough to fall in their way. The state of a province depended in this respect almost entirely on the character of the governor. If, like most of his countrymen, he was a man of energy and determination, the roads were wonderfully safe, while if he was a man of weak or indolent disposition, murders and robberies were of constant occurrence. Under the former class of governors robbers were unsparingly hunted down and summarily executed—sometimes, it must be confessed, in a cruel or barbarous manner. Governors of this kind were at least a terror to evildoers, if not always, or to the same degree, a praise and protection to them that did well.

"There is an institution in Persia, which even the most cursory account cannot pass without notice—the *chapar* or horse-post, which has probably been handed down to the present time with but little change from the days of Xerxes and Darius. Post-houses or rather post-stables, containing relays of saddle-horses, are kept up at distances varying from 20 to 30 miles apart all along the main roads radiating from the capital to the extremities of the kingdom. As a rule the horses are good. A traveller who is accustomed to hard riding, and not afraid of fatigue, can by means of the *chapar* get over the country at the rate of 80 to 100 miles a-day. He must, of course, sleep on the ground, and content himself with the barest modicum in the way of kit and provisions. *Chapar* is the express train of Persia, and I need hardly say that we found it extremely serviceable, and used it freely. I regard it with much respect, and I have probably had more experience of this thoroughly Persian institution than any other European, having chapared an aggregate distance of fully 25,000 miles. The fact that I should have done so without molestation, travelling as I did without escort, by day and by night, at all seasons of the year, speaks volumes for the good order which generally prevailed. Sometimes, it is true, I narrowly escaped, and all of our staff were not so fortunate as myself, several of them having been robbed and wounded, and two of them killed.

"The Persians are a decidedly robust, handsome race, amply endowed with the gifts of intelligence and imagination. They are of a restless, active disposition, and in this and many other respects totally unlike what Orientals are supposed to be. Grasping and unscrupulous in the pursuit of gain, they are free and even lavish in their expenditure. The rich love to surround themselves with all that is beautiful. They live in spacious houses luxuriously and tastefully furnished. Their love of fine gardens with long vistas of flowers, shrubs, trees, and fountains, amounts almost to a passion. 'Live and let live' is one of the practical mottoes of their lives. A rich man is almost invariably surrounded by a host of retainers and dependants who, with their families, live on his bounty. An acquaintance with the works of their great poets is very general. More than once, at a Persian gentleman's table, I have heard a guest either prompted to an apt quotation or corrected in a false one by one of the servants in attendance. . . ."

Such was the enterprise with which Murdoch Smith was now identified, and such the country in which he was to spend so many years. In the foregoing extract the history of the telegraph is brought down to 1865, when he became Director at Teheran. We must, however, go back to the period of his first arrival in Persia.

On the 17th of November 1863 he met Major Champain at Bushire. The officers of the Persian telegraph were fortunate in their chief. Champain had been selected in January 1862 to accompany Colonel Patrick Stewart to Persia, in response to a request on the part of the latter for a first-rate young officer. He soon showed that he possessed very great administrative ability, sound judgment, unfailing tact, and a rare faculty of gaining the loyal devotion of his subordinates, and the friendship and goodwill of every one with whom he had to do, whether European or Oriental. Murdoch Smith wrote of him long afterwards that "he was liked by all who met him and loved by all who knew him." The meeting at Bushire was the beginning of an intimate friendship which was only severed by Champain's death in 1887.

The two officers started on the journey up country on December 7, and reached Teheran on January 28, 1864. Five superintendents had been appointed to carry out the construction of the line. The work was apportioned so as to give on an average about 220 miles to each superintendent. On the line from Teheran west, joining the Persian with the Turkish and European systems, the superintendents were Lieut. Pierson, R.E., from Baghdad to Kangawar, and Mr H. V. Walton, from Kangawar to Teheran. On the line going south to the Persian Gulf they were Captain Murdoch Smith, R.E., from Teheran to Kohrud, Mr H. Man, from Kohrud to Murghab, and Lieut. St John, R.E., from Murghab to Bushire. Mr Man soon had to be invalided home, and was succeeded by Mr Hoeltzer.

Work was started at once. It soon appeared that the task which had been undertaken was one of no ordinary magnitude.

It will be remembered that the convention which authorised the construction of the line contemplated that the work was to be carried out by the Persians themselves, and only provided for the employment of one English officer in an advisory capacity. Champain's staff consisted of three officers and twelve non-commissioned officers of the Royal Engineers and six civilians, for the presence of none of whom had any provision whatever been made in the convention. Their arrival in the country was not unnaturally viewed with the very strongest sus-

COLONEL SIR JOHN BATEMAN CHAMPAIN, K.C.M.G.

picions. "The situation," as Murdoch Smith afterwards wrote, "was altogether false and unsatisfactory. A line of 1250 miles, through an extremely difficult and troublesome country, had, by hook or by crook, to be made with Persian materials, at Persian expense, by a handful of foreigners whom every man in the kingdom, from the Shah downwards, then regarded as pestilent interlopers. Looking back with the knowledge of subsequent experience, the writer is astounded at the cool impudence of the whole undertaking. The marvel is that our throats were not promptly cut by patriotic brigands." Not only were the people hostile, but the work met with active opposition from many of the local governors, who naturally regarded with dislike a new-fangled Feringhi invention which could not fail in the end to diminish their powers and privileges. Before the line was completed, many miles of it, over the most difficult part of the country, had been entirely swept away by the nomadic tribes at the secret instigation of the local authorities.

How these difficulties were faced and overcome, and the work brought to a successful conclusion, has been fully told by Sir Frederic Goldsmid in *Telegraph and Travel*. Sir Frederic kindly allows me to quote from his book the pages relating to Murdoch Smith's share of the work.

Captain Smith's report [he says] is so characteristic of the occasion, and so faithfully descriptive of the troubles a British officer can manage to surmount, when resolved to fulfil his instructions, and when placed in exceptional and quasi-unprofessional positions, that more than one extract may be found interesting.

He had left Teheran on the 26th February, and reached Kum, a distance of eighty-five miles, on the day following.

"On my arrival I was astonished to find that neither wire, insulators, nor tools had come from Ispahan, although the Persian authorities there had been instructed, . . . as early as the beginning of January, to forward them without delay. I at once sent a courier to Ispahan, on whose return I learnt that some had been sent to Kashan notwithstanding . . . instructions to the Persian officers at Ispahan to despatch all the stores for Kum, before sending any of them anywhere else. I therefore sent the Mirza . . . to Kashan with a letter to the Governor, requesting him to send on all the tools and a specified quantity of wire and insulators to Kum. On the 13th March I received wire and insulators, but no tools. These I long afterwards found had been purposely kept back by the Persian *yawar* at Ispahan, . . . with the object of preventing work in my division until he himself should join it after completion of the line from Ispahan to Kohrud. There was, moreover, no Persian officer appointed to attend to my requisitions for workmen, transport, and materials."

He applied to the Governor of Kum to get some tools made in the bazaar, and was told that orders to this effect were wanting from Teheran. When with great difficulty a supply of some kind had been obtained, he applied for workmen. First came a few old men and boys; but after repeated remonstrances he got a working party of thirty labourers.

"As these men were either very badly paid or not paid at all, they naturally enough ran away, and others quite new to the work had to be found. I at length prevailed on the Governor to . . . pay them 16 *shahis* (about 7½d.) per day, in my presence; but it was not till the 25th March that this concession was made, and mules enough provided to enable me to move out of the town, form a camp, and fairly begin work."

The Governor had introduced in his correspondence with Captain Smith a form of address marking his own superiority, which, if not a covert insult, at least was likely to be so interpreted in a country where worth is measured by position, and humility is another word for disgrace. For this a written apology was exacted and reluctantly given; but the ruler of Kum had other failings than vanity.

"Seeing a number of good poles (about 600) lying near the *chapar khanah*,[1] I asked the Governor how they happened to be there, if, as he assured me, there were more than enough laid out along the road within his territory? He replied that those I saw were the first that had been brought, but as he did not consider them good enough, he had rejected them, and sent the others now lying scattered along the road, which were much longer and better in every way. This, I afterwards found, was utterly untrue, as the poles on the road were deficient in number, most of them much too small, and none of them suitable for stretching-posts. I was therefore obliged, after nearly a month's delay at Kum, when the poles at the *chapar khanah* might have been distributed, to carry all the stretching-posts required, and many of the ordinary ones, from the town, along the line as far as the boundary of the district of Teheran, a distance of forty-five miles."

Captain Smith had barely a sufficient number of mules for the carriage of wires, insulators, and similar materials; yet had he to make his own arrangements, not only for the conveyance of poles, but for a supply of bread to the workmen. "In short," he wrote, "the Governor did almost nothing that I required, and I was only too thankful when left uninterrupted to do as best I could without his assistance."

On the 29th March arrived a *shahzadah*, or royal prince, attached by the Persian Government to Captain Smith's division, to provide working parties and comply generally with the superintendent's requisitions. . . .

Under the new *régime* matters could scarcely be said to have mended. After two days' delay, Captain Smith arranged with his Persian assistant that the men should be paid at the

---

[1] Post-house.

same rate and in the same manner as before. Work was then recommenced, but progress was slow, owing to the continued interruptions caused by want of money, want of bread, and want of poles. A government letter was shown, giving fifty of the king's mules for the service of the telegraph. But only thirty were actually forthcoming; and of these, four were riding mules for the use of muleteers, and out of the balance of twenty-six seldom more than twenty were available at a time. Twenty mules of the fifty were altogether mythical, for of them no account could be rendered. And with respect to two artillery carriages and eighteen horses, also reported at the disposal of the telegraph, their existence was not more real, for the service specified, than that of the twenty mules.

On the 5th April the Persian agent, coming to the telegraph camp, reported he could no longer pay the workmen, and proposed to revert to the system of forced labour. The superintendent refused consent to such procedure; but the prince said he could get no money from the Governor; there was no way to get unpaid work but by the use of the stick; and he could not prevent desertions.

Captain Smith explains his position in the following manner:—

"The officer to whom alone I could give my requisitions had himself no power to fulfil them, without applying to another who refused to give the necessary supplies; so that if I addressed myself to the Governor, he said he had nothing to do with me, and if to Abul Fath Mirza, the reply was that the Governor would give him nothing. The result was another stoppage of the work, and the breaking up of the working party which had been collected and partially instructed with great difficulty, and no resource was left me but an appeal to Teheran."

The appeal was made to her Majesty's Legation, whither Captain Smith at once repaired, riding in post to Teheran. He proposed that since the Persian Government required the attendance of one of their own officers in each telegraph division, the respective governors of towns within his range of superintendence should be instructed to comply with his requisitions made through the native agent, and to have the workmen daily paid in his presence. After a delay of ten days the necessary orders were procured.

We resume the quotations:—

"The tedious work of collecting and drilling a new lot of workmen had again to be gone through. In this I received no assistance from the Persian officers. Notwithstanding repeated applications, not a single man was sent either by the Governor or Abul Fath Mirza, so that, at a distance of fourteen miles from the nearest town or village, we had to get our workmen as we best could ourselves. All my requisitions were neglected in the same way, although there was now no excuse to offer of want of orders. The artillery horses and carriages remained, as a rule, in Kum, only occasionally bringing out a load of stretching-poles, and I could not obtain a single mule besides those belonging to the king, notwithstanding a special clause regarding them in the orders I had brought from Teheran. I applied repeatedly for tents for the workmen, but none were given, so that before we reached the inundation near Hauz-i-Sultan, they had to walk daily a distance to and from their work of eighteen miles. With a camp pitched near the work, and mules enough to supply it with bread and water, nearly half of each day would have been saved. . . . I never succeeded in getting more than thirty-five men, . . . and from want of mules half of them had always to be employed in carrying poles."

Circumstances occurred to change the plan of operations. It had been intended to complete the line from Kum to Teheran; but it became necessary to stop about midway, and return to the former city, thence to work back to Kashan and Kohrud. Here again the old difficulties were revived; and the newly appointed Governor of Kashan refused to lend any assistance whatever to the construction of the telegraph, as he had no orders from his Government.

Moreover, in full accordance with the verbal asseveration of this functionary, when the working parties from Kum reached the Kashan boundary, none were there to replace them, and these being withdrawn, operations were suspended for six days. In this interval, orders appear to have been received from Teheran, and the Governor was in a position to comply with the requisitions of the British superintendent.

From the 2nd to the 10th June some thirty-six miles had been completed in the new direction. A brief delay was caused by the intervention of the Muharam festival; but before the end of the month the boundary of Nathenz had been reached, and the goodwill of the local authorities in that district enabled Captain Smith to join his line, through a long rocky gorge, and in spite of physical obstacles unknown in the tracts he had lately quitted, to the line brought by his fellow-superintendent from Ispahan.

Returning to Hauz-i-Sultan, he laboured at completing the line thence to the capital. . . . We will take leave of Captain Smith with an extract from his concluding paragraph. He is speaking of the Persian agent in his camp, who had complained to him bitterly that his method of conducting business had "blighted his hopes of making what the Persians, by a quaint euphemism, call *mudakhil*, or income." Perhaps it would be better translated as "perquisites," for that is the generally-understood meaning of the word. "I had some difficulty in making him comprehend that *mudakhil* in English went by a much harder name. From the highest official down to the meanest labourer, I found that all were actuated by the same principle. When they thought it possible to make *mudakhil*, they were all activity, but when their income was interfered with by the system I adopted of seeing everything paid in my presence, and warning the villagers on no account to give 'presents' to any one, they relapsed into their usual state of obstinate indifference."

At last, on October 13, 1864, Major Champain reported to the Bombay Government the completion of a single-wire line of telegraph from Baghdad by Teheran to Bushire. In his report he writes:—

"Captain Murdoch Smith, R.E., has been perhaps more annoyed by the Persian authorities than any other superintendent. Time after time has his progress been stopped for no reason whatever, and it often seemed that it would be impossible to complete the line. To the end, however, Captain Smith laboured with the most untiring patience and unconquerable determination. His line is beautifully laid out and finished, and he deserves the greatest credit."

He also stated that the line would " in all probability be open to the public in a few days." Two serious hitches, however, had occurred.

One was on the Turkish frontier at Khanikin, where the line passed from Persian into Turkish territory. The position of the actual frontier was matter of dispute, and for some seventeen miles the line passed through a strip of debatable land. An arrangement was made with the Turkish authorities as to the point at which the lines were to meet, and Pierson joined up the wires accordingly, and worked back to Kermanshah, the headquarters of his division. The Governor of Kermanshah then wrote to him to return to the frontier and pull up part of the Turkish line, substituting Persian posts and wire; subsequently he desired him to cut the wire at the junction. Pierson replied that his duty was confined to taking measures for erecting and maintaining the line; if the Governor, he said, wished to destroy it for political reasons, he must send his own agents to do so. The Governor actually caused the wire to be cut, and it remained so for a considerable time. After much negotiation the difficulty was solved by Colonel Kemball, the British Resident at Baghdad, who hit upon the happy expedient of turning to account the telegraph poles used by the litigants respectively to represent the national interests involved; that is to say, as the Turks used iron and the Persians wooden posts for their respective lines, it was suggested that alternate iron and wooden posts over the disputed tract would illustrate a mutual understanding, or the recognition of a misunderstanding, in a satisfactory manner. This arrangement, accompanied by the exchange of *statu quo* declarations, was accepted by both parties.

A much more serious difficulty arose at the other end of the line.

When the line from Teheran to Bushire was completed at the end of September, by some inadvertence a land-line instrument had not been made over to that station, so that messages had to be forwarded to Shiraz direct from the cable office. The necessary instrument was supplied a few days later, but the Persian clerks were not considered sufficiently expert to be trusted with its working. The Minister of Public Works at Teheran thereupon sent instructions to a Persian clerk at Shiraz to prevent the English from talking with Bushire, by disconnecting their instrument. A protest on the part of Major Champain was met by a further order to cut the wire, which was carried out. He thereupon removed his instruments from Shiraz and Ispahan, disconnected those at Teheran, and laid the matter before her Majesty's Minister, Mr Alison. The situation was rendered still more serious by the conduct of the Persian authorities at Ispahan, where they had attempted forcible seizure of the instruments, and where the English superintendent had forbidden those of his countrymen under his orders to enter the city or the Persian telegraph office. For several weeks the departure of the whole English telegraph staff from the country seemed imminent. It was not till the beginning of December that the matter was settled. An arrangement was effected which readjusted the relations of the English staff to the Persian authorities. The Persian Government agreed that the English staff were to control the telegraph office, and to work the line for five months from the date of renewing correspondence with India. The Minister of Public Works was to be acknowledged as head of all telegraphs in Persia, but was to issue no orders on the lines from Teheran to Khanikin or Bushire without the consent of the English director. After five months the English were to leave the country, making over the entire line to the Persians; but it was proposed to retain one engineer officer and two assistants at Teheran in a consultative capacity for a further period of ten months. A formal apology was offered for what had taken place at Ispahan.

In the mean time, however, very serious damage

had been done to the line in the neighbourhood of Shiraz by the inhabitants, especially by the nomadic Iliats when migrating from their summer quarters in the hills to the seaboard. Lieutenant St John, who had been driven to sea by an attack of fever, on returning to Shiraz in December found that some twenty miles of the line had been almost totally destroyed. The long spans which had cost so much time and labour to erect had been cut down; out of six hundred consecutive insulators only twenty remained unbroken; and the wire was severed in pieces and lying on the ground, or confusedly festooned round the poles. Many of the poles had been used for firewood. Fortunately St John was able to trace one of the main offenders, whose position as a clan chief of the powerful Kashkai tribe made his punishment politically important. He had caused the fall of the large span across the Kothal Pir Zan by smashing a lower supporting insulator with a bullet from his gun.

By this time the difficulty with the Persian Government had been settled, and the authorities at Teheran were greatly annoyed by the news of this wanton damage. On the representation of Mr Alison the Shah was pleased to issue stringent orders for the seizure and punishment of the culprits. Mirza Jiafar Khan, second in rank among Persian telegraph magnates, was ordered to proceed at once by *chapar* to Shiraz, accompanied by a royal executioner to cut off any heads which St John might indicate. Ali Khan Beg, the offending Kashkai chief, was to be sent in chains to Teheran, and a fine of 1000 tomans (£400) was to be levied from the Ilkhani, or head of the nomad tribes, a chief powerful enough to bring into the field some 50,000 men. The Mirza duly posted to Shiraz, found and seized Ali Khan Beg, squeezed the prescribed fine from the Ilkhani, plus a second thousand for his chief in Teheran and 500 tomans for himself, and plundered the village of Dashtiarjan, where he had been insulted by the villagers. In the mean time further serious injury had been done to the line, the amount of damage having been nearly doubled. The prompt action of the Government, however, put matters on a much more satisfactory footing, and for many years afterwards less damage was done to the line in Fars, the most turbulent province of Persia, than in any other part of the country. Ali Khan Beg, after being locked up for two months, was released at St John's request, with the result of securing to the English telegraph officers the friendship of the Kashkai chiefs.

It was not till March 1865 that the damage was repaired and the line open for traffic. Before that period, however, a change had taken place in the directorship.

Colonel Patrick Stewart died at Constantinople on the 16th of January 1865. He was succeeded as Director-in-Chief of the Indo-European Telegraph by Colonel Goldsmid. Major Champain was associated with Colonel Goldsmid in the directorship, and Murdoch Smith succeeded

Champain as Director of the Persian Telegraph at Teheran, with the local rank of major.[1]

He held the appointment for twenty-three years with conspicuous success. Long afterwards, when recalling this period of his life, he said: "It would be endless to attempt to describe the difficulties by which the task that thus devolved upon me was surrounded. Imagine a country in many ways resembling the roadless lawless Highlands of Scotland as depicted in the pages of *Waverley* and *Rob Roy*, and you will have some idea of the conditions under which a telegraph line, 1200 miles in length, through a rugged, mountainous, and absolutely independent country, had to be constructed, maintained, guarded, and worked. . . . Success often seemed wellnigh hopeless. It came at last, however, very gradually, after some ten years of incessant struggling. Thanks to the tact and to the zealous and loyal efforts of our widely scattered staff, consisting chiefly of officers and non-commissioned officers of the Royal Engineers, suspicion gradually gave place to trustfulness, and enmity to friendship. . . . At last the whole line was brought into a state of general efficiency that for the last quarter of a century has compared favourably with that of the oldest and best established lines in Europe."

When Murdoch Smith was called upon to take up the duties of Director the whole enterprise was in a very precarious position. As we have seen, it had just escaped total shipwreck, and

---

[1] He became captain in 1864, major in 1873, lieutenant-colonel in 1881, and colonel in 1885.

the arrangement which had been concluded contemplated the early departure from Persia of the whole telegraph staff. Before Champain left Teheran, however, he had scored a great diplomatic success. Writing at the time, he says: "'I am off to Constantinople at once to take my dear lost friend's place. . . . A real triumph came yesterday. You remember, perhaps, that the great objection to our *last* telegraph agreement with the Persians was that we were only to remain five months after the through line was open. I tried hard for seven months, and then for six, but had to agree to five; the 'Telegraph Prince'[1] and his secretaries being our great opposers. They were jealous of us and anxious to get the complete management. Yesterday the Sertip came to me, and, after a lot of flattering palaver, asked when our five months were to begin. I replied in about ten days. He then said, 'Shall you really leave Persia when the time has passed?' 'Certainly,' was my answer. He said, 'Could you be induced to leave all the English staff here if the King desired it?' I pretended to be doubtful, and replied that that was precisely what we wished when the agreement was first drawn up, and that personally I should rejoice in such an arrangement, but that I couldn't speak as to the views of the English Government. He then confessed to me that the prince and he had been racking their brains as to what they should do if we really left. He

[1] The "Telegraph Prince" was the Itazad-u-Sultaneh, Ali Kuli Mirza, then Minister of Public Works.

allowed that our management surprised the Persians, that their receipts even now were very great from the line, and that the prince was horrified at the idea of all breaking down when we went, and at the correspondent anger of the King. He added that the prince himself had actually written to his Majesty asking him to try and prolong our stay for at least a year. Imagine my triumph! . . . Smith arrives from Ispahan to-day, and I leave for Constantinople on Monday. Oh that Stewart had survived to see our grand difficulties over!"

The Shah had begun to take a personal interest in the telegraph. On January 21, 1865, he paid a visit of some two hours' duration to the telegraph office at Teheran, conversing there through the wires with the governors of Shiraz, Ispahan, Kashan, Kum, Hamadan, and Kermanshah. He expressed himself much pleased with the arrangements, and was impatient to be able to communicate with Europe and India.

The political difficulties, however, were by no means over. The Persian authorities were simply feeling their way. They had already, at the instance of certain foreign Legations, sent secretly to Europe for a staff of telegraphists to take the place of the Englishmen when the five months expired. A number of these arrived from Paris and Constantinople shortly after Champain's departure. Still, the great point had been carried; a fairly secure footing in the country had been obtained. It remained with the telegraph officers to make that footing a permanent one.

For this task the new Director was excellently qualified. Had the post been filled by a man of the aggressive John Bull type, success would have been hopeless; but Murdoch Smith, besides being a thoroughly efficient telegraph officer, possessed in a rare degree the qualities which the position required — tact, patience, a sympathetic understanding of Oriental character, and a singularly winning personality. He succeeded beyond expectation.

The Shiraz line was soon got into working order again, and by the beginning of March through communication was open. By this time the opposition to the telegraph had greatly abated. The Government at Teheran was becoming reconciled to the idea of a permanent English staff; the people were becoming familiar with the presence of Englishmen; and the hostility of local authorities was much less violent.

On August 1, 1865, Colonel Goldsmid arrived at Teheran for the purpose of negotiating, if possible, a new telegraph convention. The negotiations dragged on for months. It was not till the 23rd of November that the convention was signed. The Persian Government agreed to attach a second wire to the poles already erected between Bushire and Khanikin, the work to be done under the direction of an English officer and staff, the wire, 200 new posts, insulators, and instruments to be supplied by the British Government at a reasonable cost, recoverable in five years. It was further agreed that an English telegraph officer and staff, not exceeding fifty persons, exclusive of families, should be engaged for five years from the opening of communications through the second wire, in organising the line and giving instruction in telegraphy. At the conclusion of that period the line was to be made over to the Persians. The yearly receipts were to be credited to Persia up to 30,000 tomans (£12,000), any surplus to be made over to the officers of the English Government for the cost of that establishment.

An incident which took place during the negotiations, and which did a good deal to help them forward, amusingly illustrates the ways of diplomacy at Teheran. Some time before this a question had arisen as to which much serious diplomatic discussion had taken place. The Ministers of the European Powers were in the habit of attending the annual races at Teheran. The places allotted to them in the grand stand were on the ground floor, immediately under the room occupied by the ladies of the Shah's harem. It was considered that these places were not befitting the dignity of those who were invited to occupy them, and that they ought to be changed to the upper floor. Reams of foolscap were expended on the subject, and for some years the members of the *corps diplomatique* absented themselves as a body from the annual races. At last it was announced that an amicable settlement had been effected. On the next race day the representatives of the Great Powers proceeded towards the course. An advance party, which included Murdoch Smith, was sent forward to reconnoitre, but returned to inform their Excellencies that instead of any elevation in position having been effected they had been merely transferred from one room to another on the same floor. The diplomatists with one exception returned in high dudgeon to their respective Legations. Negotiations were opened, and ultimately the offended dignity of Europe was satisfied and peace restored. The authorities were specially anxious to smooth down the ruffled plumage of Her Britannic Majesty's Minister, and their conciliatory attitude made itself felt in the negotiations which resulted in the convention.

The convention was an excellent bargain for the Persians; it gave them a free wire for local use, a maximum annual royalty of £12,000 for the right of transit enjoyed by the foreigners, and the ultimate reversion of the entire property.

On the completion of the convention the Director-in-Chief, accompanied by Murdoch Smith, travelled down country to Ispahan, and thence on December 18 started on a journey through Beluchistan with the object of surveying the country in order to determine as to the practicability of constructing a land line between Ispahan and Karachi. The story of their trying journey through snow and desert has been told by Sir Frederic Goldsmid in *Telegraph and Travel*. On January 21, 1866, the two officers parted at Sabristan, a few stages east of Karman. After three weeks' separate wandering, they met again at the fishing village of Charbar, whence they steamed along the coast to Gwadur, and continued their route by sea to Karachi. They reached Karachi on the 20th of February, and thence proceeded to Bombay. The Director-in-Chief had to proceed to Calcutta, to make his report to the Government of India, and at the suggestion of Sir Bartle Frere, then Governor of Bombay, Murdoch Smith accompanied him. A most enjoyable trip round India ensued, which Murdoch Smith always recalled with great pleasure. They crossed Southern India by rail, embarked at Madras, and reached Calcutta on the 2nd of April, to find that the Government had gone to Simla. After visiting Delhi, Lucknow, and Cawnpore, they reached Simla, and were most kindly received by Sir John Lawrence, then Viceroy. On leaving Simla they proceeded by Amritsar and Lahore to Multan, and thence down the Indus by steamer to Karachi, and so back to Bombay.

They had reported favourably as to the feasibility of the proposed land line through Beluchistan, and it had been approved of by the Indian authorities, but it was never carried out. Subsequent negotiations, however, with the Persian Government resulted in a short convention signed at Teheran on April 2, 1868, of which the outcome was the construction of a land line from Gwadur to Jask on the Beluchistan coast, and the laying of a second cable from Jask to Bushire, the telegraph station at Mussendom on the Arab coast being at the same time transferred to Jask.

An interesting episode of this tour was a visit to Wajid Ali Shah, the dethroned King of Oudh, in his palace at Garden Reach, Calcutta. Among

Murdoch Smith's valued relics was a small silver cup given him by the King as a souvenir of this visit.

In May Colonel Goldsmid left for England and Murdoch Smith returned to Teheran.

Before proceeding to speak of his personal life in Persia, it will be convenient here to narrate shortly the subsequent history of the Persian Telegraph.

Steps were at once taken to proceed with the construction of the second wire in terms of the convention. The necessary stores reached Bushire on September 2, 1866. Work was at once commenced. Matters were not so bad as they had been during the construction of the original line, but still the difficulties were endless. Dry-rot and white ants had made havoc among the telegraph poles. A large number of poles had already been replaced, and for a great part of the line every pole had to be taken out and examined. No amount of pressure could induce the Persians to replace the decayed or useless poles. There was great difficulty in getting beasts of burden, and in the province of Fars there had just been an epidemic among the mules. The work, however, was resolutely pushed on, and on the 1st of August 1867 Murdoch Smith reported to the Government of Bombay the completion of the new lines from Bushire to Teheran, and from Teheran to Karmanshah.

Colonel Goldsmid, writing officially to the Government of Bombay on October 21, 1867, said:—

"The completion of the work at all in eighteen

months must afford abundant proof how much has been achieved by the unfailing energy and perseverance of the English superintendents and their assistants, on whom the onus of labour fell. . . .

"As regards the services of Major R. Murdoch Smith, for more than two years Acting Director of the Persian telegraphs, and his immediate assistants,—notably Lieutenants St John and Pierson, whose reports are submitted to Government,—I am convinced that it would be difficult to find officers better adapted for the delicate and often arduous and trying duties which they are called upon to fulfil in Persia. I can certify from personal experience that Major Smith's testimony to the character of his assistants is no other than the expression of an impartial and unbiassed judgment. And I can further certify that the encomiums which he has passed upon these officers would be no less deserved if applied to his own case."

It will be remembered that the Turkish line by Baghdad and Fao had been opened in the end of 1864. A stream of telegrams at once poured in, but the want of efficiency in the lines across Europe and Asiatic Turkey caused great delay and confusion in their transmission. Matters became worse than ever when in 1866 the Russian and Persian Governments joined their local lines at the Caucasian frontier and announced that a new route for Indo-European messages had been established *viâ* Russia. There were now three routes open, the Anglo-Turkish by Fao and Baghdad, the Anglo-Persian by Teheran and Baghdad, and the Anglo-Russian. On none of them, however, was there a staff in any way competent to deal with international English telegrams. Transmission was very slow; the state of confusion in which the messages did or did not reach their destinations was appalling, as may well be imagined when it is remembered that on the three lines they had opportunities of being translated and retranslated by ignorant clerks into English, French, Dutch, German, Italian, Greek, Bulgarian, Wallachian, Servian, Russian, Turkish, and Armenian. An illustration may be given of the chaotic state of international telegraphy at this time. Shortly before Major Champain left Teheran a telegram had been sent from India to the effect that the director of the Punjab railway had been struck by paralysis, and that some one should be sent at once to replace him. In its devious course towards London it had been translated into Persian and back again into English, and finally reached the Secretary of State in the form of a report through the Embassy at St Petersburg, from the English Legation at Teheran, that the director of the telegraph at Teheran had been paralysed. The word "Punjab" had in Persian been mutilated into *inja* (here); the place of origin had dropped out, and "Teheran" been inserted for "Lahore"; while some intelligent telegraphist, knowing there was a *telegraph* but no *railway* in Persia, had given the message its final correction by substituting the one word for the other. A repetition which was called for from Constantinople and Baghdad confirmed the report! Fortunately, international telegraphy was still as slow as it was inaccurate, and almost as soon as the message (by that time twenty-six days old) was communicated to Champain's father, letters of later date arrived from himself.

Still worse was the hopeless confusion of dates. A message dated, say, the 1st of the month, might as likely as not be overtaken and passed on the road by a message dated the 2nd, 3rd, or 4th. A merchant at Calcutta might get a telegram giving him the London prices of the day before, while his neighbour's latest, received at the same time, might be a week or ten days old. This intolerable state of things led the eminent engineering firm of Siemens Brothers, at the head of which was the former President of the Royal Society, Sir William Siemens, to conceive the idea of a special through line from London to Teheran, to be made and worked by an English company for the transmission of Indo-European messages alone. The firm's relations with the Governments of Germany and Russia, together with the active assistance of Major Champain, who went to St Petersburg and had an audience of the Czar on the subject, enabled them to obtain concessions to construct and work a line across those countries exclusively for Indian messages. A similar concession was obtained from Persia for the section between the Russian frontier and Teheran. An English company, called the Indo-European Telegraph Company, was then formed to take over the concessions and carry them out. On January 31, 1870, the new line was opened between London and Teheran, where it joined the already existing Government line.

In the mean time submarine telegraphy had made enormous strides, thanks chiefly to the genius of Lord Kelvin, and in 1867 the Eastern Telegraph Company was formed for the purpose of laying a submarine line the whole way from England to India. In 1870, almost simultaneously with the opening of the Indo-European Company's line to Teheran, came the opening of the Eastern Company's to Bombay. In 1878 the Indian Government entered into a joint-purse agreement with both companies. Since that time the telegraphic communication with India has been regular, rapid, and unintermittent, and the Government and the public have the great advantage and security of two entirely different telegraphic systems uniting the Indian empire with London—namely, the Indo-European *viâ* Lowestoft, Emden, Berlin, Warsaw, Odessa, Kertch, Tiflis, Teheran, Bushire, and Karachi; and the Eastern *viâ* Falmouth, Gibraltar, Malta, Suez, Aden, and Bombay. To these must be added the original route through Baghdad and Constantinople.

On December 2, 1872, another telegraph convention with Persia was signed. It was to last for twenty-three years, being the full period of the Siemens concession. It laid down the terms on which the international traffic was in future to be worked, the system by which accounts were to be settled, the duties and responsibilities of the English staff employed in the country, and the protection to be accorded them by the Persian authorities. This convention, together with that which had been concluded in 1868 providing for the Gwadur-Jask extension already referred to, was on the occasion of Murdoch Smith's mission to Persia in 1887 extended to the year 1905. They have since been further extended to 1925.

As to the efficiency attained by the telegraphic service, it may suffice again to quote Murdoch Smith's Geographical Society paper. "Some considerable time," he says, "after through-communication had been opened, a hope was expressed (in 1867, to the best of my memory) that the service might eventually be so improved that telegrams would reach their destination correctly and regularly within a maximum of *three days* from their original dates. This opinion, however, was thought at the time to be too utopian. Messages between all parts of the United Kingdom and all parts of India (not merely those between London and the Presidency towns) *now* reach their destinations within an average interval between their reception at one end and their delivery at the other of less than an hour and a half. In an average of only one word in about two hundred does even the most trivial mistake occur in transmission. And it must be remembered that the telegrams are almost entirely either in code or cypher, which, as compared with ordinary language, adds enormously to the chances of error, as well as to the time required for transmission. Were this degree of speed and accuracy attained with a small amount of traffic, it would still, I think, bear favourable comparison with that of any telegraph system in the world. But the traffic to which those averages apply amounts to the large total of nearly 1000 messages a-day.

"Of the far-reaching effects which this constant stream of rapid communication has had, and has, on the Government, the commerce, and the general condition of India, I shall not attempt to form an estimate. One effect on this country is patent to all—viz., the greater and more widely spread knowledge of India, and the greater interest taken in her affairs. Every noteworthy event is at once telegraphed to the press at home, and in every Monday's copy of the *Times* appears an exhaustive summary of the week's Indian news accompanied by such commentary as the events seem to call for. It may perhaps surprise you to be told that those interesting telegrams are altogether unpadded, and that even to the punctuation—the use of inverted commas, for instance—they are printed absolutely *verbatim*."

The establishment of the telegraph has profoundly affected the social and political condition of Persia and our relations with that country. A very remarkable appreciation of the effect which it has produced was placed on record in 1892 by Mr George Curzon, now Lord Curzon of Kedleston and Viceroy of India, in the closing chapter of his well-known book on Persia. It forms part of the result of a minute and exhaustive study of Persia and Persian questions, and its importance is of course greatly enhanced by the position which the writer has since attained.

From whichever point of view we regard its operation [says Mr Curzon], the influence of the telegraph has been enormous. I am disposed to attribute to it, more than to any other cause or agency, the change that has passed over Persia during the last thirty years, and the results of which I have chronicled in these volumes. To begin with, the telegraph for the first time brought Persia into contact with Europe, with the result of making her a member of the comity of nations. . . . But for the electric telegraph she would have lingered drowsily on, plunged in the self-satisfied stupor from which how many an Oriental kingdom and khanate has only been aroused to find itself upon the brink of doom, and would have rotted slowly away until the Muscovite trumpet rang its final summons in her ear, and Europe was invited as a spectator to the funeral feast. Whatever of civilization, or reform, or regeneration has been introduced into Persia in the last quarter of a century may indirectly be attributed to the influence of the telegraph. . . .

Secondly—and this consequence has been scarcely less momentous or considerable than the first—to the introduction of the electric telegraph into Persia, followed as it has been by the spread of subsidiary lines throughout the country, must be attributed, even more than to the personal character of the sovereign or the altered spirit of the times, that consolidation of the royal authority which has made Nasr-ed-Din Shah the most powerful monarch of Persia since Nadir Shah. With a few rare exceptions, the licensed independence of the great border chieftains is at an end. . . . The telegraph has also very much impaired the administrative independence of provincial governors. . . . Not the least, therefore, among the indirect services rendered by England to the reigning Shah has been that gift by which he has been enabled to colleot his annual revenue with a precision very welcome to his economical instincts, to suppress local disorder or frontier turbulence, and, within the contracted limits of the modern Persian kingdom, to find himself everywhere acknowledged supreme.

Thirdly must be ranked the friendly relations that have been developed by the social and official contact of nearly thirty years between Persians and Englishmen. Scattered throughout the country, where they are brought into frequent connection with all classes of the people, from a governor passing along the highway to his official post to the peasants of the neighbouring villages; constantly riding to and fro along the lines; possessed sometimes of a little medical knowledge, and willing to dispense a modest charity; above all, absolutely superior to bribes, the English telegraph officers in Persia may be considered mainly responsible for the high estimate in which English character and honour are held in that country. They are often made the unofficial arbiters of local disputes; the victims of injury or oppression fly to the telegraph office as a sort of *bast*, or sanctuary, where they are free from pursuit; and in the great towns the officers of higher rank are the friends, and sometimes the advisers, of governors and princes. If we contrast this state of affairs with the conditions under which the first engineers and sappers entered the country, in the face of daily obstruction, insult, and danger, we can arrive at some appreciation of the good work that has been done.

CHAPTER VII.

LIFE IN PERSIA.

TEHERAN IN THE 'SIXTIES—DR WILLS'S VISIT TO MURDOCH SMITH—THE MAJOR'S DERVISH—"ASHES ON MY HEAD!"—TEHERAN FESTIVITIES—"SHE STOOPS TO CONQUER"—LEGATION BUILDINGS—MARRIAGE—THE *CORPS DIPLOMATIQUE*—MRS MURDOCH SMITH'S ILLNESS—VISIT TO EUROPE—PAPER AT UNITED SERVICE INSTITUTION—CHAPARING ADVENTURES—PERSIAN JUSTICE—ST JOHN AND THE LIONESS—STARVING SOLDIERS—THE SADDLE AND THE PRINCE—THE "TRANSIT OF VENUS"—THE FALCKENHAGEN CONCESSION—POLE-SHOOTING—RUSSIAN INFLUENCE—*TANZIMAT*—MURDOCH SMITH'S RELATIONS WITH THE PERSIANS—THE MUKHBER-ED-DOWLEH—ADMINISTRATIVE METHODS—A POLYGLOT WORLD.

THESE great results represented many years of strenuous and anxious work on the part of all concerned. In Persia Murdoch Smith was from 1865 onwards the inspiring force and the guiding mind of that work so far as it was done by the British Government. He planned every detail of it; he grappled with difficulty after difficulty with unfailing resource and unfailing good humour; he organised victory out of the most unpromising materials. Before he laid down the reins of office he had not only organised the Persian Telegraph, but had succeeded in the far more difficult task of changing the entire attitude of the Persians, from the Shah downwards, towards the telegraph and through it towards this country.

In tragic contrast to the record of success presented by his official career is the story of his personal life during the same period, which opened with brilliant prospects of happiness, but before he left Persia had been overshadowed by the darkest clouds of calamity.

Teheran in the 'Sixties was still an entirely Oriental city. Nasr-ed-Din Shah had been on the throne since 1848, but few of the changes which during his reign revolutionised the appearance of the Persian capital had as yet been effected. It was still surrounded by its embattled mud wall. The streets were narrow and foul, with open drains in the middle. Poplar-planted avenues, gas-lamps, and tramway lines were still in the future. The city was still the city of Fath Ali Shah—the city of Hajji Baba—where black eunuchs held sway over secluded beauty and the dervish sat begging at the great man's door. The European population was a mere handful; it did not amount to more than some fifty persons all told, chiefly the *personnel* of the English, Russian, and French Legations.

The enjoyment of life in such surroundings depends entirely upon a man's own point of view. To one man such a place is a mere penal settlement, a place where life has to be endured as philosophically as may be from furlough to furlough, until the arrival of the happy day of return to European civilisation. To another it is a wonderland of endless interest.

To Murdoch Smith it was the latter. The duties

of his new office included work of the most varied and exacting kind: correspondence with the Government of Bombay, under which his department was placed, negotiations with the Persian authorities, and endless financial and administrative detail; but he found time to work hard at the Persian language, to interest himself in Persian art, history, and social life, and to enjoy all that was to be had in the way of sport and of social amusement.

He built a house in Teheran, and another at Gulahek, the hill village some six miles out of Teheran where the British Legation has its summer quarters. When Dr C. J. Wills, on his appointment to the telegraph staff, went out to Persia with Sir Frederic Goldsmid in 1867, they were for a fortnight at Teheran the guests of Murdoch Smith, who is the "Major S——" of that most entertaining of travel books, *In the Land of the Lion and Sun*. Dr Wills has placed on record some impressions of his visit, and I gladly avail myself of his permission to quote from them here.

When we reached Major S——'s house [he writes], on the outside the prospect was not inviting, but no sooner were we inside than everything was comfortable: good doors, good windows, carpets of great beauty, *chairs*,—only try to do without these for a few days, and then, and then only, does one appreciate their comfort,—big settees and divans, and a host of smart and attentive servants. Tea and pipes at once; a warm bath, much needed, in prospect, and above all, the freedom from the morning's call to boot-and-saddle at an unearthly hour.

No sooner was breakfast over than messages were for ever arriving for my chief as to what time he would receive this grandee or that friend; and shortly the ceremonious visits

TEHERAN.

commenced. I was, of course, only too glad to see what a Persian visit was like.

To be a successful entertainer in Persia it is imperative to be a master in the art of compliment, as the conversation itself is generally trivial; but the exact amount of compliment must be meted out with a careful hand, according to the visitor's rank. By no means should the thing be overdone, as an excess of good treatment, over and above what the caller is entitled to, merely lowers the recipient of the visit in the guest's estimation.

Of course I did not at once appreciate the differences of the intonation in the *Bismillah!* or invitation to be seated, but I saw that great differences were made in the position of the guest, in the duration of his visit, and whether he were pressed to stop or not, and in the rising and advancing to receive him, or the refraining from so doing. . . .

By five all the visitors had gone; we dined at seven, and I retired to sleep in a comfortable bed.

At about five next morning I am roused by—

"*Chai, sahib*" (tea, sir); and a lordly individual, with huge mustachios, a black lambskin cap, a brown cloth inner coat, a blue cloth outer coat, a broad belt, and a long *kummer* (or straight broad-bladed sword), dark-blue *shulwar* (what an American calls pants, and an outfitter pyjamas), and his stockinged feet,—his shoes were outside my door,—places a cup of tea, some twice-baked sweet biscuit, of delicious crispness, and some marmalade at my side and departs. He soon returns with a second cup of tea and a *kalian*.

As I am a griffin, he draws my attention to the latter being —" Welly good thing, *kalian*."

He then goes through a pantomime suggesting sleep, talking all the time to me in Persian. I take his advice.

At eight he wakes me, and I find he has a warm tub ready for me. I dress once again in the clothes of ordinary life, and go down, to find no one about, for Major S—— has gone to the office, and taken the Colonel with him. . . .

We visited the telegraph office, and looked round the Major's garden, returning to breakfast at eleven, and we sat down to a substantial *déjeûner à la fourchette*, with country wines, and tea for those who preferred it. It was followed by the inevitable *kalian* and coffee.

I wanted much to see the Zoological Gardens, but we were told that the Shah had turned the beasts loose. We, however, decided to go, and we found it so—they were all loose.

The leopanther, a cross between the lion and panther, a lovely animal like an immense cat, very tame, allowing one to pat him; two lions, a bear, two tigers (young ones), walking about with the antelopes and wild sheep. I must say the presence of the tigers was not quite pleasant. . . .

In the evening we dined at the English Mission,[1] where there is a billiard-table—my last game for some time, I fancy. . . .

I had been regularly robbed of my rest, after the first few dreamless nights that one has at the end of a long journey, by a sort of hooting sound, followed by cries of "*ya huc, h-u-u-u-c.*" These noises were repeated at irregular intervals all through the night, and I found also that they occurred in the daytime whenever Major S—— entered or left the house. They proceeded from the Major's dervish, and they grew louder and more frequent day by day. . . .

Major S——, as an undoubted personage, had a dervish sent to his house. He had suffered from the infliction before, and had bought himself off on that occasion by a gift of 50 *kerans* (£2), but this time he was determined to grin and bear it, thinking that by making a stand he would escape a similar infliction in the future.

The chief of the dervishes indicates to his subordinates the houses that they are to besiege, and they are allotted to the various members of the fraternity according to seniority —the King, the Prime Minister, the Chancellor, and so on downwards.

When I say that every man of standing had his dervish, it

---

[1] The English Legation or Embassy is always called "The Mission" in Persia, by the members of it, and the English in the country.

will be seen that there were many of the brotherhood at that time in Teheran.

Every foreign Minister had one at his door, and I am sure that any Persian of consideration would have been very loth to be without this very visible sign of greatness.

The Major's dervish was to be found in the street day and night, in or beside his so-called tent; this consisted of some two yards of thin canvas, pegged into the wall at the side of the outer gate, and held down by three pieces of string. The dervish sat by day on an antelope-skin, and by night (if he ever did sleep) slept on it in his clothes.

As any one, visitor or host, entered or left the house, a shrill blast was blown on a buffalo-horn, and the man emitted his monotonous "*Huc—yah huc*" and extended his palm. He had a small pot of live charcoal before him; and smoking, and his so-called garden (a sort of playing at gardening, six twigs of box-tree being planted in a little heap of dust, and an orange being placed between each), occupied a good deal of his time.

The annoying part of it was that he was *always there*, and that we could never forget or fail to notice this fact, from the persistent salutations of "*Salaam, sahib!*" smilingly given, or the eternal cries and blasts of the buffalo horn, by which he made night hideous and the day unbearable. As time wore on, and the New Year approached, the blasts and cries became more prolonged and more frequent, and the whole household became more and more depressed. We all knew that the servants were providing the man with two square meals a day and unlimited tobacco, of course quite contrary to orders.

But I think the greatest sufferers were myself and a friend, whose bedroom window was above the so-called tent of this demon in human form. Patience has its limits, and one morning we determined to, as we hoped, induce our bugbear to shift his quarters. We emptied our two tubs into one, and carefully choosing our moment, suddenly emptied the contents on the tent.

Down it came on the head of the dervish, putting out his

fire-pot, and producing a very free succession of invocations to saints.

But, alas! when we went out in the morning, hoping to find him gone, we were received with "*Salaam, sahib!*" and a solo on the horn that for volume, Harper, of trumpet fame, might have vainly attempted to emulate.

We slunk off, but vowed further vengeance. The next day we determined on a baptism of fire, and we carefully stoked our *mangal*, or brazier, till it gave off a fine red heat, and was quite full of live charcoal. At that time, when there were few fireplaces in the rooms of Persian houses, it was usual to employ these braziers to warm the rooms.

We did not impart our design to the Major, who would doubtless have disapproved, but as soon as the coast was clear, and we were sure that the dervish was in his tent, we prepared for action.

We had got the brazier into position, when the wretch commenced one of his frantic solos; down came the contents, some twenty pounds of live charcoal and wood-ashes.

The dervish laughed at such things, and blew a defiant blast; but in a moment the charcoal, having burnt through the tent roof, descended on his flowing locks, and, amidst deriding shouts of "*Khock ber ser um!*" (Ashes on my head!), a favourite form of imprecation with Persians, from my companion, the dervish emerged considerably the worse.

We were delighted, and felt that we had been at last too many for him. Though our minds were not quite free from visions of a severe wigging from the Major, we felt we had triumphed, and hurried down to tell our tale.

We then found that the dervish had exhausted even the Major's patience, and had received his present and gone. We maintained a discreet silence. Whether the Major heard of our two attacks I never knew, but the man was gone—tent, garden, fire-pot, oranges, and all. Perhaps the treatment he got was considered too bad; anyhow, *he was gone*, and we ceased to hear nightly "the voice which cried, Sleep no more."

Another of Murdoch Smith's many guests at Teheran was Mr Richard Helme, whose acquaintance he renewed long afterwards in England. The acquaintance became an intimate friendship, and in later years Sir Robert was a frequent guest in Mr Helme's house at Walthamstow.

After the early Chatham and Halicarnassus days he never kept a diary, and he preserved very few papers of any kind relating to his life in Persia. Fortunately, however, a considerable number of his letters to Sir Frederic Goldsmid, and to Sir John Champain, who in 1870 succeeded Sir Frederic as Director-in-Chief in London, have been preserved. They relate chiefly to details of telegraph work which would now interest the reader little, but they also give not a few side-lights on the writer's life in Persia.

To Colonel Goldsmid.

TEHERAN, *December* 22, 1868.

... We have been having great doings here socially. Teheran is quite gay. I suppose you heard of the ball I gave at Gulahek in September, on which I (foolishly perhaps) spent £200. It was a grand success, and was in fact the prettiest ball I ever saw. Here we had a charade one night which went off so well that we were encouraged to become more ambitious. We are now getting up *She Stoops to Conquer* for New Year's Eve, and all Teheran is invited. The house is full of carpenters, builders, tailors, and what not, as Pierson and I want to astonish the Vizier Mukhtars, who seem to leave the leadership of the European society entirely to us. We are rigging up a nice stage with all the accessories of footlights, &c., and the dresses are of the most correct and gorgeous description. Our audience will number about fifty. After the play we shall have supper, for which we have knocked three rooms into one upstairs, and are going to decorate elaborately. During supper the stage will be cleared away in the drawing-room for a ball, with which the evening's amusements will terminate. There is tremendous excitement on the subject throughout Teheran, and I am sure the thing will go off with great *éclat*. We have remodelled the play a little, and cut out Tony and Mrs Hardcastle, but what is left makes a capital comedy.

Mrs Baker is Miss Hardcastle.	Lawrence is Hastings.
Miss Baker ,, Miss Neville.	Baker ,, Sir Ch. Marlow.
Pierson ,, Marlow.	Myself ,, Mr Hardcastle.

We have immense fun at the rehearsals, as you may fancy. How I wish you were here!

We have hunting once a-week, and dancing once a-week at Baker's. In fact you would hardly know Teheran. It is getting quite civilized. I have sent for a mail phaeton for four-in-hand, a basket phaeton for a pair, and a clothes-basket. By the time you come to Teheran I hope to give you a drive *comme il faut*. Champain is getting the carriages built in London. I have got four very fine grey horses and am beginning breaking them in.

A letter from Champain to Sir Frederic Goldsmid gives us an amusing glimpse of the Gulahek dance.

"Smith has written me a tremendous long letter," he says, "describing a grand ball he gave at Gulahek. There were no less than 12 ladies and 40 men! They seem to have enjoyed it hugely, and danced from 9 P.M. till breakfast. Smith seems a little smitten by a fair Russian, married and therefore harmless! He has asked me to buy and send out a mail phaeton and pony carriage to Baghdad, with a list of etceteras as long as your arm. Extravagant dog."

The performance of *She Stoops to Conquer* was an immense success, notwithstanding the absence of Tony and Mrs Hardcastle, and the fact that not a few of the audience were entirely unacquainted with the English language, so that polyglot leaflets containing the argument of the play had to be provided for their instruction. One wishes that Goldsmith's ghost could have been there.

On the night of the theatricals Murdoch Smith became engaged to Miss Eleanor Katherine Baker, daughter of Captain John Robinet Baker, R.N. Her brother, Dr James Baker, who was cast for the part of Sir Charles Marlow in the play, was at this time attached to the telegraph staff, and Miss Baker had been for some time in Persia on a visit to him and his wife.

To Colonel Goldsmid.

TEHERAN, *Jan.* 1869.

. . . I need not tell you I am frightfully in love, the happiest man, &c., and all the rest of it. My trotting off to Bushire in these circumstances and at this season is not therefore a pleasure trip exactly, but for the above reasons and some others I should greatly prefer going to not going. If you cannot come now to Bushire can you come up to Teheran and so home? That would, indeed, be a pleasure to all of us. If you come after March I hope you will find me a steady married man, and I am sure my wife will do all she can to make your stay agreeable. There is a bother about *how* to get married, there being no duly authorised official here. Mr Alison has sent to the F.O. for what is necessary, and I hope all will be ready by March, otherwise we must go to Tabriz or elsewhere to get the ceremony legally performed. . . .

Teheran is a perfect whirl of gaiety. Our theatricals on New Year's Eve were beyond a success. It was universally voted the grandest entertainment and soirée that Teheran ever saw. Our theatre *per se* was quite a bijou and our dresses scrumptious. And everybody seemed to think we acted like so many Garricks. The supper, at which all (50) sat down at one table, was beautiful. After supper we had a stunning ball, which was kept up till five in the morning. This and my Gulahek ball have made the swells at last do something. Last Friday we had a capital ball at the Russian Mission. On Tuesday week there is a fancy-dress one on the grandest possible scale, which Mr Alison gives. His preparations are going on regardless of expense. I don't suppose it will cost him much under £1000. It is given in the special honour of my true love, so that it is rather hard both to her, Mr A., and myself to have to tear myself away. On 15th February another ball by the French Minister.

Teheran is quite unrecognisable. Instead of grumbling you hear nothing but, "How gay and jolly Teheran has become!" And people all know that they have the telegraph to thank for it. . . .

In 1868 it was decided to erect new buildings for the British Legation, to replace the old Mission buildings in the southern part of the town, which dated from the days of Sir Gore Ouseley. In June 1868 Murdoch Smith was requested to undertake the general superintendence of the buildings and control of the expenditure connected with the operations. He conducted the somewhat difficult arrangements relating to the acquisition and delimitation of the site for the new buildings; and the enclosure of the Legation grounds was carried out under his professional direction. The bringing in of the water-supply to the Legation was also carried out by him, a difficult piece of professional work, which necessitated constant attendance during the hottest months of the year, which lay entirely outside the scope of his official duties, and which was carried out in a manner which received the high appreciation of the British Minister. In February 1869, however, it was decided to reconstruct on iron posts the telegraph line from Teheran to Bushire, and at the same time to erect a third wire throughout the same line. The extra work which this entailed rendered it impossible for him, consistently with the performance of his proper duties, to continue the superintendence of the Legation buildings.

The work was accordingly handed over to Captain Pierson, and the fine buildings now occupied by the English Minister were designed by that officer. The desolate and stony ground surrounding the Legation was in a few years transformed into a beautiful and luxuriant garden with fine trees and fountains; a striking example of what the climate and soil of Persia can be made to produce by judicious irrigation and careful culture.

Murdoch Smith's marriage to Miss Baker took place in the Legation on March 18, 1869.

To Colonel Goldsmid.

GULAHEK, *June* 2, 1869.

... My wife and I are as happy and jolly as possible here, barring the usual worry and bother incidental to my position in this bothering country. I hope some day or other to have a year or two's repose in Europe on furlough. ...

GULAHEK, *August* 24, 1869.

... Here I have been interrupted by the arrival of the Indian mail with the usual amount of horrid documents from the Acct.-Genl. My whole time almost is taken up in simple accountant's work, which gets more and more complicated every day. ...

I have just returned from Lar, where I spent a few days with my wife to recruit our health after the heat and endless office work. If I write you stupid letters set it down to the Acct.-Genl. & Co.

at Bombay. I loathe the very sight of pens, ink, and paper. . . .

St John, who left the day before yesterday, you have of course seen, and got all the news from him. I am very glad Pierson is coming back married to such a nice girl. Persia is becoming *abād*.

GULAHEK, *September* 22, 1869.

. . . The new Russian Minister has arrived, Mr Beger (I don't know how to spell his name). He seems a very nice sort of man. Also a new second secretary in place of Serjepowtovski, appointed consul at Resht. . . . These are, I think, all the changes among your old friends of the Corps Diplomatique. The Persians are also pretty much *in statu quo*. The cholera has at last almost if not quite disappeared. The peculiarity of it this year was that it attacked the villages and country districts almost more severely than the towns. At Tedjrish, for instance, it was worse than in Teheran, and in the villages belonging to the Ispahan Government they say 11,000 people died of it, some places being quite depopulated. None of our people have had it, but four Europeans died here. . . .

I have some hope of seeing you all next summer. My privilege-leave will be due in October, but I am writing to Bombay to ask to be allowed to forestall it by two or three months to permit of going and coming by the Volga, a mid-winter journey by the Black Sea being all but impossible for a lady. It will be hard lines if I am refused so small a favour, especially as my privilege-leave would be due *now* had I not, from regard solely to the interests of the service, remained here last time more than a year after my first was due. . . .

TEHERAN, *October* 19, 1869.

. . . Two men, Mr Read and Mr Goodfellow, are here on the part of Mr Brassey, the English contractor, to inquire into railway prospects in Persia. I fear they will hear little that is encouraging.

I have been kept exceedingly busy since I wrote last. Correspondence and accounts are becoming so voluminous that I can hardly stir out of my office. . . .

The new Russian Minister, Mr Beger, I like very much, and fancy that he will prove much superior to Mr Giers, although, as you know, he was always most friendly to us. Mr Beger, whose mother, I believe, was English, is much more English in his style, habits, and manners than any Russian I have seen. We have begun by being very good friends, and I trust we may continue so. Zinoview goes home shortly to look out for another post. The French Mission is simply *nul*, one sees or hears nothing of them more than if they were not in existence. Querry is at Tabriz acting consul-general, Tholozan is here as of old. . . .

Soon after this time a sad misfortune overshadowed Murdoch Smith's happy married life. In November 1869 his wife was expecting the birth of her first child. When out driving she sustained a slight sunstroke, which brought on premature confinement. The child, a son, only lived for a single day, and Mrs Murdoch Smith's illness ultimately resulted in partial paralysis of the left side.

In September 1871 he came home on two years' furlough, accompanied by his wife. Eminent specialists were consulted in London as to her illness. They agreed in stating that entire recovery was not to be expected, but held out hopes that with the birth of other children some improvement in her health might be looked for. These hopes were in some measure realised, but for the rest of her life she remained to a great extent an invalid. It is not difficult to imagine what this meant to the brilliant girl who had been the belle of Teheran society, and to her devoted husband.

The winters of 1871-72 and 1872-73 they spent at Coblenz, where Murdoch Smith renewed his acquaintance with German and German literature, which he had known well in his college and Chatham days, and where he made some pleasant and lasting friendships among the officers of the Ehrenbreitstein garrison. The summer of 1872 was spent in visiting some of the battlefields of the then recent Franco-German war.

In March 1873 he read at the United Service Institution a paper on *The Strategy of Russia in Central Asia, from a Persian Point of View*, dealing with the advance of Russia from the great base of the Caspian, and the position of Persia as regards that advance, and with the actual and possible relations of England towards the latter country. Based as it was on an intimate personal knowledge of the regions concerned, the paper attracted considerable attention at the time, and some of the forecasts which it contained have since been strikingly justified by the facts.

Before he and his wife left England a second son, Hugh, was born at Blackheath. They returned to Persia with the child by way of Sweden and Russia in the summer of 1873.

To Sir Frederic Goldsmid, K.C.S.I.

TEHERAN, *December* 31, 1873.

Many thanks for your note by the last English mail. I need not say with what interest I shall receive your History of the Telegraph. I hope it will have the success which *d'avance* I am sure it deserves.

There is nothing very new here, where, although men may come and men may go, *mudakhil* and villainy go on for ever. One very good thing, however, has happened. Mirza Saeed Khan has at weary last been kicked out of his vizarat and given the congenial and appropriate post of Keeper of the Shrine at Meshed. The Mushir ed Dowleh (the late Sadr Azem) has been made Minister for Foreign Affairs in his place, a very good appointment so far as England is concerned. It is of course a snub for the Russians, who had M. S. K. under their thumb. The Shah lately announced his intention of going on a pilgrimage to Meshed, I presume to purify himself and please the mullahs. Both objects being, I should think, hopeless after his utter defilement in Europe, I now hear that he has given up the idea.

A WET WINTER.

The winter hitherto has been excessiv[e] and snowy, so much rain has not fallen for [years]. Do you remember our trouble with the roofs [in] '66-'67? This year it is the same thing. Ceilings tumbling down and rain pouring in everywhere. Hardly a house in Teheran has escaped. The French Minister (in our old house) was nearly buried alive the other day, and the Turkish Minister returned from a dinner-party to find his bedroom a shapeless heap of ruins. We have got off rather cheaply. Sir Joseph[1] was kept trotting about his house all night, and has hardly yet recovered from the effects of such a derangement of his usual regularity.

I prefer Taylour Thomson[2] to our old friend poor Mr Alison. He does not seem at all inclined to cave in to the Persians. Socially he is very agreeable and hospitable. . . .

The new French Minister, M. Mellinet, is exceedingly nice. All the others are nearly as you left them.

I leave in three weeks or so for Bushire on inspection. It will be fearfully cold. The line is working very well, but I have had rather a job to keep the rotten old wooden posts on their legs during this severe weather.

My wife and the youngster are both well. We had a beastly time of it on the Caspian coming out. We passed Enzelli twice without being able to land. . . .

[1] Sir Joseph Dickson, physician to the British Legation at Teheran.
[2] Mr (afterwards Sir William) Taylour Thomson became British Minister at Teheran on the death of Mr Alison in 1872.

but at the same time the most
nportant, of Murdoch Smith's
sisted of his frequent journeys
nd down the line. His inspection
ran to the sea and back, covered
les, most of it over bare desert.
These journ... he invariably made by *chapar*, or horse-post. His description of this institution, the express train of Persia, has already been quoted. *Chapar*-riding at the best is not a luxurious manner of travelling. It means long hard days in the saddle, and comfortless nights in bare, and generally filthy, *chapar-khanahs*, or post-houses. His journeys had to be made at all seasons and in all weathers. In Persia this meant exposure to great extremes of temperature, to blazing sun in summer, and in winter to deep snow and intense frost. He used to tell a story of how when home on furlough he ordered from his London tailor a coat for winter chaparing. It was of ample proportions, and made of the thickest obtainable pilot-cloth, lined with heavy fur. When he went to try it on he observed that the tailor's fitter seemed very anxious to make some remark. At last he said in a hesitating manner, "But, sir, is not this a *rather* heavy garment for a hot climate?" The tailor's idea of the Persian climate is somewhat widely shared. At certain seasons of the year it is the most delightful climate in the world, but in many parts of Persia the winter is of arctic severity. At the mountain telegraph stations the clerks in charge were sometimes snowed up for weeks, and travelling was a matter of no small difficulty and danger.

Crimes of violence were not frequent, life and property being on the whole probably safer than in most other parts of the East. Still this element of danger was by no means absent, especially in times of famine or disturbance. In 1872, the year of the great famine, Dr C. J. Wills, then stationed at Shiraz, was carried off by brigands, and narrowly escaped with his life. On two occasions telegraph employees were murdered; one of these was a line inspector, Sergeant Collins, R.E. He was robbed and murdered about fourteen miles from Shiraz during Dr Wills's residence there. Three of his murderers were, after considerable trouble, arrested and thrown into jail at Shiraz. Dr Wills gives an account of their subsequent fate, which may be quoted here as a characteristic specimen of Persian justice:—

Mirza Hassan Ali Khan, C.I.E.,[1] then British Agent at Shiraz, had to bring considerable pressure on the Persian authorities to get justice done, but was at last successful. Of course there was no moral doubt as to the guilt of the

---

[1] The Nawab Hassan Ali Khan began his career in the telegraph service, and was for some time on Sir Robert Murdoch Smith's staff. He was for many years British Agent at Shiraz. He was employed as assistant to Colonel Sir Oliver St John on political duties, under Sir Donald Stewart, during the Afghan war, and was present at the battle of Maiwand. Afterwards he accompanied Sir Peter Lumsden on the Afghan Boundary Commission. Ultimately he became second Oriental Secretary to the British Legation at Teheran. After his retirement from Government service he resided in London. I was indebted to him for valuable help in collecting materials for this book. He died at Monte Carlo on March 29, 1901. His body has been taken to be buried at Kerbela, the holy city of Shiah pilgrimage; it seems a strange ending for a man whom one knew as a member of the St James's Club.

three murderers, but to bring it home to them definitely was no easy matter. To cause the men to be executed was simple enough; the Governor of the town would have been quite pleased to oblige in such a trifling matter; but no example would be made, and the men would be looked on as martyrs, who had suffered from pressure brought by the English Minister at Teheran. In a civilised country these men would doubtless have escaped, but in Persia, Justice, though at times very blind, is never slow unless her palm is greased. Great dissatisfaction was felt among us all that these men should be allowed to escape, yet there seemed no way of bringing the matter home to them. At last artifice was used by the Governor. I was not present, but substantially what took place was the following, and my informant was well posted, and said he saw it all. The three men being brought into the Governor's presence, he smilingly asked them how they liked prison. Of course they immediately began to assert their innocence, and to call heaven to witness it. "Ah, my friends," said the Governor, "I, too, am a Mussulman. We are all Mussulmans here—an unbeliever more or less does not much matter. I shall not really punish but reward you. That you killed the Feringhi there is no doubt; I *must* punish you *nominally*. I shall cut off a joint from a finger of each of you; but your dresses of honour are ready. Clothed with these you will be immediately liberated; and now, my children, tell me all about it; how did you manage it, eh?" The astonished and delighted prisoners fell into the trap, and vied with each other in giving the details. "The European fired twice from one pistol—may we be your sacrifice—and we all fired at once, rushing in on him. He was but a European. We trust in the clemency of your Highness—may we be your sacrifice," &c. The Governor had now succeeded in bringing the murder home to the three men. From this they did not deny it, but gloried in the fact, gloating over the details. In a few moments they were taken into the public square and their throats cut.

Dangers from wild beasts had also to be reckoned with. On two occasions employees of the telegraph were killed by lions. In March 1867 Captain St John had a very narrow escape. He was riding up one evening from Shiraz to his camp at Mian Kotal. He had just entered the oak-forest south of Dashtiarjan when a lioness emerged from the wood some thirty yards in front of him. St John's horse stopped, so did the lioness, and for a few seconds they stood looking at each other. Then St John cracked his whip and gave a loud shout, but instead of sneaking back into the forest as he expected, the lioness charged down hill and sprang at the horse's throat. She missed her spring, and came down under St John's stirrup. He had no weapon except a small revolver. He spurred his horse, but the animal was paralysed with fear and would not move. Next moment the lioness sprang on the horse from behind. St John jumped off. The horse plunged violently, knocking him in one direction and the lioness in another. The horse trotted away, the lioness charged after him, sprang upon his quarters, and both disappeared among the trees. St John lost no time in climbing a convenient oak-tree. To stay there meant spending a bitter March night on the top of the tree, so after a little deliberation he decided to follow the horse. Half a mile down the road he found him bleeding from a wound in the quarter, and in such a state of terror that he could not be approached. The lioness had disappeared. St John accordingly walked back to the nearest village, but no bribe would induce any one to come out that night with torches to find the horse. Next morning he was found grazing quietly. His quarters and flanks were badly scored with claw-marks, but he had only one serious wound. This St John sewed up, and in a week the horse was as well as ever, though he bore the scars of his adventure for the rest of his life.

Along the main highways there were few villages, chiefly owing to the fact that roadside villages were subject to the exactions of the Shah's troops when on the march. Lack of discipline often rendered these warriors more terrible to their friends than to their enemies, and the mere presence of a regiment was regarded as a calamity. On one occasion Murdoch Smith witnessed a scene amusingly illustrative of the relations between troops and villagers. Near the border of Irak and Fars, on the highway between Ispahan and Shiraz, is a large village called Yezdi Khast, built on a precipitous wall-sided rock, to which the only access is by means of a small plank bridge at one end. Arriving there one day he found the planks removed and the rock surrounded by hungry soldiers, whose promises and threats were alike unavailing to obtain admittance. From every balcony high up on the top of the rock hung baskets in which the soldiers, officers as well as men, were fain to deposit in advance an exorbitant price for the provisions which they required.

One of his chaparing adventures was the subject of a well-known story. On one occasion shortly after the famine of 1872, when post-horses were scarce and bad, he was riding up the line towards Teheran.

His horses broke down between two post-houses. Out of three animals, one was barely able to crawl. As much of the baggage as possible was piled on him, and the rest was divided between Murdoch Smith, his servant, and the post-boy. Murdoch Smith's share was his heavy English saddle and bridle. Hanging his helmet on his back by a string round his neck, he balanced the saddle on his head, hung the bridle over his arm, and stepped out for the next post-house. Soon he outdistanced his attendants, who lagged behind with the jaded animal. Presently he met the Prince Governor of Shiraz, who was travelling in the opposite direction. On recognising him the Prince pulled up his horse and exclaimed, "God is great and Mohammed is His prophet!—but, Ismit Sahib, what *are* you doing?" "Chaparing to Teheran," was the reply. "Yes, but—in the name of Ali—how? Explain," said the Prince. Murdoch Smith laughed and quoted the line of Firdusi, "*Gahi pūsht ber zeen, gahi zeen ber pūsht*" (sometimes the saddle bears the back, sometimes the back bears the saddle). The Prince was delighted with the apt reply, and ordered one of his suite to dismount and give Murdoch Smith his horse.

Bushire, where the Persian line meets the Gulf cable, was the southern terminus of his inspecting journeys. When there he was generally the guest either of the British Resident, Colonel (now Sir Edward) Ross, or of Mr Robert Paul, of the firm of Gray, Paul, & Co. Both became his lifelong friends; the latter was perhaps the most intimate friend of his later life.

On account of his wife's invalided state and her need for his constant care and attention, he was always unwilling to be absent from Teheran for a day longer than was absolutely required by the exigencies of his duty. His *chapar* journeys were therefore always made at the highest possible rate of speed, the longest possible marches being undertaken in all weathers. This, of course, added greatly to the fatigue and exposure which his tours of inspection involved. He used to say long afterwards that they had knocked years off his life.

To Colonel Champain.

SHOOLGESTOON, *February* 7, 1874.

If the *gholam* has not stuck in the Dehbeed snow we ought to meet him to-morrow, so I scribble a line to you from this interesting and important city. Percy Haig, the young doctor, is with me to see the country, in which object I fear he will fail, as we have hitherto seen little but a wild waste of snow. We are now approaching the worst bit of all, the district about Khani Khorreh and Dehbeed, over which not a single caravan has passed for the last month. The *gholam* on his way down was more than a week getting from Abadeh to Dehbeed. He at last got through by some roundabout road where there was less snow. Over the Kohrood hills we waded on foot with eight men in front tapping the soft snow to find the narrow track of hard snow beneath. If you slipped off the track down you went any depth. At Ispahan I stayed three days. So far

I find the line in good order, except in some places where the wooden poles must be replaced as soon as possible. I will hurry up the iron posts to the weak points as quickly as possible. . . .

TEHERAN, *December* 31, 1874.

A happy New Year to you, and many of them.

As you already know by telegraph, I have just come back from Bushire. The journey was rather a grind, as the horses beyond Ispahan were few and frightful. Of course I had lots of spills, but am back sound in wind and limb. I saw the Hissam-es-Sultaneh both on my way down and back. He is doing something towards stopping pole-shooting, which still goes on. Walker and I all but fell into the hands of the same robbers who attacked Napier's caravan in spring. . . .

The German astronomers are back here on their way to Europe from Ispahan. I put them in direct communication from their observatory at Ispahan with Teheran, Berlin, and Karachi, so that the relative longitude of all these places is now accurately fixed. . . .

I have just seen a copy of the Tabriz railway concession to the Russians. At the last moment the Russians gave up the guarantee which the Persians had been stickling at. Roughly the concession gives the Russian company the line for seventy years, after which it becomes the property of the Persian Government; the line to be 5-feet gauge; the Persian Government to beg the Russian to make the line from Tiflis to Julfa, and to allow the two to be joined across the Araxes; the necessary land to be given free, and 100 metres on each side; the right of exploiting any coal mines that may be found within 100 miles of the line; a mixed commission to settle all disputes; General Falckenhagen to have four months in which to consult his colleagues and say definitely if he abides by the concession or chucks it up; the line to be made in five years; caution-money to be lodged in a Russian bank to the extent of 100,000 ducats, which will be paid back one-fourth when earth-works are completed, one-fourth when sleepers are laid, one-fourth when rails are laid, and one-fourth when the line is opened; special clauses regarding supply of water and making new *kanats* or repairing old ones; the Russian company to have the refusal of any other railway within 100 English miles of the Tabriz one: *the cooks, coffee-makers, and sherbet-makers at the stations to be Mussulmans, separate compartments for women, and special places at all stations for prayer!* This last article strikes me as very dodgy on the part of the Russians, as another which provides that mosques and the tombs of saints are to be exempt from demolition. The capital to be 3,440,000 Russian ducats in shares and debentures. The Persian Government to be in no way responsible with reference to the capital or dividends. There are twenty-seven articles in the concession, but the above is the *mutlab* of the whole. . . .

Hugh is becoming very amusing, and begins to chatter away at a great rate. Everybody says he is a marvellous beauty. . . . I have heard nothing more of the Belgian service of gold plate.

The German astronomers referred to in this letter were the members of the expedition which had been sent to Persia by the German Government to observe the transit of Venus. On their way between Tabriz and Teheran they met a solitary European lady riding in the opposite direction,—a member of the English colony, who was as clever as she was beautiful. Having been long resident in Persia, she was fearlessly riding alone, a long way ahead of her caravan. The Germans marvelled at such an apparition in such a dreary waste — wondered she wasn't afraid — wouldn't she let some of them stand by till her servants and baggage came up? No, she was quite at her ease, and usually in her travels was far ahead of her attendants, whose mules, more heavily laden, could not keep her pace. "And now, gentlemen," she said, "who are you, and where are you bound for?" They introduced each other; one was the astronomer, another the photographer, another the archæologist and naturalist, and so on, and they were going to Ispahan to observe the transit of Venus. The lady smiled, started her pony, and waved her adieux, saying, "To observe the transit of Venus. Ah!—well, you can go home now, gentlemen, *your duty is done.* Good-bye." The fair vision disappeared at a canter towards the horizon, and it was said that the Germans did not see the joke till a long time after Venus had disappeared from their ken.

The Falckenhagen concession was one of the many railway concessions whose bones strew the wayside of modern Persian history. General Falckenhagen was a retired Russian engineer officer who, ostensibly on his own account, but in reality backed by the Russian Government, endeavoured to obtain authority for a line from Julfa on the Perso-Russian frontier to Tabriz, in connection with a Russian line from Tiflis to Julfa. The terms at first proposed by him were too exorbitant to be entertained by the Shah, even under the strongest Russian pressure, but a modified concession was ultimately granted in 1875. The project fell through owing to lack of funds. "Sir H. Rawlinson," says Lord Curzon, "said of the Falckenhagen concession, which, however, he did not name, 'There can be no question that the interference of the Russian Government in this matter has far transcended the limits of advice or even solicitation tendered by a friendly Power, and has given a rude check to the Shah's independent authority.'"

The "Belgian service of gold plate" refers to a characteristic incident connected with the Shah's visit to Europe in 1873. The Shah had bought a number of valuable pictures from certain Belgian artists, without, however, paying for them at the time. It is no easy matter to get money out of a Persian Court official, and when the Shah returned to Persia the price of the pictures, a large sum, was still unpaid. It was scarcely a matter for diplomatic action, so Murdoch Smith, whose personal influence with the Persian authorities was well known, was asked if he could do anything. He took the matter up zealously, and finally succeeded in obtaining payment in full for the pictures. The delighted artists in the first exuberance of their gratitude talked of presenting him with a service of gold plate. Their testimonial, however, ultimately took the more modest form of a bronze inkstand and a pair of vases.

"Pole-shooting" was a form of mischief which for years was the cause of great trouble. Long after general opposition to the telegraph had ceased the line continued to suffer from wilful damage that was mischievous rather than malicious. Its most annoying form was the sportive habit that prevailed in some provinces, where every man carried arms, of using the poles and insulators of the telegraph as targets for ball-practice. On one occasion when riding through a pole-shooting district, Murdoch Smith was joined by a stalwart tribesman who seemed very proud of the long gun which he carried. "That is a fine gun of yours," said the Director. "Does it hit hard?" "Oh yes," said the man, "it shoots straight and hits very hard indeed." "What do you call hard?" was the reply. "Standing at one telegraph pole, can you with that gun send a bullet through the cast-iron socket of the next pole?" But the tribesman was not to be caught. With a broad grin he answered innocently, "I never tried." At last even this playful cause of serious trouble was suppressed.

To Colonel Champain.

TEHERAN, *January* 28, 1875.

... The Russians having got their railway concession without a Persian guarantee, have now returned to the question of getting one. They ask for a guarantee of nominally 3, but somehow or other practically 6, per cent, and although I believe the papers are not yet actually signed, I hear the Persians have given in. ... I hear they have tipped very largely, one man getting as much as 40,000 tomans. ... General Falckenhagen left a few days ago, so I suppose the whole affair is settled in spite of Lord Derby's support of Baron Reuter's protest. The whole thing appears to me a very direct slap in the face to England. It is surely high time the English made up their minds regarding the whole Eastern and Central Asian Questions. Meantime we are drifting steadily into a new set of complications in both. Turkey is at the end of her credit; Roumania is becoming altogether independent; Egypt is getting on in the world; and Russia is now preparing to annex Azerbaijan after swallowing up Turkestan. Russia is covered with railways, while Turkey is worse off in every way than she was twenty years ago. ...

Everything is now Russian here, more so even than in old M. S. K.'s time. I have long thought that the Mushir humbugged old T—— egregiously, and now the Russian railway, in spite of Lord Derby's protest, proves that I was not far wrong. It was considered high treason at the Mission to say a word against the Mushir, and now they have their reward. . . .

To-day is Hugh's birthday, so that he is just two years old. He talks away at a great rate and is very amusing.

TEHERAN, *February* 24, 1875.

. . . The wilful damage goes on apace. I have only just received a detailed return I called for, for the year 1874, in the course of which I observe that 213 posts were bulleted. . . . We had on 1st January 1875 303 damaged ones. . . . The damage, far from stopping, is increasing and spreading. Until last year the damage was confined to the country below Kazerun. We now have 39 new poles bulleted between Kazerun and Shiraz. It has only been by means of the greatest *zahmet* that we have been able to keep the line open to Bushire through the winter. A violent storm at any moment might bring down the whole of the 303 cracked and bulleted posts now on the line. I see the Indian Government have at last written to London about it. . . .

Tholozan and all your friends here are flourishing. Lansquenet, which I don't myself indulge in, is in great force for some time back, particularly at the Russian and Turkish Legations. Mr Beger has been very ill, but is now somewhat better. I believe his lungs are organically affected. He goes away as soon as the Volga opens, and they talk of Zinoview as his successor. It lies, I believe, between him and Ouroussoff. . . .

Hugh is becoming great fun and grows visibly. . . .

Dr Tholozan, the Shah's French physician, friend, and adviser, was one of Murdoch Smith's most valued friends. His well-deserved and well-exercised influence over the Shah did much for the cause of progress in Persia during the many years in which he enjoyed the intimate confidence of the sovereign.

To Colonel Champain.

GULAHEK, *August* 9, 1875.

... The Shah still gives out that he is going soon to Shiraz and perhaps Bushire, but until he starts there is of course nothing certain. Yahia Khan has arrived at Shiraz as governor, where he has replaced the Hissam, now on his way to Teheran. ...

The *Tanzimat* or Reform, a ridiculous new-fangled system of local *medjlises* to control the governors, lately introduced with much parade, has had only a few months' existence. It was abolished the other day. The *medjlises* were composed not of local magnates but of men sent from the different departments of Government from Teheran, the result of which was easy to foresee—viz., that each district in the country would have half-a-dozen hungry leeches to satisfy instead of one.

Robberies have again been rife in Fars, owing probably to the interregnum following the Hissam's recall. Yahia Khan I like very much personally, but I fear he is not the man to keep Fars in order. Before leaving Teheran he called on me and said he would do his very utmost for the protection of the telegraph. I have more faith, however, in the wrought-iron sockets you are sending us than in any efforts, even if sincere, of the Persian authorities. . . .

Murdoch Smith always got on well with the Persians. As chief of the telegraph he had direct access to the Shah's Ministers at all times, and the unique position he held outside diplomatic circles predisposed them to accept his views as unbiassed by political interests or motives. Mr J. R. Preece, now H.M. Consul at Ispahan, who was for many years a member of his staff, and who knew him intimately both officially and personally, writes :—

"His well-known integrity, justness, and straightforwardness — qualities much appreciated by the Persians—gave him a very strong position in Teheran. He was well known to all the members of the Government, by whom he was esteemed and consulted, and by none more than the late Mukhber-ed-Dowleh, the Minister of Telegraphs, and head of many other departments. This Minister, who was the most trusted of all the Ministers of the late Shah, was ever a firm friend and ally of Smith ; he used to come to him for advice in all his difficulties, and would consult with him on various State matters. Between the two men there was a very sincere and deep friendship, which was only severed by the death of the Mukhber-ed-Dowleh. Through him Smith became personally known to the late Shah, who thought very highly of him. Smith spoke Persian fluently and correctly, and Arabic, Turkish, French, German, Italian, and Spanish.

He was popular with the various nationalities represented at Teheran, and his hospitable house, open to all, was kept up in a style second only to that of the British and Russian Legations. He believed and impressed on all his staff that it was their duty to live well and properly represent England."

The Mukhber-ed-Dowleh, Ali Kuli Khan, was Minister of Public Instruction, Telegraphs, and Mines, and was for many years Murdoch Smith's neighbour in Teheran. The latter never spoke of him but in terms of the highest esteem. "The Mukhber," he writes to Champain in September 1875, "is not a bit spoiled by his elevation. It is a great blessing to have such a Persian to deal with. I know of no other like him in the country. He generally consults me in all his difficulties, and I do what I can for him."

Few men can have had more experience of the faults of the Persian Government and of the Persian character, yet in 1887 we find him writing to Sir Owen Burne: "The country is not so badly governed as people suppose. Life and property are, as a rule, wonderfully safe, and the remarkable freedom of speech and behaviour which prevails does not indicate that the people are cowed by oppression. . . . The people are one of the finest races in the world, physically and intellectually. They are imbued with a strong sense of nationality, and through their art, literature, and general culture exert an influence in the East out of all proportion to their military power."

The qualities which command respect—honesty,

H.E. THE MUKHBER-ED-DOWLEH, K.C.I.E.

capacity, incorruptibility—are happily so common among English officials in the East as to be taken for granted. Those which evoke personal friendliness—tact, sympathetic understanding of another's point of view, however remote from one's own, scrupulous courtesy to men of all ranks and all races—are perhaps not quite so universal. With these qualities Murdoch Smith was amply endowed. He thoroughly understood the value of the soft answer that turneth away wrath. Duing the years spent in the Levant he had served an invaluable apprenticeship to the East. The "d——d nigger" method of dealing with Orientals was utterly repugnant to him. He always tried to make the best of every man, to take him as he found him, and rather to give him credit for the good qualities which he possessed than to contemn him for the lack of those which he did not possess. Nearly every man, he thought, has a good side to his character somewhere; in dealing with him it is one's business to find out that good side and appeal to it. So every race has somewhere the virtues which correspond to its defects; it is better to dwell upon the virtues than on the defects. In a lecture written after his return to England there is a passage which characteristically illustrates this habit of mind. Readers of books of Persian travel are familiar with the idea that that country is the very Fatherland of liars. This is how the facts struck Murdoch Smith. "The untruthfulness," he says, "with which they are so freely credited is not altogether a vice. Much of it is a mere form of politeness, arising from an innate dislike to saying what is disagreeable, and it ceases to deceive those who are familiar with their ways. Their ever-active imagination accounts for as much more of it as it does for the poetic and artistic instincts by which they are so eminently distinguished. Instead of untruthfulness, I should say politeness was one of their most striking characteristics—a politeness somewhat formal in character, inherited from a long line of polite ancestors. Even an insult often assumes the garb of a compliment. A typical instance which came under my observation during my recent visit to Persia is perhaps worth quoting. Two servants who were accompanying me from Teheran to the Caspian fell into an angry dispute about something or other as we rode along. At last one exclaimed indignantly, 'So then you call me a liar!' To which the other, assuming a look of blank astonishment, replied, 'I call you a liar! God forbid! It is only that I, your humble slave, am unable to believe you.'" Now this incident did not strike him as being in the least absurd; he used to speak of it rather as an example by which some of his own countrymen might do well to profit.

His methods were certainly justified by their results, and by the regard in which he was universally held. He carried a similar spirit into his administrative work. Near the end of his term of office he had occasion to correspond with Champain about a serious matter of discipline. In one letter the Director-in-Chief had commented on the mildness of Murdoch Smith's rule, with the suggestion that it might be well to employ somewhat severer methods. In Murdoch Smith's reply the following passage occurs: "I am certainly averse from punishing people as long as it may be avoided, and prefer relying on the better side of even indifferent characters. I may be wrong in this, but I do not think so. Not once but fifty times the staff, jointly and individually, have exerted themselves to the utmost and gone out of their way to please me, much to the advantage of the service. The general state of this section is the best test of the state of discipline in which I keep it."

"In his relations with his staff," writes Mr Sidney Churchill, who knew him well, "from the highest to the lowest he treated every one as a gentleman. I never heard him use a swear word or get excited with any one, and God knows he had enough to try the patience of a hundred Jobs."

The subordinate telegraph staff was of the most cosmopolitan nature, including Englishmen, Germans, Persians, and Armenians. As an instance of the polyglot character of his surroundings in those days, Murdoch Smith used to recall the case of a Mr and Mrs H——, who between them spoke six languages, but who at the time of their marriage had not a single language in common. H——, who was an old warrant officer of the Indian navy, and who was afterwards in the employment of an English commercial firm, was the hero of a famous Persian yarn. He was richly blessed with daughters. A young Englishman named P—— became attached to one of the younger daughters, and approached H—— with a proposal for her hand. H—— was quite satisfied, and said he would be pleased to have him for a son-in-law. P——, who had not happened to mention the name of the particular daughter to whom his proposal applied, expressed himself delighted, and assured his prospective father-in-law that he would do his best to make a good husband to Polly. "What—what—Polly?" said the old gentleman; "no, no—none of your d——d picking and choosing—*take 'em as they come.*" The best part of the story is that the young man was quite content to "take 'em as they came," and obediently married the eldest daughter.

CHAPTER VIII.

WORK FOR THE SOUTH KENSINGTON MUSEUM. LATER YEARS IN PERSIA.

PURCHASES FOR THE SCIENCE AND ART DEPARTMENT—M. RICHARD—THE PERSIAN COLLECTION AT SOUTH KENSINGTON — THE SHAH'S INTEREST IN THE MUSEUM — HIS PRESENTS—DOMESTIC TROUBLE—ILLNESS—THE TELEGRAPH AND THE WAR IN EGYPT—INTEREST IN COMMERCIAL ENTERPRISE—THE KARUN RIVER QUESTION—DEATH OF MRS MURDOCH SMITH—THE TRAGEDY AT KASHAN—A DARK TIME—THE AFGHAN BOUNDARY COMMISSION — ON THE BRINK OF WAR—THE SHAH'S SWORD OF HONOUR — A CHANGE OF FORTUNE—ESTIMATE BY HIS CHIEF OF MURDOCH SMITH'S SERVICES TO THE TELEGRAPH.

IT was during his visit to England in 1871-1873 that Murdoch Smith's connection with the Science and Art Department began. On his return to Persia he was requested by Sir Henry Cole, then Director of the South Kensington Museum, to spend £100 on objects of Persian art for the Museum. The money was spent in the purchase of some old Persian faience, a suit of damascened steel armour, and some fine pieces of engraved metal work. These were so highly appreciated that he was asked to spend another £100 for the Museum, and then a further sum of £250. At the same time he began the series of reports on Persian art objects which at the request of the Department were periodically forwarded to South Kensington during the whole of his stay in Persia.

There was at this time resident in Teheran a certain Monsieur Jules Richard, who held an appointment as instructor in French and translator to the Shah. He had for many years been a nominal Mohammedan under the name of Mirza Reza, and many more or less authentic stories were told about him. He was said to have embraced Islam under the most romantic circumstances, and he made no secret of the fact that he used to go to Hamadan every spring and return with two new wives, whom he divorced when the time for his next annual excursion came round. In short, he was a very Oriental personage indeed. He certainly was an excellent judge of Oriental art, and possessed a very fine collection of Persian art objects of all kinds—the fruit of nearly thirty years of research, for which his position as a Mussulman offered special facilities. In 1875 Murdoch Smith induced M. Richard to agree to give the Museum the refusal of his collection, and himself prepared a detailed catalogue of it, which he forwarded to South Kensington with a strong recommendation that the whole collection should be bought. His proposal was submitted to the Committee of Council on Education, and was at once adopted. "I am directed to assure you," wrote Mr Cunliffe Owen, now Director of the Museum, on March 15, 1875, "that my Lords have learned with much satisfaction the success of the efforts already made by you on behalf of the Museum, and it is on this account that they have so promptly decided on taking advantage of your present recommendation." The purchase was effected for the sum of £1778, 7s. 3d., and soon afterwards a further purchase of wall-tiles to the extent of £400 was made from M. Nicolas, secretary to the French Legation at Teheran. The purchases were despatched by caravan to Bushire on July 24. Murdoch Smith succeeded in obtaining from the Sipeh Salar Azem an order that export duty on objects sent to the Museum should be remitted, and that the cases were not to be opened in the customhouse—an arrangement which not only saved much money and much damage, but rendered it possible to export various semi-sacred objects, such as mosque tiles and the like, which otherwise might not easily have been got out of the country. The cases reached London safely in December, and were received with the utmost satisfaction by the authorities. "Those who have seen the collection," wrote Mr Cunliffe Owen, "are wild with delight, and your name is regarded more than ever as that of a public benefactor. . . . As to the success of your purchase, we have had offers of £10,000, and it is said the collection would fetch £15,000 to-morrow. This information may best repay you for all your labours."

The collection included ceramic ware, wall tiles, metal work, arms and armour, manuscripts, musical instruments, engraved gems, enamels, paintings, embroideries, carpets, and other art objects of all kinds, all good of their kind, and in many cases of the utmost beauty and value. A feature of special interest was the splendid collection of old Persian faience *à reflet métallique*, the beautiful lustred ware the making of which has long been a lost art, and which is now practically unobtainable at any price. It was opened to the public in April 1876, and evoked very great interest and admiration. The *Times* and all the leading newspapers devoted long articles to the exhibition, fully appreciating the great beauty, interest, and value of the exhibits. Much surprise, too, was expressed at the extremely moderate prices at which they had been obtained. Not a few protests were received by the Museum authorities from dealers and collectors, both in this country and abroad, against the publication of the prices, which they feared might depreciate the value of their wares. The skill and judgment which Murdoch Smith had shown in his purchases and the valuable service which he had rendered to art and to the country were universally recognised.

At the time at which the Persian collection was opened a Handbook of Persian Art, which he had prepared at the request of the Committee of Council on Education, was issued by the Department. After passing through several editions it still remains the official manual on the subject.

His position as an expert in Persian art was now made, and during the remainder of his stay in Persia he had practically *carte blanche* to buy for South Kensington, and devoted most of his spare time to that object. A great number of important and costly purchases were made. Many of these were made through M. Richard. He had also the assistance of Mr Sidney Churchill, whose knowledge of Persian art, history, and literature were of great value.

A very great service which Murdoch Smith rendered to art students, architects, and designers was the obtaining—a task of no small difficulty—of a splendid series of full-size coloured drawings of the tile mosaic decoration of the Mosque of the Madrasah-i-Madir-i-Shah at Ispahan, built by Shah Sultan Husein in 1710. Some of the panels of these drawings are over 25 feet in length. They have only recently been mounted and shown at South Kensington.

He also succeeded in interesting the Shah and his Ministers in the Museum. Yahia Khan, the Mushir-ed-Dowleh, brother-in-law of the Shah, presented a piece of gold brocade and a very beautiful silk velvet carpet. The Mukhber-ed-Dowleh gave a valuable illuminated manuscript. A number of reproductions of articles in the Museum had been sent out to Persia to be used by Murdoch Smith as presents, at his own discretion. The best of these, a large gilt and enamelled vase, he reserved for the acceptance of the Shah. He intimated to his Majesty that the Museum had sent a vase for presentation to him, and requested that he might be informed whether it would be accepted, and if so, in what manner the presentation should be made. The presentation is described by Murdoch Smith in a report to the Director of the Museum (December 23, 1876).

"His Majesty," he writes, "was pleased to grant me a private audience, at which I presented the vase and explained its history. I took the opportunity of explaining the general scope of the South Kensington Museum, and gave a short description of the Persian collection which it now possesses. I recalled to mind the remark of the total absence of Persian productions made by his Majesty on visiting the London International Exhibition of 1873, and pointed out that, thanks to the efforts of the South Kensington Museum, the artistic manufactures of Persia were now for the first time brought under the eyes of Europe, not in a transitory manner, but as an integral part of a permanent museum in London, with branches in other parts of England. Such a special exhibition, I stated, was not only an honour to Persia, but was eminently calculated to stimulate her art industry and her commerce with the great markets of Europe. I added that the Museum had sent the present, which he had been pleased to accept, in recognition of the facilities which his Majesty's Government had offered in the transport and shipment of the articles I had purchased in the country.

"His Majesty was evidently highly pleased both with the attention shown by the Museum and with the object presented, and requested me to convey his best thanks to the donors. Before leaving, his Majesty told me he had already heard of the Persian collection in London, and had ordered that a suitable collection of Persian textile fabrics should be got together and given me for presentation to the Museum."

Several valuable specimens of textiles were accordingly sent. These were afterwards supplemented by further similar gifts from his Majesty.

The result of Murdoch Smith's work for the Department may be seen in the magnificent Persian collection now exhibited in the Victoria and Albert Museum. In taking leave of this branch of his work one may quote a passage from the introduction to the Illustrated Catalogue of the specimens of Persian and Arab art exhibited at the Burlington Fine Arts Club in 1885. The introduction was written by Mr H. Wallis, one of the greatest authorities on such subjects. "It must never be forgotten," he says, "that students of Persian art are deeply indebted to Colonel Murdoch Smith. To his promptitude, energy, and sound taste the country owes the large collection of Persian art objects at South Kensington."

His domestic troubles were now thickening fast. Between 1875 and 1881 five children were born, three sons and two daughters. Exposed as they were to the conditions which at the best life in an Oriental city involves, their health was a source of constant anxiety.

"We have had a very bad month or two of it in our house with illness," he writes to Champain in August 1875. "The baby's smallpox was at one time very serious, and still keeps us in a sort of quarantine. . . . I had a little fever myself, . . . and now little Hugh has been very ill with dysentery. . . . I have charge of the little fellow myself. He is a little better to-day, but I have been up for the last four nights with him. The heat since the beginning of July has been unusually great, which I fancy has been the cause of a good deal of the illness lately prevalent in and about Teheran." . . .

Hugh died in November 1876, and Alan, born in July 1876, died in January 1877. They were laid in the little burial-ground at Teheran, where Charles Scott, Sir Walter's younger son, lies, far from Tweedside. A month later Murdoch Smith writes to Sir Frederic Goldsmid: "My wife and myself both thank you very much for your kind sympathy in our bereavements. The loss of Hugh is terribly grievous, and it seems as if we should never get over it. . . . I have just finished building a new house in Teheran at the north end of the Lalehzar garden. . . . It is very comfortable and commodious, but, alas! two of those for whom I built it are for ever gone." . . .

Not long after his return from England in 1873 his wife's mother, Mrs J. R. Baker, became an inmate of his house. Owing to her daughter's invalid condition it was on her, the beloved "Granny," that the care and education of the children chiefly fell. She died in 1884, having survived her daughter by a few weeks. A friend of this period who must not be forgotten was Eliza Priest—now Mrs Gray—who had accompanied the family on their return from England, and who, until her marriage some years later, acted as nurse to the children and as maid to Mrs Murdoch Smith. No services are greater, surely none are more deserving of appreciation and gratitude, than those rendered by a kind and faithful nurse, above all when they are rendered in a distant land, and amid strange and trying surroundings. That unforgotten debt of gratitude is here recorded.

The expenses of a large family and of so much illness were now bearing somewhat heavily on his finances. He writes to his sister, Mrs Mather, in September 1879: "This autumn I have a year's leave due to me, but I can't afford to take it. With a family the expense of going and coming, besides the year in Europe, is ruinous. I should be very glad of a rest and change, but being impracticable there is no use thinking about it." His correspondence and accounts of this period show that no small proportion of his income was being spent in acts of unobtrusive benevolence. He loved to spend money on others. We have seen how in the early Persian days he liked to entertain splendidly. Extremely simple in his personal habits, in charity and in hospitality he was always open-handed.

In 1879 he lost a valued friend. "I was greatly shocked," he writes to Mrs Mather, "to see the death at the battle of Ulundi of one of my best friends, Captain Wyatt-Edgell of the 17th Lancers. Three years ago he stayed a month or six weeks with us here and afterwards accompanied me to Bushire. I had a long letter from him from the Cape on his way with his regiment to the front, written a few days before his death. He had everything this world could give him, estates of £20,000 a-year, heir to an old peerage, splendid abilities, youth, health, and everything, now all gone in a war with obscure savages. He had taken a great affection to me, which it was impossible not to return, he was so thoroughly good in every way.

T

It seems all the harder that he was the only officer killed in the battle."

Soon after this time he began to suffer from attacks of lumbago—an exceedingly trying ailment in view of the amount of rough travelling and exposure which his work necessitated. A letter to Mrs Mather in February 1881 describes a terrible journey. . . . " I got back," he writes, " to Teheran on the 19th January, after a very unfortunate and rather painful journey of two months. I left with Colonel Champain and his brother-in-law, Mr Currie, on the 21st November, marching stage by stage with mules and our own horses, servants, &c. When 700 miles from Teheran and about 100 from Bushire I got a very severe attack of lumbago which laid me up without power of moving myself, even of turning myself in bed." All the way from Teheran he had been in great anxiety about his wife, who was down with an attack of fever. "At one time," he continues, "I was so anxious that I rode back thirty miles to the nearest telegraph-office to get news in detail. Finding her then somewhat better, I went back and caught up the others near Ispahan. We then had extremely bad weather — rain, snow, &c. — for a fortnight. On Christmas Eve at a village I was laid up with the lumbago. At the same time the track down a mountain precipice just in front of us was washed away in a landslip caused by the heavy rains, so that no animal, and not even a footman, could pass. After three days' delay Champain and Currie at last started for Bushire by a circuitous mountain path on foot. I remained three days more in bed, until I could crawl with help, when I started to return to Shiraz, about 100 miles off. I was afraid of the passes getting closed by snow and my being kept till they opened in spring. In four days I got to Shiraz, but such a journey! I had every day to be lifted on to a mule and *packed* in with pillows, &c., and thus carried over what is probably the worst road in the whole world. The pain and fatigue were very great. At Shiraz I again lay two days in bed and started for Teheran (still dreading the closing of the passes on my way) in a *takhteravan*—that is, a sort of litter or palanquin carried between two mules. In this way I travelled about 150 miles, when I resumed horseback, left my caravan, and came on the remaining 450 miles *chapar*. At Kohrood Pass, nearly 9000 feet above the sea, the snow was very deep, but I got over all right by getting a lot of villagers to go in front and find a practicable track by plodding or 'sounding' the soft drifts with long sticks. . . . My back, which was very weak and painful the whole way, is nearly quite well again. I am now struggling through my arrears of office work accumulated during my absence." . . .

He was now beginning to look forward to his retirement from the service, and his letters of this period are full of plans for the future. His idea was on quitting the army to emigrate to New Zealand, buy land there, and make a home for his family in the colony. The event, however, was to happen far otherwise.

Another daughter, Jeanie, born in April 1881, died in the following November.

In the early part of 1882 he had a very severe attack of dysentery. For many weeks his life was despaired of. As soon as he was well enough to travel he came home on leave accompanied by his wife and his eldest child. They spent the summer in Scotland, returning to Persia in the autumn.

On November 10 he writes from Teheran to Sir Frederic Goldsmid :—

... "We got back to Persia all right in the end of August after a very hot fatiguing journey. I am now nearly all right again, but not quite. I had a very long painful illness with (for about two months) almost no hope of recovery. My wife had a dangerous illness just after our return, from which, however, she recovered just in time for her confinement eight days ago—a daughter this time.

"During the war in Egypt we had all the telegraphing between East and West, over 1000 messages a-day. We never had a hitch the whole time. Even the telegrams between Alexandria and Suez passed this way. This was a crucial test of the efficiency and usefulness of our line, which is now one of the best in the world. Any recognition of the twenty years' hard uphill work it has cost to bring it to its present state is of course not to be expected." ...

Telegraph construction in a distant country is not the kind of work which appeals to the imagination of the public, and the men who made the Persian Telegraph always felt that their long and arduous services were scarcely appreciated at home. Murdoch Smith certainly shared this feeling. He never gave expression to it, however, except in the most intimate of private correspondence or conversation. No man was ever less of a grievance-monger. A story which used to be told of him may perhaps without indiscretion be repeated here. On one occasion he was attending the levee of an exalted military personage. He arrived very late, and the great man greeted him wearily with the question, "Well, and what's *your* grievance?" "I haven't any grievance, sir," was the reply. "*Thank God for that!*" piously ejaculated his Royal Highness.

Murdoch Smith was now a recognised authority not only on Persian art, but on Persian affairs in general. He took the keenest interest in the advancement of commercial interests in Persia, and no enterprise of any importance was undertaken without first seeking his counsel and guidance. In February 1883 he prepared a memorandum on the question of the navigation of the Karun River, a subject which was yearly becoming of greater importance to British commerce in view of the closing by Russia of the northern trade routes into Persia. It was owing largely to the encouragement and support which Mr George Mackenzie received, solely from him, on his pioneer journeys through the Bakhtiari country, that we are indebted for the opening of the Karun to navigation and the consequent establishment of direct communication between Shuster and Ispahan. He was an ardent advocate of the construction of a light railway, or failing that good roads, from Shuster to Hamadan and Kermanshah, which would open up vast and rich grain-producing districts, and thereby add materially to the revenues of the Persian Imperial Treasury. This scheme, so much to be desired in the interests of Persia herself, at one time assumed definite shape, but failed through the opposition of the Russians in Teheran and the supineness of the British authorities in London.

In 1883 he also drew up for the War Office a report on the strength, organisation, and equipment of the Persian army.

His youngest child, a daughter, was born at Teheran in November 1883. Mrs Murdoch Smith's confinement was followed by a serious illness, and she died on the 30th of November.

What her loss meant to the husband who had loved and tended her so devotedly for fourteen years, cannot be written here. Six weeks after her death he writes to Champain: "Time has not yet brought me any alleviation of the pain and misery of my life. I sometimes feel as if I could not live, but the sight of the children nerves me to bear my burden without utterly giving way under it."

Five children survived—two boys, Hubert and Archie, and three girls, Kathleen, Isabel, and the baby Nellie. In any case the elder children must soon have been sent home for education. Their mother's death now rendered their immediate departure necessary.

When home on leave in 1882 Murdoch Smith had paid a long visit to Mrs Mather at Dunoon. She was now a widow with a young family. It was arranged that the children should make their

MRS MURDOCH SMITH.

home with her, and a house in Merchiston Bank Terrace, in the southern suburbs of Edinburgh, was taken for the joint establishment. In the beginning of March Murdoch Smith, accompanied by the children and by Dr Odling of the telegraph staff, left Teheran for Bushire. His intention was to march down country to the sea, then to accompany the children as far as Karachi, and see them safely on board the ship which was to convey them to England. On March 11 he writes from Kum: "I have got so far all fairly well with the children on our way to Bushire. The youngest infant is not well, but otherwise all are well." Before Kashan was reached the whole of the children, with the exception of Isabel, were seriously ill. The illness proved to be diphtheria. In the *chapar-khanah* at Kashan they lay for a few dreadful days struggling for life. Hubert, the eldest boy, died on the 19th of March, Archie on the 20th, and the baby on the 21st. Mr Churchill came out from Teheran and took them back to be laid there beside their mother. When the little girl was well enough to travel, the dreary march to the sea was resumed. A divergence from the route to visit Persepolis had been planned in order that the children should take home with them the recollection of a visit to the wonderful ruins of "The Glory of the East." It is characteristic of the man that notwithstanding the terrible blow which he had received, he carried out this excursion rather than disappoint his little daughter, and for a night the tents of the caravan were pitched among the pillars of the Hall of

Xerxes. In due time Karachi was reached; the ship carried the children away to England, and the sorely stricken father returned alone to the empty house in Teheran.

The year which followed was a very dark time. He had lost nearly everything that he had lived for; everything that had made success worth having seemed gone. Attacks of lumbago added bodily suffering to his mental grief, and before him stretched the prospect of five more lonely years in Persia before he could hope to come home for good. But he went bravely on with his duty. "I knew him," writes Mr Churchill, "under the most trying circumstances, when his wife and children died, and when he was down on a journey with lumbago, but I never knew him to lose his temper, his courage, or his equanimity." Fortunately there was a great deal of official work to be done in 1884. A new line from Teheran to Kum was in progress, and the Afghan Boundary Commission threw a great deal of extra work on the telegraph staff. Murdoch Smith's long letters on telegraph business to his chief show the same keen interest in work as ever, the same resourcefulness, the same mastery of detail.

To Colonel Champain.

TEHERAN, *March* 19, 1885.

... This week is the anniversary of the dreadful one I spent last year at Kashan. To-day little Archie died, to-morrow Hubert, and next day

Nellie. I don't find that Time has yet done much for me.

The Afghan affairs are of course much talked about. I suppose it will end in the Russians retaining Penjdeh and Pul-i-Khatun and the frontier being drawn south of those places. You can imagine what a mass of cipher telegrams have been passing to and from Lumsden. I am very glad we have a good clerk like Gray at Meshed as things have turned out. I have put on an extra clerk at Teheran specially for Meshed work, doing with one less at Shiraz. Without an extra man here the Meshed work could never have been got through. As it is it goes with regularity and correctness, in fact not a single repetition has ever been asked for. During last month the Legation telegram bill to the company and ourselves must have been about 3000 tomans. . . .

I can't get rid of this last attack of lumbago, which seized me the day I arrived in Shiraz last June. It is not acute, but is very irksome and depressing, as it keeps me in constant dread of being laid up. I have tried all sorts of remedies — "massage," liniments, electricity, and cautery with red-hot iron—but all in vain. In fact they did more harm than good. I now let it alone and take a quick walk of four or five miles every evening. This for the time makes the back tired and painful, but with rest the feeling soon goes off. In other respects my health has much improved during the last three months. For about a year I did not know what it was to sleep half an hour consecutively. Now I sleep fairly well. . . .

In the spring of 1885 the Penjdeh affair had brought us to the edge of war with Russia. The state of political affairs gave unusual value and significance to a very distinguished mark of honour which Murdoch Smith received from the Shah on the day of No Ruz, March 21, the Persian New Year's Day—the gift of a valuable sword of honour, which he received special permission to accept. A similar sword was sent to Colonel Champain. The firman which accompanied the sword was in the following terms :—

Since the Illustrious Colonel Smith, the Head of the Telegraph of the mighty English Government, has pleased our Royal Mind with his honesty of disposition and excellence of character, and during the time of his residence at Teheran has acted with rectitude and uprightness of conduct, and his good wishes towards this sublime Government have been brought to our august notice by the exalted Ministers of this Illustrious Kingdom, therefore, merely by way of Royal kindness as regards the aforesaid, in this auspicious year of the Hen,[1] We honour and exalt him by the grant of a sword adorned with gold. It is decreed that the Illustrious Ministers of this auspicious Government shall consider him the possessor of this distinction.

Dated Month Rajabu'l Murajjab 1302 = May 1885.

[1] The expression "the year of the Hen" is a curious relic of antiquity. It refers to the ancient Turkish method of reckoning time, said to have been brought by the Turks from Tartary into Persia. Time is divided into cycles of twelve years, each year having a separate name, the "year of the Mouse," "year of the Bull," "year of the Leopard," and so on. This method of reckoning is now only preserved in certain formal Government documents in Persia. It is entirely unknown in Turkey.

To Colonel Champain.

TEHERAN, *March* 30, 1885.

... Before you get this I suppose the question of peace or war will be settled. If war, I should like to volunteer my services for it in any capacity, but hesitate on account of my want of strength. My back keeps in exactly the same state, one day better, another worse, but never well, and always threatening to lay me up altogether. I have not attempted to ride since I arrived in Teheran in December. If there is no war, I should like to go on privilege-leave in the end of June. ... Of course if there is war my services are entirely at the disposal of the Government and yourself wherever they may be wanted. How war would affect the company's line I don't know. Günzel at Tabriz seems to think that cipher messages would be stopped, but that otherwise things would go on as usual. In any case the Gulf line will be more than ever important, and the Turkish line might perhaps be improved and utilised for Government messages. It would never do to trust entirely to the Eastern. Persia, I have no doubt, will remain neutral. Perhaps we may have to resume charge of the Teheran-Khanekin line, for which provision is made in our convention. To make the line good we should want wire (there is only one wire now) and insulators. ... Many poles would, of course, have to be renewed.

It would be difficult to exaggerate the importance of the work we have done for the Boundary

Commission. The line is of course very shaky and often broken, but by having a smart man always ready at each end the telegrams to and from Lumsden are at once got through immediately communication is restored. In this way an enormous telegraphic correspondence has been got through without error and generally without delay. . . .

On No Ruz day the Shah sent me my sword. It was evidently sent with the idea that I should wear it at the salaam. But there was no time to arrange with Thomson about my going, so I am now waiting for the Shah appointing a time for me to go and thank him. Yours is not quite ready yet, but they say it will soon be so, when it will be given me to send you. The firmans also are still to write. It was evidently an afterthought sending me mine on No Ruz. It is very handsome, far more so than I expected. The blade is a curved Khorassan one of fine water. The hilt and scabbard, which is covered with dark-blue velvet, are mounted with massive repoussé gold, of which there must be something like £80 worth. Roughly, therefore, the sword may be estimated at 100 guineas. I have never heard of anything of the kind being given to a European before. . . .

TEHERAN, *April* 6, 1885.

. . . Your sword has not come yet, but I expect it every day. Last week the Shah gave me a private audience, at which he was extremely gracious. I was introduced by the Foreign Minister and the Mukhber. The Shah spoke in the most flattering way of my services, &c., &c., and spoke in the same way about me to different Ministers and people after I had gone. He asked very kindly about the children, how many I had left, where they were, who was taking care of them, &c. I thanked him for his great kindness in giving special orders last year about the funeral of the three who died at Kashan. He then talked about the Afghan Boundary, about the Mahdi, and so on. He seemed much astonished when I told him the Ameer had arrived in the Viceroy's camp, and was at first hardly inclined to believe it. The conversation lasted about half an hour. The Mukhber is giving me a dinner in honour of the occasion to-night.

The general idea here is that there will be no war, an opinion strongly held by the German and Austrian Legations. Everybody says that whatever happens Persia will be neutral. . . . My back still bothers me a great deal. Yesterday it seemed better than usual, but to-day it is rather worse. I wish I could find a remedy. . . .

A change of fortune now came, which was to shape the course of his remaining years. Now that his boys were dead the New Zealand project had been given up. The directorship of the Museum of Science and Art at Edinburgh had just become vacant through the death of Professor Archer. Murdoch Smith was of course intimately known to the authorities of the Science and Art Department, and in particular to Sir John Donnelly, who in 1884 had succeeded Sir Francis Sandford as secretary of the department. His reputation as a classical archæologist had been made before he went to Persia; the work which he had done in that country for South Kensington had given him an equally high reputation as an authority on Oriental art; and he was known as an excellent administrator. He was asked by telegraph if he would be willing to accept the vacant appointment. An appointment which not only offered interesting and congenial employment at home for many years to come, but would take him to the very place in which he had made a home for his children, was a piece of unlooked-for good fortune. He intimated his willingness to accept it if offered. His name was accordingly submitted to the Lord President of the Council, and on May 2, 1885, he was appointed by Lord Carlingford to the vacancy. Having made arrangements for the discharge of his duties in Persia, he came home on furlough, and at once proceeded to Edinburgh to take up his new office.

This record of his life in Persia may be fitly closed by quoting his chief's estimate of the services which he had rendered. In a letter to Sir Juland Danvers, then secretary to the Public Works Department of the India Office, written in November 1886, Sir John Champain said: "It was fortunate for the eventual success of the enterprise that such a man as Lieut. Murdoch Smith succeeded to the appointment of Director. Owing to his unusual tact, his unfailing temper in the most trying circumstances, and his courage and perseverance, difficulties were gradually surmounted, and hostile opposition converted first into indifference and then into friendly feeling. . . . The success of the through Indo-European route to the East is in a great measure due to the unremitting labours of Smith. No European in the country is more highly respected and esteemed by the Persians of all degrees. His Majesty the Shah has a strong personal regard for him."

CHAPTER IX.

THE EDINBURGH MUSEUM. MISSION TO PERSIA IN 1887.

THE EDINBURGH MUSEUM — RECEPTION IN EDINBURGH — LIGHTHOUSE CRUISE — THE QUEEN'S BOOK — DEATH OF SIR JOHN CHAMPAIN — APPOINTED DIRECTOR-IN-CHIEF OF THE INDO-EUROPEAN TELEGRAPH — THE JASK AFFAIR — MISSION TO PERSIA — PRESENTS TO THE SHAH AND HIS MINISTERS — THE KARUN RIVER — VISIT TO INDIA — RECEPTION BY LORD DUFFERIN — SETTLEMENT OF THE JASK QUESTION — JOURNEY TO TEHERAN — MR CECIL SMITH'S ARCHÆOLOGICAL WORK — RECEPTION AT TEHERAN — AUDIENCES OF THE SHAH AND HIS MINISTERS — EXTENSION OF THE TELEGRAPH CONVENTIONS — PRESENTATION OF BAND INSTRUMENTS TO THE SHAH — THE DIAMOND SNUFFBOX — ARDUOUS RIDE TO ISPAHAN — THE ZIL-ES-SULTAN — RETURN TO TEHERAN — FAREWELL TO PERSIA — MR NICOLSON'S DESPATCH — LETTER FROM LORD SALISBURY — K.C.M.G. — RETIRES FROM THE ARMY.

THE Edinburgh Museum of Science and Art is the northern counterpart of the great institution at South Kensington. It grew out of the old Edinburgh Natural History Museum, which was established in 1812, and was in 1855 transferred by the Town Council to the Department of Science and Art, then under the Board of Trade. In 1857 the Museum was transferred with the Department of Science and Art to the Committee of Council on Education, with the reservation of certain privileges in favour of the University of Edinburgh. The fine buildings in which the Museum is now accommodated were commenced in 1861; the first portion of the building was opened to the public in 1866, and a second portion in 1874. When Murdoch Smith became Director the third portion, completing the buildings, was in process of erection.

He entered on his duties in June 1885. He had the entire administrative charge of the Museum, his second in command being the Curator, Mr Alexander Galletly. The Natural History section of the Museum was under the scientific charge of Dr R. H. Traquair. Murdoch Smith was cordially received in Edinburgh, and soon mastered the details of his new work, and began to find himself at home in his new surroundings.

Soon after his arrival he enjoyed one of the pleasantest experiences which can befall a man in the way of Scottish hospitality; he received an invitation to join the Commissioners of Northern Lights in their annual cruise on board the *Pharos*. Readers of Lockhart's *Life of Scott* will remember Sir Walter's diary of his lighthouse cruise, the cruise to which we owe *The Pirate* and *The Lord of the Isles*, and of which he wrote that during it "I have enjoyed as much pleasure as in any six weeks of my life." The voyage nowadays is made under more luxurious conditions than in Sir Walter's time. "I wish you were with us here," Murdoch Smith writes to Champain from Douglas Bay on July 26, 1885. "The ship is a splendid sea-boat, built specially for rough seas, and fitted up as a yacht. The kitchen and cellar are of the very best, and there is a genial party of ten on board. The weather has been perfect. We sailed from Greenock on the 22nd, anchored the first night in Brodick Bay, then next night in Loch Ryan, then at Peel, and last night here. To-morrow night we anchor at the Mull of Galloway, the anchorages after that being Sanda, Campbeltown, Sound of Islay, Earraid, Fort William, Tobermory, Loch Hourn, Stornoway, Lochinver, Loch Eriboll, and Strome Ferry. We finally arrive at Oban on the 8th August. We visit some lighthouses every day. Some of them are most interesting. The scenery of most of the route is superb."

Shortly before Murdoch Smith's return from Persia Queen Victoria's *Leaves from the Journal of our Life in the Highlands* had been translated into Persian by command of the Shah. He had brought with him a copy of the translation, which he had caused to be specially bound, and had offered through Sir Philip Cunliffe Owen for her Majesty's acceptance. The Queen was greatly pleased with the volume, and Sir Henry Ponsonby wrote as follows:—

BALMORAL, *November* 13, 1885.

MY DEAR COLONEL,—I am commanded by the Queen to assure you that it has given her Majesty great pleasure to receive the Persian translation of her book, and I am desired to convey to you the Queen's best thanks for your kindness in having this copy prepared and for presenting it to her Majesty.—Yours faithfully,

HENRY F. PONSONBY.

Murdoch Smith was not yet done with Persia. He still held his Teheran appointment, from which he had two years' furlough. He had elected for continuous Indian service, and under the terms of a then recent Royal Warrant he had still to put in four months of service in the East in order to qualify for Indian pension. He accordingly applied to the Science and Art Department for special leave to return to Persia in May 1887, in order to complete the necessary service, undertaking to make suitable arrangements for the discharge of his duty in his absence, and at the same time offering to utilise the opportunities afforded by his journey for the benefit of the Museum. His request was readily granted, and he made arrangements accordingly.

Before the expiration of his furlough, however, new circumstances had arisen. In the winter of 1886 Sir John Champain was very seriously ill. For many years he had suffered from acute attacks of hay fever, which developed into chronic asthma. During the last few years of his life the asthma became complicated with bronchitis. He was frequently urged, but always in vain, to take some months' complete rest in a genial climate. At last, in December 1886, he was definitely ordered to the south of France, and it was arranged that Murdoch Smith should during his absence act for him as Director-in-Chief of the Indo-European Telegraph.

Champain left England on the 10th of January. His brilliant career was now very near its close. His last letter to Murdoch Smith was written from Cannes on the 15th of January. "My dear old Smith," he writes, "I can only write a very short letter, for I am as weak as a rat. I *have* had a buster. Probably the pestilential atmosphere of our hermetically sealed first-class compartment, Paris to Marseilles, damaged me, and then I caught an awful cold. But how *can* one possibly help it? Thermometer inside the carriage 120° and air poison. Thermometer outside zero!! or not much more. Then one *had* to turn out occasionally, and also for coffee in a draughty station at 6 A.M. But thank God I am here! It is like Gulahek climate in April. Perfect. . . . I hope I am a shade better to-day. . . . But when one can't sleep or eat or stop coughing it isn't quite satisfactory. . . . I can never thank you enough for what you are doing, for I should have gone out very soon.—Ever yours affectionately, J. B. C."

Champain died at San Remo on the 1st of February, and Murdoch Smith hurried thither to pay the last offices of friendship. He contributed to the *Royal Engineers Journal* of March 1, 1887, a sympathetic and affectionate notice of the career of his old friend.[1]

On Champain's death Murdoch Smith was appointed to succeed him as Director-in-Chief of the Indo-European Telegraph. In the circumstances, and in view of the fact that Murdoch Smith's appointment was in the meantime of a provisional character, no difficulty as to his accepting it was raised by the Science and Art Department.

While Murdoch Smith was acting Director-in-

---

[1] Recently reprinted in Sir Edward Thackeray's *Biographical Notices of Officers of the Royal (Bengal) Engineers* (Smith, Elder, & Co., 1900), pp. 235-252.

Chief a question had arisen between the British and Persian Governments which had caused considerable feeling on the part of the latter. It will be remembered that in 1869 the land line along the Mekran coast had been extended from Gwadur to Jask, where it joined the Gulf cable. Jask thus became an important telegraph station. When the Indian naval station was withdrawn in 1879 from Bassadore on Kishm Island, the company of sepoys, 100 strong, which had been posted there, was moved to Jask, and barracks were erected by the Indian Government for its accommodation.

At that time [says Lord Curzon] the promontory of Jask was unoccupied, save by the English telegraph station, and its ownership was not strictly determined, the tribes along the coast and in the interior being Beluchis, who claimed independence, and the Persian authority being as yet precariously established in those parts. When the telegraph station had been first opened at Jask in 1869 the cape was a barren piece of sand to which no claimant turned a thought. This tiny military settlement remained unnoticed and unobjected to until 1886, when the Persian Government, hearing that a small trade had sprung up since the arrival of the English, sent an agent to establish a custom-house. This individual detected an opportunity of personal distinction which was not to be missed. In a highly coloured report he represented the English as exercising sovereign rights upon Persian territory, and acquiring undue political influence over the Beluchi tribes (the village sheikh received a few rupees a-year for the preservation of the wire running through the district), and himself as having by valiant measures restored seventeen townships to the Persian allegiance. He received his decoration, and subsided into satisfied obscurity. The two local sheikhs, however, who were quite innocent of anything in the nature of a conspiracy, were carried off in chains, and were only released after a long imprisonment. Meanwhile the Shah appealed to the Indian Government to withdraw the sepoys.

The matter was referred to London, and Murdoch Smith was sent for by Lord Salisbury to be consulted with regard to it. He laid the facts before his Lordship, and being invited to express his views as to the proper course of action, suggested that the sepoys should be at once withdrawn, as Jask was undoubtedly in Persian territory, being a long way to the west of the Perso-Baluch frontier delimited by Sir Frederic Goldsmid in 1872.

Ultimately he was requested to proceed to Persia and arrange matters on the spot, combining his journey with a tour of inspection of the Gulf and Persian lines. He then suggested that this would be a very favourable opportunity to send out some complimentary presents to the Shah and other exalted personages in Persia, in acknowledgment of the support and assistance which the Indo-European Telegraph had received from them since its establishment in 1863. This suggestion was adopted by the authorities of the India Office, and the purchase of the presents was entrusted to Murdoch Smith. Knowing the Shah's taste for military music, he, after taking counsel with Mr Zavertal, bandmaster of the Royal Engineers, purchased for his acceptance a set of instruments for a military band of sixty men. These were specially made by Messrs Boosey & Co. A pair of fine rifles and a dressing-bag were bought for the Zil-es-Sultan, the Shah's eldest son; a carriage for the

Mukhber-ed-Dowleh; and a magnificent dressing-case for the Shah's sister, the wife of Yahia Khan, the Foreign Minister.

Murdoch Smith was further entrusted by the Foreign Office with certain political duties relating to the negotiations for the opening to navigation of the Karun River and other matters which need not be specified in detail.

Before his departure he made a further suggestion that he might with advantage be accompanied by Mr Cecil Smith of the British Museum, in order that the latter might have an opportunity of examining some likely fields for archæological research in Southern Persia. This proposal was carried out through the good offices of Sir Juland Danvers. Sir Juland asked Murdoch Smith to breakfast to meet his (Sir Juland's) brother-in-law, Mr W. H. Smith, who had then just become First Lord of the Treasury. The matter was talked over, and no difficulty was raised with regard to the requisite funds.

After a final interview with Lord Cross on the 17th of March, Murdoch Smith, accompanied by Mr Cecil Smith, left London on the 25th, and travelling *viâ* Brindisi arrived at Karachi on the 14th of April. A few days were spent there in inspecting the telegraph store-houses, workshops, and offices. He then proceeded to Simla, where a cordial reception by Lord Dufferin awaited him. He lunched and dined with his Excellency, and on both occasions Persian affairs were discussed at considerable length. A week was spent at Simla in the enjoyment of much hospitality from the members of Government, and in the discussion of telegraph and other matters with the officials concerned. Returning to Karachi, he embarked on board the telegraph steamer *Patrick Stewart*, and after visiting Gwadur arrived at Jask on the morning of May 10.

In the mean time a highly satisfactory agreement with regard to Jask had been made by Mr (now Sir Arthur) Nicolson, H.M. Chargé d'Affaires at Teheran, with the Persian Government. It was provided that the promontory of Jask for a distance of some 900 yards from its point should be assigned to the English telegraph station; that it should be occupied solely by telegraph employees, whose supplies were to be freed from customs duties; and that it should be exempted from Persian jurisdiction. Murdoch Smith had been met at Karachi by a telegram from Mr Nicolson, asking him to meet the Persian agent on the spot at Jask, and adjust the delimitation of the ground thus allotted, and other details. On reaching Jask he found the agent, Mirza Hidayet, awaiting his arrival. After a couple of days of somewhat difficult negotiation, the boundary of the telegraph settlement was satisfactorily adjusted. The sepoys were withdrawn and sent down the Gulf by the mail steamer which called on the 12th of May. A proposal had been made to replace them by a police guard; but on Murdoch Smith's suggestion this had been abandoned, as the station was not exposed to any special danger of disorder, and he thought that the policemen would be regarded by the Persians as merely soldiers under another name. The settlement which had been made gave entire satisfaction both to the British authorities and to the Persians. The former retained all that was really necessary for the telegraph service, while the wounded *amour propre* of the latter was fully satisfied.

After leaving Jask Murdoch Smith proceeded to visit Fao, at the head of the Gulf, to inspect the telegraph station there, and at the same time to have a look at the fort which the Turks were in course of constructing at the mouth of the Shat-el-Arab. He then returned to Bushire and started on his journey up country. The presents had been landed at Bushire and were already on their way to Teheran by caravan. Murdoch Smith overtook them at Shiraz. It had been his intention to stop at Ispahan, and there make the presentation to the Zil-es-Sultan, and then to proceed to Teheran; but on reaching Shiraz he was met by a letter from Mr Nicolson to say that the Zil had gone away into Irak to spend Ramazan, and would not return to Ispahan till the end of the month of fasting, which was then just begun. The Shah, on the other hand, was spending Ramazan at Teheran, but was going away immediately afterwards to places where it would be difficult, if not impossible, to get to him. As Mr Nicolson was anxious that Murdoch Smith should see the Shah and have one or two private audiences, the only feasible plan was for him to *chapar* up at once to Teheran, afterwards, at the end of Ramazan, return to Ispahan to see the Zil, and finally go up again to Teheran. He accordingly decided to leave his caravan at Shiraz and push on at once.

Mr Cecil Smith was left behind at Shiraz. On the way up from the sea he had made notes on the antiquities seen at Sharpur and elsewhere, and from Shiraz, which is the centre of a district of great archæological interest, he made numerous excursions to Persepolis, Naksh-i-Rejid, Istakhr, and other places. An important result of his journey was the acquisition by the British Museum of a series of casts of the Persepolis sculptures. He reached Ispahan on June 16. When there he planned an expedition to Mal Amir, near Shuster; but this had to be abandoned on account of the dangerous state of the Bakhtiari country. He afterwards followed Murdoch Smith to Teheran, and accompanied him on the homeward journey. The results of his researches were embodied in an interesting report to the Trustees of the British Museum, dated October 6, 1887.

In the mean time Murdoch Smith had pushed on to Teheran as rapidly as possible. He arrived there on the 8th of June, after a hot and fatiguing ride of 620 miles. "When I started from Shiraz," he writes on the following day to Sir Juland Danvers, "I was rather afraid of my old enemy lumbago, which was still bothering me, but I got on all right, and after riding the 620 miles in nine days, I arrived here yesterday with my back stronger and less painful than when I left Shiraz. I have been greatly pleased at the kind reception I have had everywhere. Last night the Mukhber-ed-Dowleh, hearing of my arrival, sent word that he was coming to see me, but I forestalled him by going to call on him. This being Ramazan, I knew he would be up late, so I went about ten and stayed till after midnight. He received me most cordially,—in fact affectionately,—and I was equally pleased to see him again. During all these twenty-four years of constant intercourse, official and private, we have never had a single disagreeability." Next day he went out to Gulahek, where the British Legation was in summer quarters.

He remained at Teheran till the 5th of July.

Sir Henry Rawlinson once characterised the history of England's relations with Persia as made up of hot and cold phases. At this time they were in the middle of a hot phase. Under the management of Mr Nicolson, who came as Chargé d'Affaires in 1885, the relations between the British Legation and the Persian Court had been of the most cordial nature, Mr Nicolson himself being regarded with special personal friendship by the Shah. On the 6th of May a great reception had been held at the British Legation in honour of the Queen's Jubilee. It had gone off with the utmost success. At supper Yahia Khan had proposed her Majesty's health in the most cordial terms, and that of the Shah had been proposed by Mr Nicolson. The friendly feeling of the Persian authorities had been greatly increased by the satisfactory settlement of the Jask affair. Murdoch Smith accordingly found himself received with the greatest cordiality.

On the 11th of June he was received in audience by the Shah, Mr Nicolson, Mr Churchill, and Yahia Khan being present. He preserved some interesting notes of what passed.

"H.M. asked me," he writes, "whether I had come from London or India. I said I had come from London *viâ* India. In reply to further remarks I said I had while in India gone to Simla, the geographical position of which at H.M.'s request I described. He asked if it was a large city. I said no, that it could hardly be called a city. It was the *yelak* or summer quarters of the Viceroy and Government of India. He asked about the climate, if the air was like that of Shemran (the summer quarters of Teheran). I said it was not so cool and bracing as Shemran, but was more like the climate of Teheran itself. At this H.M. laughed and said, 'Teheran a *yelak!*' I said Teheran would be thought an excellent *yelak* in India. He recurred once or twice to the subject, much amused at the paradoxical idea of Teheran being a *yelak*. He then asked if there was an *ordū* or military camp at Simla. I said, 'No, there is only a small detachment to furnish a few sentries.' Asked if there was a railway to Simla. I explained how it was situated in this respect, and that a railway to Simla itself would be very difficult, the mountains being as steep as at Elburz (immediately behind the palace where we were). He asked how people got up. I said in carriages, to which he remarked, 'Oh, then there is *une chaussée—une route carrossable.*' He asked about the vegetation, &c., which I described. When I mentioned the *kāj* (Persian for fir) he said, 'Yes, *sapins.*' (H.M. I observe is still in the habit of helping his interlocutor by translating an occasional word or phrase into French.)

"H.M. then inquired about the health of the

Viceroy, and asked about his age, his habits, whether he was a sportsman, &c. I said that when I visited Simla H.E. had just come from a *shikar* excursion. He asked what sort of *shikar*. I said tigers, leopards, deer, and other big game. He said inquiringly and with much animation, 'Ha! Tigers!' I said, 'Yes, H.E. had been shooting in the jungles which were the very home of the tigers.'

"H.M. then asked what news from Afghanistan. I said some tribes, Ghilzais, were in rebellion, and Mr Nicolson told him that the two commanders-in-chief of the Amir had now joined their forces against them. H.M. then asked me about new railways in that direction, whether there was one to Kelat. I said, 'No, but there is one to Quetta from Sukkur on the Sind railway.' He asked one or two questions about its position, how far it was from Kandahar, &c. When I said it was some 20 or 25 *farsakhs*, he said, 'But that is a long way from Herat, how will you send troops there?' I said, 'Yes, it is a long way.' He asked if the railway was not to go on to Kandahar. I said I did not know, and in answer to a further remark (which I did not quite catch) as to the attitude of the Afghans to the railway, I said that if our Government continued the railway to Kandahar the Afghans would greatly benefit by it. Mr Nicolson then told H.M. he got Afghan news regularly from India, and that as much of the news in the newspapers was made up, he would communicate the authentic news to H.M. if he wished, to which his Majesty replied, 'It is very necessary.'

"H.M. then remarked to me that from India I

had gone to Jask. I said, 'Yes, I went there specially.' The Foreign Minister then said I had there made the settlement which H.M. had been pleased to approve of. H.M. said, 'Yes, it is very good.'

"In the course of further conversation I told H.M. that I had observed that from Kazerun and Shiraz to Teheran the crops were everywhere good, but that in the Bushire plain they were bad owing to want of rain.

"After we had taken leave H.M. called me back to ask how long I was staying, to which I replied eight or ten days.

"Throughout the audience H.M.'s manner was particularly cheerful and genial, and he appeared to be in very good humour. He seemed to me to look younger and to be in better health and spirits than when I last saw him two years ago."

On the same day, and again on the 14th, Murdoch Smith had interviews with the Amin-es-Sultan, Mirza Ali Askar Khan, the young and capable Minister who was then practically Prime Minister, and who now occupies the position of Grand Vizier, the present Shah having recently conferred upon him the title of Atabeg Azim, meaning the Father of the People,—an exceptional mark of favour and distinction. During the following fortnight he had further interviews with the Persian Ministers, meeting in all cases with a most friendly reception.

The convention of April 2, 1868, which provided for the extension of the Beluchistan land-line to Jask, expired on April 2, 1888, and the matter of its renewal had been before the British authorities.

The difficulty which had arisen with regard to the telegraph station at Jask might have proved a serious obstacle to negotiations for this purpose. In view of the satisfactory settlement of that difficulty, and of the exceedingly friendly attitude of the Persian authorities, it appeared to Murdoch Smith that a suitable opportunity now presented itself for obtaining the renewal, not only of the Jask Convention, but of the general Telegraph Convention of 1872, which would have expired in 1895. He accordingly made this suggestion to Mr Nicolson. The requisite authority was obtained from home by telegraph, and negotiations were opened, with the most satisfactory result. The matter was referred by the Shah to the Mukhber-ed-Dowleh, who expressed his willingness to frame his answer in whatever sense Murdoch Smith desired. The latter proposed that the existing conventions should be prolonged till January 31, 1905, the date of the expiry of the Indo-European Company's concession. To this his Excellency readily assented, and agreements providing for the prolongation of the conventions to that date were signed by Yahia Khan and Mr Nicolson on the 3rd of July. The position of the English telegraph in Persia, the political and general importance of which has already been sufficiently dwelt on, was thus secured for another eighteen years. It may be added that by agreements dated January 7, 1892, the conventions have been further prolonged to January 31, 1925.

The one constant factor which has to be taken into account in all British enterprise, public or private, in Persia is the "stubborn and selfish antagonism of Russia,"—the phrase is Lord Curzon's. When it is remembered that that antagonism was at this time represented in Teheran by so distinguished a personage as Prince Dolgorouky, the importance of the service which Murdoch Smith had rendered will be obvious.

The caravan bearing the presents reached Teheran on the 26th of June, having left the Zil-es-Sultan's present at Ispahan. The carriage for the Mukhber-ed-Dowleh had been sent by way of Baghdad and Kermanshah, and did not arrive until after Murdoch's Smith's departure from Persia. Anticipating this, he had provided himself with a sketch of it, with which the Mukhber expressed himself highly gratified. The presentation to Yahia Khan took place on the 27th of June, and a public audience for the presentation of the band instruments to the Shah was fixed to take place at the summer palace of Sahibkranieh on the 2nd of July.

During the summer and autumn of 1887 a series of interesting letters on Persian affairs were contributed to the columns of the *Scotsman* by Mr J. J. Fahie of the Telegraph Department. In one of these, dated Teheran, July 25, he gives the following account of the ceremony at Sahibkranieh:—

Evidently wishing to attach to this simple function as much importance and significance as possible, his Majesty departed considerably from the custom usual on such occasions. He was arrayed in a dress resplendent with jewels, and was attended by several of his Ministers of State, and a crowd of chamberlains and other officers. Amongst the former were his Royal Highness the Naib-es-Sultaneh, Minister for War, and the Ministers for Foreign Affairs, for Telegraphs, for Police, and for Revenue and Commerce. The latter, known as the Amin-es-Sultan, occupies the high position of the Shah's guide, philosopher, and friend, and, although quite a young man, is practically Grand Vizier of Persia.

On entering the audience-chamber the Shah, so I am told, looked neither to the right nor to the left, where the instruments with their cases and other accessories were laid out on shawl-covered trays, but fixed his eyes on Colonel Smith, and so kept them until the first formalities of presentation had been gone through. This, it appears, was intended to signify that the gallant officer was himself the object of consideration for the moment, a compliment which he richly deserved, since for the last twenty-four years he has been a loyal servant of the Shah.

Colonel Smith, who adds to his many other accomplishments that of being a good Oriental scholar, then made a speech in Persian, which I find fully reported in the official *Gazette*. In translating it into bald English it must necessarily lose a few beauties of expression in which the vernacular so much abounds, but in substance it was as follows:—

"On behalf of the English Government I have the honour to offer for your Majesty's acceptance this set of musical instruments as a slight expression of their grateful thanks for your Majesty's many and gracious kindnesses towards the English Government telegraph department in Persia. Thanks to your Majesty's constant care and solicitude, the Persian telegraphs have attained to a high state of efficiency; while under your sheltering shadow its officers and employees of all ranks have lived in peace and security. For twenty-four years this happy state of things has existed, to the advancement of the trade of the world, and to the mutual advantage of Persia and England. At the same time, the English Government would wish your Majesty to regard this present as a mark, however slight, of their great regard and sincere friendship for your Majesty's Government and person. It is their earnest desire that your Majesty's auspicious reign may last for many years, and that the power and independence of the oldest Government in the world may continue and increase."

In reply his Majesty said: "I accept with much pleasure this fresh mark of the friendship of the Government of the Queen-Empress, which I greatly prize, and which I cordially reciprocate. I wish you, therefore, to convey to her Majesty's Government my warm thanks for their handsome present, as well as for the friendly sentiments they have expressed towards my person and Government."

His Majesty was also graciously pleased to add, as regards Colonel Smith himself, that he was not ignorant of his long services in connection with the telegraph department, which were as valuable to Persia as they were to his own country; and to mark his appreciation of his conduct, and as a souvenir of Persia, which he had served so well, his Majesty presented the gallant officer with a gold snuff-box encrusted with diamonds. I may remind your readers *en passant* that it was only two years ago that the Shah presented Colonel Smith with a magnificent sword of honour on the occasion of his leaving the telegraphs in Persia to assume the post of Director of your Science and Art Museum.

The Shah then minutely inspected the instruments, and for nearly an hour kept up a desultory conversation which was marked by his well-known urbanity of manner, and full of allusions to old friends in England, amongst others to Sir H. Rawlinson and the late Sir J. Bateman Champain, whose death he greatly deplored.

The diamond snuff-box was accompanied by the following letter from the Foreign Minister:—

Mon cher Colonel,—Sa Majesté le Shahinshah, mon auguste Maître, a bien voulu vous donner un souvenir de sa haute bienveillance. Je m'empresse de vous envoyer une tabatière enrichie de diamants, et vous verrez par là, mon Colonel, une nouvelle preuve de la sympathie de sa Majesté à votre égard. En vous envoyant mes sincères félicitations, je reste votre invariablement dévoué,

YAHIA.

Immediately after the audience the Shah signed the draft declarations for prolonging the two Telegraph Conventions, thereby formally authorising the Foreign Minister to sign those documents, which was done on the following day.

On the 5th of July Murdoch Smith started on his return journey to Ispahan to make the presentation to the Zil-es-Sultan. One of Mr Fahie's *Scotsman* letters may again be quoted.

> Your readers [he says] can hardly conceive the hardships of such a journey. From Teheran to Ispahan and back is a distance of 600 miles, over a desolate country, with miserable accommodation *en route*. This journey had to be accomplished on post-horses in a fierce July sun. At one place Colonel Smith, on arriving, had the choice between bitterly salt water and the stinking dregs of a tank in which the surface drainage from winter's rains is stored. Preferring the pangs of thirst to the risk of fever or cholera, he refrained from both from morning till evening, and then rode on another stage of twenty-eight miles before tasting a drop of water.
>
> At the best of times a journey from Bushire, in the Persian Gulf, to Teheran, is a painfully weary undertaking of nearly 800 miles, all of which must be done on horseback; but in the height of a fierce Persian summer, and with a repetition of 600 miles of the worst part of the road, it becomes a task requiring courage and endurance, for which the Victoria Cross might fittingly be awarded.

Referring to the journey in a despatch written at the time, Murdoch Smith characteristically says: "I was rather glad that I had to make it, feeling sure that, undertaken as it was for the sole and express purpose of presenting the gifts, it would give them a double value in the prince's estimation."

H.R.H. Sultan Masud Mirza, the eldest son of the Shah, commonly known by the title of the Zil-es-Sultan or Shadow of the King, was at this time very generally regarded as the most powerful subject in Persia. At a very early age he had been made Governor of Ispahan, and afterwards of Shiraz. Province after province was added to his dominions until he attained the position of a powerful sovereign. He had proved himself a resolute and capable administrator. He controlled an army of over 20,000 men, who were maintained in a high state of efficiency, and well provided with artillery and with breech-loading rifles. From the fact that his mother was not of royal origin he did not hold the position of heir-apparent, but it was widely believed that in the event of his father's death he would be a formidable candidate for the throne. He professed, at all events to English ears, the most liberal and Anglophile sentiments. He was exceedingly well informed as to European politics, and was at no pains to conceal his contempt for the *mullahs*. The friendship of so important a personage was naturally regarded as a desirable object by the European Powers. The French Government had just sent him the Grand Cordon of the Legion of Honour, and very shortly

H.R.H. THE ZIL-ES-SULTAN, G.C.S.I.

after Murdoch Smith's visit he received the G.C.S.I. The Zil's ambition, however, overleaped itself. In February 1888 he was deprived of all his governorships except that of Ispahan, and of all but a fragment of his army, and ceased to be a prominent political figure.[1] On the assassination of Nasred-Din Shah in 1896, Muzaffer-ed-Din, the Zil's younger brother, being the son of a princess, succeeded to the throne.

On reaching Ispahan Murdoch Smith was received by his Royal Highness with the utmost distinction. On the 14th of July he was received in private audience in the prince's garden, when a long and interesting conversation on political affairs took place. The prince expressed great interest in the Indian army, and the warmest admiration of Sir Frederick Roberts, to whom he said that he had sent "a greeting and hand-shaking as from one soldier to another."

Murdoch Smith at once set out on his return journey to Teheran. On arriving there he was met by a courteous message from Yahia Khan, conveying the compliments of the Shah, with his Majesty's good wishes for his homeward journey. In reply he begged the Foreign Minister to express to his Majesty his gratitude for his gracious message, and for the many favours which he had received from him. "Je prie votre Altesse," he continued, "de lui offrir mes hommages respectueux

---

[1] An interesting account of the character and present political position of the Zil-es-Sultan is given by Mr Wilfrid Sparroy in a recent article, "The Elder Brother of the Shah," *Blackwood's Magazine*, August 1900.

et l'assurance de mon dévouement. Je me rappelerai toujours de son beau royaume hospitalier où j'ai passé les meilleures années de ma vie, et auquel je porte le plus vif intérêt."

These words were his last farewell to Persia. On the 28th of July he started for home by way of Baku, Constantinople, and Vienna.

On reaching London he found that the value of the services which he had rendered was fully appreciated both by Lord Salisbury and Lord Cross. He had brought with him copies of the Jask agreement as finally settled and signed, and the two protocols, or declarations, prolonging the Telegraph Conventions; and he had materially helped forward the negotiations as to the Karun River, which in the following year was opened to navigation.

On the 9th of September a copy of the following despatch from Mr Nicolson to Lord Salisbury, relating to Murdoch Smith's personal services, was sent to him by Sir Philip Currie:—

TEHERAN, *July* 28, 1887.

MY LORD,—I have the honour to report that Colonel Murdoch Smith leaves here to-day on his return to England. Colonel Smith has met with a very cordial and flattering reception from the Shah, the Zil-es-Sultan, and the Persian Ministers, who all very highly appreciate his personal qualities and the services which he has rendered during his lengthened residence in Persia.

The stay of Colonel Smith was necessarily somewhat limited, but he has in the short time that he has been here greatly promoted the several projects we have in view, and has done excellent service in bringing clearly before all who are in authority the friendly intentions and feelings of her Majesty's Government towards Persia.

I should mention to your Lordship that Colonel Smith has not spared himself in the performance of his duty, as after a long and arduous ride from Bushire to Teheran he returned again by post to visit the Zil-es-Sultan at Ispahan, a task not to be undertaken lightly in this great heat.

I should like also to express my personal gratitude to Colonel Smith for the great assistance he has cordially rendered to me, and for the benefit that I have derived from his accurate knowledge of this country and its people.—I have, &c.,

A. NICOLSON.

A few days later he received the following letter:—

FOREIGN OFFICE, 12th *September* 1887.

SIR,—I have received through her Majesty's Chargé d'Affaires at Teheran the reports drawn up by you of your interviews with various high officials of the Persian Government, . . . and have been in communication with the Secretary of State for India on the subject.

I have now much pleasure in conveying to you the entire approval by her Majesty's Government of the judicious language employed by you on the occasion in question.—I am, sir, your most obedient humble servant,

(*For* THE MARQUIS OF SALISBURY),

J. PAUNCEFOTE.

He also received from the Permanent Under Secretary for India, on November 2, a letter expressing Lord Cross's "special satisfaction" at the prolongation of the Telegraph Conventions, "the successful accomplishment of which was due to the great tact and judgment shown by yourself in conducting with the Persian authorities the delicate negotiations on the subject."

On November 29 Lord Cross wrote to say that in recognition of Murdoch Smith's services her Majesty had been pleased to appoint him a Knight Commander of the Order of St Michael and St George, and a similar intimation was shortly afterwards received from Lord Salisbury, the honour having been granted on the recommendation of both Ministers.

His K.C.M.G. was announced in the list of New Year honours for 1888, and was gazetted on the 10th of January. On December 31, 1887, he retired from the army with the honorary rank of major-general.

CHAPTER X.

LIFE IN EDINBURGH.

AMALGAMATION OF INDIAN AND INDO-EUROPEAN TELEGRAPH DEPARTMENTS — MURDOCH SMITH RESIGNS DIRECTORSHIP — RETURNS TO EDINBURGH — WORK AT EDINBURGH MUSEUM — ADDITIONS TO THE MUSEUM — THE SHAH'S VISIT IN 1889 — A PICTURESQUE CEREMONY — CONTINUED INTEREST IN PERSIA — PAPERS ON THE KARUN RIVER — THE BOARD OF MANUFACTURES — EDINBURGH FRIENDSHIPS AND OCCUPATIONS — SPEECH ON ART — EFFECT OF THE REFORMATION ON ART AND MANNERS IN SCOTLAND — DOMESTIC LIFE — HOLIDAYS — ST GILES'S CATHEDRAL — CHARACTER — THE LAST YEARS — THE END.

WHEN Murdoch Smith returned from Persia the India Office had under consideration the subject of the amalgamation of the Indo-European and Indian Telegraph Departments. During his journey he had given this question his most anxious attention, and had fully conferred with the Indian officials regarding it. His return and report on the subject were awaited before any action was taken. After full consideration he expressed an opinion in favour of amalgamation, chiefly on the ground that the office of Director-in-Chief of the Indo-European department, to which he had succeeded on Champain's death, was not any longer necessary, and involved needless expense to the public. Amalgamation was accordingly decided upon, and he tendered his resignation, which was accepted with effect from February 15, 1888. The office has since been re-established under somewhat different conditions.

Henceforward his work lay at the Edinburgh Museum.

At the Museum there was a great deal to be done. The west wing, which was in course of erection at the time of Murdoch Smith's appointment, was finished in 1888. It was appropriated to the accommodation of the Reference and Patent Libraries attached to the Museum, of mechanical and engineering models, of the Oriental and ethnographical collections; and of the specimens and maps collected and prepared by the Geological Survey to illustrate the geology of Scotland. The rearrangement of all these objects, and the carrying out of the necessary changes in the organisation of the Museum staff, was the work of many months. It was not until 1890 that the whole of the collections in the west wing were thrown open to the public.

The routine work of museum administration does not offer much material to the biographer. The annual reports of the Director, with their lists of donations and purchases, statistics of attendance of visitors, and details as to the registering, labelling, and arranging of specimens, represent a great deal of accurate and laborious work, but do not contain much in the way of incident. It may perhaps suffice to mention a few of the more notable additions to the Museum made during Sir Robert's period of office.

His chief interests naturally lay in the departments which had been the field of his own earlier work, those of Oriental art and classical archæology. One of the first pieces of work which he took up after his appointment was the formation, by purchase and by loan from the Science and Art Department, and from private individuals, of a Persian section containing typical collections of most of the forms of Persian art, ancient and modern, including wall tiles, glazed earthenware, metal work, armour, textiles, carving, caligraphy, enamelling, and painting—a collection which on a smaller scale is very fairly representative of the great collection at South Kensington. When in Persia he had rendered valuable services to Monsieur and Madame Dieulafoy when they were engaged in their famous excavations at Susa. For these services he had received the thanks of the French Government, and they bore fruit in a valuable addition to the Museum,—reproductions of two large panels of enamelled bricks from the Palace of Darius at Susa, which were presented by the director of the Louvre, where the originals now are. These panels, which formed part of a great frieze, are decorated with life-size coloured figures of archers of the King's Guard, the Ten Thousand Immortals of Herodotus, and form a beautiful and striking ornament to the hall of the Museum. A series of casts from the sculptures of Persepolis made by Lord Savile's expedition in 1891 may also be noted. A descriptive guide to the whole collection, written by Sir Robert, was issued in 1896.

The presentation of the Cyrene Dionysos by the Trustees of the British Museum has already been mentioned. A number of the other discoveries at Halicarnassus, Cnidus, and Cyrene were represented by casts, including a fine reproduction of a column and a portion of the entablature of the Mausoleum from the original in the British Museum. Owing to the great height of the central hall of the Museum in Edinburgh, it was possible to erect the column and entablature to their full height, as in the original building, which had not been feasible in the Mausoleum Room of the British Museum. A series of water-colour drawings by Mr R. P. Pullan, illustrating the excavations in Asia Minor, was also purchased.

A very fine series of reproductions of mediæval and Renaissance sculpture and architecture was added, perhaps the most notable of these being a cast of the figure of Christ at the west door of Amiens Cathedral — the famous "beau Dieu d'Amiens"; reproductions of Peter Vischer's bronze statues of King Arthur and Theodoric from the tomb of the Emperor Maximilian at Innsbruck; and two beautiful large-scale models of Renaissance interiors, one of a room from the "Paradiso" of Isabella d'Este in the old palace of the Gonzagas at Mantua, and the other of the Cappella Portinari, or Chapel of St Peter Martyr, in the Church of Sant' Eustorgio at Milan.

The industrial department of the Museum was also largely extended, numerous additions being made to the collections illustrative of manufacturing and industrial processes. Many fine models of machinery were made in the Museum workshops.

In 1894 an exceedingly important addition was made to the scientific part of the Museum by the acquisition, partly by gift and partly by purchase, of the rich collection of Scottish minerals formed by Professor Heddle of St Andrews, numbering upwards of 7000 specimens. The acquisition of this unique collection, made at a time when the oldest lines of railway in Scotland were in course of construction, was due entirely to Sir Robert's personal initiative. He urged that such a collection once broken up could not easily be brought together again, so, with the aid of a few patriotic Scotsmen in London, a private subscription was started to enable the Museum to take advantage of the generous terms on which the collection was offered. The funds thus raised were subsequently augmented by a grant from the Treasury. The specimens were arranged under the superintendence of Professor Heddle himself, and were incorporated with the collection, chiefly the gift of Mr Patrick Dudgeon of Cargen, previously in the Museum. The result, known as the Heddle-Dudgeon collection, is regarded as one of the finest national collections in existence of the minerals of any single country.

Nasr-ed-Din Shah paid his last visit to Europe in 1889. When in Scotland he was the guest of Lord Hopetoun at Hopetoun House, and on July 23 he paid a visit to Edinburgh. The Corporation decided to give him an official welcome, and it was arranged that it should take the form of a reception and luncheon in the Museum and the presentation

of a civic address. The reception was made the
occasion of a picturesque function, and the Director
took no small trouble to carry out the ceremony
with appropriate detail. It took place in the new
west wing of the building, in which the Persian
collection had just been placed. Among the decora-
tions of the hall appeared a portrait of the Shah,
which had been presented to Murdoch Smith in
1874 by the Mukhber-ed-Dowleh, and a water-
colour drawing, by Sir John Champain, of the
valley of the Lar, a favourite summer resort of
the Persian Court. On the table at luncheon were
Shiraz wine and *gez* from Ispahan, the favourite
sweetmeat of Persia. The Shah was delighted with
his reception, and at meeting an old friend in the
person of Sir Robert, to whom he was so anxious
to talk that he was with some difficulty induced to
carry out the details of the civic programme. After
luncheon he walked with him round the galleries of
the Museum. "In the course of conversation," says
the *Scotsman's* account of the proceedings, "his
Majesty frequently expressed his admiration for
Edinburgh and everything he had seen, both of
the city, its situation, and its buildings, and more
than once observed how much he had enjoyed his
whole trip in Scotland. He remarked that the
Scottish people seemed to him to have shown a
wonderful amount of energy, not only in their
own country, but wherever they went, and that
Scotland appeared to him to stand in the same
relation to the United Kingdom that Azerbaijan
did to Persia."

Although no longer officially connected with

Persia, Sir Robert continued to take an active interest in that country. He was from time to time consulted by the Government with regard to Persian affairs. He was specially interested in the opening to navigation of the Karun River, which took place in 1888, and which he regarded as fraught with great possibilities for the development of British trade and British influence in Western Persia. The matter was one in which he had long been interested. As has been mentioned, he had in 1883 written a memorandum on the subject. On his return from Persia in 1885 his views regarding it had been directly brought under the notice of Lord Salisbury, and during his visit to Persia in 1887 he had done much to forward the opening of the river. On February 13, 1889, he delivered to the London Chamber of Commerce an address on *The Prospects of the Development of British Trade with Persia consequent on the Opening up of the Karun River;* and on May 3 he read to the Society of Arts a paper on *The Karun River from a Commercial Point of View.* The latter paper obtained the silver medal of the Society, and was characterised by so eminent an authority as Professor Vambéry as "perhaps the best paper hitherto published on the subject." He was a member of the Royal Geographical Society and of the Royal Scottish Geographical Society, and in both bodies was a recognised authority on Persia. The paper on *Telegraphic Communication with India,* which has been largely quoted in an earlier chapter of this volume, was read to the Scottish Society on December 13, 1888.

On April 13, 1889, he delivered at the South Kensington Museum a lecture on *Persian Art in its Relation to Persian Life and Character*, and a number of lectures on Persian subjects were from time to time delivered in Edinburgh. He also contributed to *Chambers's Encyclopædia* the articles "Persia" and "Persepolis."

He was always ready to be of service to members of the telegraph staff. In 1890 we find him in communication with Mr Curzon about some alleged grievances, and a good deal of correspondence passed between them with reference to Mr Curzon's book on Persia, then in preparation.

In 1892 he was appointed by the Crown a member of the Board of Manufactures. The "Commissioners and Trustees for Managing the Fisheries and Manufactures in Scotland" date from 1727. They have long outlived their original function, which was the administration of the fund provided, in terms of the Treaty of Union, for the encouragement of fisheries and manufactures in Scotland, as an equivalent for the customs and excise duties imposed upon Scotland towards the payment of the English national debt. Scottish manufactures no longer need "encouragement," and the Board is now entirely concerned with art and art education. In it are vested the National Gallery of Scotland, the National Portrait Gallery, and the Museum of Antiquities. Its membership has always included some of the most distinguished Scotsmen of the day. Among Sir Robert's colleagues on the Board were some of the most valued friends of his later years—the late Marquis of Lothian, who as a young man had served in Persia; Lord Kinnear, Lord Justice-Clerk Macdonald, Sir William Muir, Sir George Reid, Mr J. R. Findlay of Aberlour, and Sir Arthur Mitchell. He took great interest in the work of the Board, and became one of its most assiduous members. He was specially interested in the management of the Scottish National Portrait Gallery, and was on terms of intimate friendship with Mr Findlay, the founder of the Gallery. On Mr Findlay's death in 1898 Sir Robert succeeded him as chairman of the Portrait Gallery Committee. He had during Mr Findlay's lifetime initiated the movement for placing in the Gallery the fine memorial portrait of its founder, by Sir George Reid, which it now contains.

In many other ways he took part in the public and intellectual life of Edinburgh. His connection with the Royal Scottish Geographical Society has been mentioned. He took an active part in the work of the Cockburn Association, the protection of the beauty and historic interest of Edinburgh. He was a member of the Royal Society of Edinburgh, and of the Society of Antiquaries of Scotland; of the latter he was elected a vice-president in 1897. He was for many years honorary president of the Edinburgh Association of Science and Arts, and did much to further the object of that body, the promotion of technical knowledge relating to the industries of the city.

In December 1890 he was asked to open an art gallery in his native town of Kilmarnock. The speech which he delivered on this occasion is of no small interest as expressing his views as to the function of art and its place in human life. . . . "We all know, more or less," he said, "what is meant by the term Art, although few of us, probably, could state precisely in what we consider true art to consist. Speaking of his own special form of it, Shakespeare, that most consummate artist for all time, says the actor must hold a mirror up to Nature. What he thus said of the Drama may be said with equal truth of all true art. Poetry, for instance, is worthy of the name, not when it follows the artificial whims and fancies of the day, but only when it strikes a natural chord deeply seated in the human heart. The painter and the sculptor must constantly and continuously turn to Nature for inspiration and guidance. To revert for a moment to Shakespeare's metaphor: the mirror may be bright but distorted, it may be smooth but blurred. The reflection we behold in it, even though of dazzling brilliancy, may be twisted by the morbid fancy of the artist, or, however true in some respects to Nature, may be smudged by the impurity of his imagination. It is only when the mirror itself is a true plane that the image is neither dwarfed, deformed, nor exaggerated; it is only when its surface is bright and unsullied that the image is truly beautiful. Metaphors, however, if pushed too far, are proverbially apt to mislead. True art must indeed always hold a mirror, but, in its higher developments, it must do something more. Its function is not only to reflect, but to select and discriminate, to analyse, to illustrate, to interpret, to impress.

Above all, its highest and most essential function is to lift us out of the miry slough of gross and sensuous materialism. It is only in proportion to the degree in which that object is attained that excellence in any form of art is to be truly estimated. In considering the question of the position which art occupies, or ought to occupy, in the life of man, that deeply suggestive text, quoted at a crisis of His earthly career by our Divine Master Himself as a foil to the temptations of the evil one, comes readily to our minds: 'It is written, Man shall not live by bread alone, but by every word that proceedeth out of the mouth of God.' Every word—that is to say, everything whereby He has manifested His attributes and His will in the material universe around us and in the spiritual world within us—all the infinitely varied beauties, animate and inanimate, of earth and sky and sea, and all that is great or noble or beautiful in the thoughts of the mind and in the emotions of the heart. True art, therefore, whose highest and most essential function it is, as we have seen, to interpret and impress upon us those manifold and often mysterious words proceeding out of the mouth of God, is a necessary and indispensable ingredient in the nourishment and development of the higher life of man. 'It is written, Man shall not live by bread alone.' That great decree applies to communities not less than to individuals. What, for instance, but ruin has followed the track of those rude but powerful hordes of Tartars, Turks, and Mongols who from time to time have swept over many of the fairest portions of the globe? Or, to take the case of a great empire with which our own has not infrequently been compared,—what has become of the highly civilised but essentially materialistic Phœnicians, of their numerous colonies, of their widespread commerce, of their long unchallenged maritime supremacy, of their great capital Carthage, the rival of Rome itself? All have vanished,

> And, like the baseless fabric of a vision,
> . . . . .
> Left not a rack behind.

Every nation, on the other hand—Egypt, for instance, or Assyria, or Persia, or Rome, or, above all, Greece—every nation of the past by whom art was sedulously and successfully cultivated, even now, after the lapse of many centuries, 'being dead, yet speaketh.' As it has been in the past so it is now in the present, and so must it infallibly be in the future. That nation or that community which either sinks into, or which never rises above, pure materialism, is already foredoomed to ignoble decay and ultimate extinction. The decree is eternal and immutable, 'Man shall not live by bread alone.' In this connection I should like to say a word regarding our own country, more especially Scotland, which does not yet occupy that position among the civilized nations of the world to which the character and gifts of her people entitle her to aspire. To understand the reason for this we must go back to the time of the Reformation, when, through the action of various causes which it is now unnecessary to specify, an unfortunate and unnatural severance took place between those two great influences for good, art and religion. The fanatical fury that then burst forth against what the Reformers called idols and idolatry soon fell upon every other form of art as well. Beauty of every kind came to be associated in men's minds with sin, and art in every form with the wiles and snares of the devil. Even in manners (an effect from which we are still suffering) politeness was considered synonymous with hypocrisy and subserviency, and rudeness with independence. From such a horrible association of incongruous and antagonistic ideas we are at last beginning in a timid and tentative way to emancipate ourselves, thanks chiefly to the genius of two of our countrymen, Burns and Scott, for whose genius, and for its vivifying effect on our national life, we can never be too thankful. It will be long, however, before Scotland is entirely free from the effects of the baneful prejudices of three centuries' duration. One particular form of art was long considered, and by some, perhaps, is still considered, specially sinful above all others— viz., the dramatic. The prevalence of that opinion was, I think, a great national misfortune, because it nipped in the bud, or stunted in its early growth, every artistic impulse in the youth of our land. Imagination, that most precious of God's gifts to man, was steadily and sternly repressed from earliest infancy. Acting, or as children call it, playing at, pretending, is, as every one must have observed, the favourite pastime of all happy well-conditioned children. Why, then, should such an innocent and healthful play of the child's imagination be checked and its natural development into dramatic art arrested? Such a course affects not only the Drama, against which it is undoubtedly directed, but all true Art, which, to use a favourite French expression, is one and indivisible. A far wiser course would be the systematic cultivation of the very earliest symptoms of the dramatic faculty. I see no reason, in fact, why every school should not have its stage as well as its playground. To take no higher ground than that of simple utility: how can we reasonably expect to compete successfully with other nations in the art of design, for instance, on which our position as a manufacturing country so largely depends, if we begin in the educating of our children by ignoring the very faculty of their nature, imagination, by the exercise of which originality in design is alone attainable? I have taken the case of the Drama, not from any idea of its superiority above other forms of art, but simply because it is the one toward which our earliest impulses seem to tend, and therefore to be one which, in the upbringing of the young, it is most important to foster and encourage. But so also with every other form of art, due regard being had to the tastes or aptitudes of the individual. What I plead for is this, that in giving our children a knowledge of the three R's and a smattering of popular science, we should not forget that all the aims and objects of their lives are not compressible within the four corners of the multiplication table, nor should we, in their education and upbringing, neglect the very highest and most precious faculty of their beings. To the want of imagination, or rather to the neglect and repression of it which characterised the system so long dominant in Scotland, is due, I am firmly convinced, much of the drunkenness, pauperism, misery, degradation, and crime by which we are surrounded." . . .

The lack of amenity in Scottish life was a subject on which he felt strongly. Himself the most courteous of men, and having lived long among the most courteous people in the world, he often deplored the existence of the too familiar type of Scot which Mr Cunninghame Graham has sketched for us in the mates of the *Atlas*:—" Glasgow men, well educated, reading 'improving' books; one of them with a master's certificate, and all so boorish in demeanour that till you knew them it appeared that they were mad." In another speech at Kilmarnock, nine years later, he returned to the subject. Speaking on education, at the opening of the new buildings of the Kilmarnock Academy in February 1899, he said: "Boys should early be taught not simply obedience, but civility, politeness, and general deference to their elders and superiors. In the course of my public service it has come within the scope of my personal observation that the sterling qualities of many a young Scotsman are obscured, and his chances in life heavily handicapped, by a certain dour gruffness of speech and manner which he has been foolishly brought up to regard as one of the minor virtues."

In 1888 he and his sister removed their joint household from Merchiston to a large house in Chalmers Crescent. Mrs Mather's children were now growing up, and in 1890 the joint establishment was broken up, and Sir Robert bought a house, No.

17 Magdala Crescent, in the west end of Edinburgh, where he lived for more than eight years.

They were very quiet and happy years. Time had done much to heal his great sorrow. He had interesting and congenial work. His health was better than it had been for long, and he was happy in the affectionate companionship of his daughters. He had made many friends, and in Edinburgh society he found himself a distinguished and welcome guest. His old love of music and the theatre revived. Museum business took him abroad from time to time; two much-enjoyed journeys to Italy were made in the company of his elder daughter. Every autumn brought a long holiday, generally spent in the Highlands — in Arran, on Loch Tay, on Loch Awe, or in Strathspey, — to which from year to year he looked forward with unfailing pleasure. Strathspey became the favourite resort, and for several autumns he was the tenant of Craggan Cottage, near Grantown. There he loved to entertain his old friends.

No record of his Edinburgh life would be complete which omitted some reference to his connection with St Giles's Cathedral. With what is sometimes called the religious world he had not much in common. He walked in all simplicity in the old ways of the faith. He believed, and acted on the belief, that a man's religion should show itself rather in conduct than in words. Theological questions interested him little; ecclesiastical controversies even less. In the old High Church of Edinburgh, with its beautiful services and great historic memories, he found a congenial atmosphere, and he was in cordial sympathy with the manly and rational preaching of his friend Dr Cameron Lees. In 1893 he became a member of the kirk-session. Sunday after Sunday, in fair weather and foul, so long as health permitted, he was to be seen in his place in the chancel, and it was seldom indeed that he failed to take part as an elder in the duties of the quarterly celebration of Holy Communion.

It was in 1894 that I made his acquaintance. In the autumn of 1896 I was his guest at Craggan, and in the following year his daughter Kathleen became my wife. From that time forward I lived in constant intimacy with him, seeing him nearly every day.

The remembrance of that friendship remains a possession for ever. When Patrick Stewart died at Constantinople in 1865 a friend at the Embassy wrote of him: "So much knowledge, intelligence, earnestness, kind-heartedness, and winning simplicity can rarely be united in the same person, and in him there was no other side to the picture." The words might have been written yesterday of Murdoch Smith. "Winning simplicity," — one might search the language in vain for a phrase which should convey with such felicitous exactness the impression which his memory recalls. After all those years of successful work, of travel, of administration, and of diplomacy, he had kept the chivalrous and tender heart of youth. His punctilious old-world courtesy of manner was the expression of the utter unselfishness which was the dominant note of his whole nature. Unwearying zeal in the public service; devotion to those whom he loved; constant thought of how to do a kind act; unfailing fortitude in sorrow and illness;— these one recalls as the familiar aspects of that noble character. In his house there stood a cast of the beautiful bust of the Emperor Antoninus Pius which he had found at Cyrene in his youth. It was one of his most valued household gods. That lofty and serene presence seemed congenial to the atmosphere of the house and to the character of its master, to whom one might well apply unchanged the words which were written of Antoninus by his great successor. "Remember," writes Marcus Aurelius, "his constancy in every act which was conformable to reason, and his evenness in all things, and his piety, and the serenity of his countenance, and his sweetness, and his disregard of empty fame, and his efforts to understand things, and how he would never let anything pass without having first most carefully examined it and clearly understood it; and how he bore with those who blamed him unjustly, without blaming them in return; how he did nothing in a hurry, and how he listened not to calumnies; not given to reproach people, nor timid, nor suspicious, nor a sophist; with how little he was satisfied, such as lodging, bed, dress, food, servants; how laborious and patient; his firmness and uniformity in his friendships; how he tolerated freedom of speech in those who opposed his opinions; the pleasure that he had when any man showed him anything better; and how religious he was without superstition.

"Imitate all this," soliloquises Aurelius, "that

thou mayest have as good a conscience, when thy last hour comes, as he had."

At Christmas 1898 his younger daughter went to school in Paris, and he became an inmate of my house. He was now in sadly failing health, and found it no small effort to carry on the work of the Museum. He would scarcely have been able to do so had it not been for the constant help and loyal support which he received from Mr D. J. Vallance, who, on the death of Mr Galletly in 1894, had become curator of the Museum.

During the early days of the Persian telegraph his eyesight had been seriously injured by surveying work in the Kum desert. The result was a slowly progressive affection of the retina, which in his later years caused no small trouble and anxiety. The frequent failure to recognise his friends which resulted from this infirmity was to a man of his scrupulous care for the feelings of others a source of great distress, and latterly detracted much from his enjoyment of society. His constant fear was that the affection should reach such a stage as to entirely incapacitate him from reading and writing. Happily this did not occur, but during his later years he found continuous reading a great strain, and took much pleasure in being read to. The literature of speculation and introspection interested him little, but of the literature of action and affairs he never tired,—Motley, Macaulay, Lord Roberts's *Forty-one Years in India*, Captain Mahan's books, Lord Malmesbury's *Memoirs of an Ex-Minister*, Sir Herbert Maxwell's *Life of Wellington*. Among the novelists Scott and Thackeray remained his favourites always, and of all novels I think he liked *The Newcomes* best—

> Perchance as finding there unconsciously
> Some image of himself. . . .

Indeed one could not be in his company for an hour without thinking of the Colonel.

He loved children always, and understood them. In his little grandsons he found a source of unfailing interest and pleasure.

Ever since his return from Persia he had been subject to occasional feverish attacks. These were attributed to malaria, from which, like most Europeans in the East, he had suffered to some extent during his Persian service. In the summer of 1898 these attacks became periodical. With the change to the Highlands in the autumn they disappeared, but returned in the following winter. When on a visit in London at Christmas-time he had a very bad attack.

His last public appearance was in February 1899, when he went to Kilmarnock to open the new buildings of the Academy, his own old school, and to receive the freedom of his native town, an honour which he very highly appreciated. On the morning of the function he was far from well, and it was with no small effort that he got through the day's engagements. My wife and I had accompanied him to Kilmarnock with the intention of spending a few days at Ayr after the ceremony. When we reached Ayr he was very ill, and a severe attack of gastritis developed. It was nearly five weeks before he was able to return to Edinburgh. Then the periodical attacks of fever came back. He derived great benefit from a visit to Folkestone in the spring and early summer, and in the autumn was well enough to enjoy a rambling holiday with his younger daughter in the Lake Country and the West Highlands. Next winter, however, the fever returned. Early in 1900 his medical advisers came to the conclusion that the attacks were due to a local cause which might call for surgical interference. In the case of a man of his age a serious operation was, of course, regarded as a last resource. A visit to Bridge of Allan in the spring brought about a temporary improvement, but this was followed by a severe relapse, and it was reluctantly decided that operation was necessary. He was accordingly brought back to Edinburgh, and the operation took place on the 16th of May.

It was entirely successful in accomplishing its object, but the strain on a man of Sir Robert's age and in his state of health had been very severe, and for some days he lay between life and death. Gradually, however, he began to gain ground. By the end of June he was well advanced on the way to convalescence, and there was talk of his soon being able to leave town.

On Sunday the first of July he was for the first time allowed to go out. He was taken in a bath-chair into Queen Street Gardens. It was a beautiful summer day; the trees of the garden were in full leaf; the sunshine and the soft air gave keen pleasure to the invalid, so long shut up in a sick-room. His children and grandchildren were with him. It seemed that the disease from which he had suffered so much was conquered at last. He said that he had not felt so well for years. To all human foresight it appeared that a peaceful and happy old age still lay before him.

It was otherwise written. On that same night he had a paralytic seizure, from which he never recovered. He died early in the morning of Tuesday, the 3rd of July 1900. On the following Friday he was buried in the Dean Cemetery.

He has left to his country the results of a long and strenuous career of public service, and to all who knew him the remembrance of a personality of rare distinction and charm. To those who knew him best his name will ever sadly recall the words of the Persian poet: "Wherever I may wander I shall write with my tears, *O my friend, your place is empty.*"

APPENDIX

APPENDIX.

REPORT ON THE MAUSOLEUM.

From *Papers respecting the Excavations at Budrum, presented to both Houses of Parliament by Command of Her Majesty*, 1858, pp. 16-21.

Lieutenant R. M. Smith, R.E., to Vice-Consul Newton.

BUDRUM, *June* 1, 1857.

SIR,—In the course of excavating the north side of the site of the Mausoleum, a number of squared blocks of marble were found, which, from their peculiar appearance and similarity to each other, led to a more minute examination of them. This examination has been productive of some very important results regarding the dimensions and construction of the ancient building.

To understand this properly it will be necessary first to state what is known regarding the building from the description of it by Pliny.

One of its principal features was a pyramid, consisting of twenty-four steps, which supported on its summit a *quadriga*, or four-horse chariot, sculptured in marble, by an artist of the name of Pythis. Regarding the dimensions of the building Pliny says, "Patet ab austro et septemtrione sexagenos ternos pedes, brevius a frontibus, toto circuitu pedes quadringentos undecim; attollitur in altitudinem viginti quinque cubitis; cingitur columnis triginta sex." "It extends 63 feet on the north and south sides, is shorter on the fronts, and has a total circumference of 411 feet; it is raised 25 cubits in height; it is surrounded by 36 columns." He further adds, "Hæc adjecta, centum quadraginta pedum altitudini totum opus æquavit." "This [viz., the *quadriga*] being added, the whole building equalled 140 feet in height."

Speaking of the height of the pyramid, he says that it equalled in height the lower part, and must therefore have been 25 cubits, or 37½ feet high.

A variety of circumstances made it evident that the blocks of marble I have already mentioned formed the steps of the pyramid.

The manner in which they are dressed shows that they have been steps, and the position in which they were found, that they had fallen from a height.

Further proof of their belonging to the pyramid is given by the fact that a colossal horse, evidently one of the four of the *quadriga*, was discovered among them. Besides this, nothing else which could be identified as part of the pyramid has been found, and it is impossible to believe that such a mass as it must have been could have totally disappeared, especially as parts of all the rest of the building have been discovered.

These blocks have a uniform depth of 11¾ inches. In breadth there are two classes, some being 2, and others 3 feet broad. Their lengths are various, but average 4 feet. One of the long sides 11¾ inches broad, being polished, has evidently formed the face of the step. The upper side has one part polished and the other rough-cut, the polished surface forming the tread of the step. This side has been dressed in this way, as it would be unnecessary to polish the part of the stone covered by the step above. In every instance the boundary of the polished and rough-cut parts is clearly defined by a well-marked line parallel to the edge of the step. The two polished surfaces forming respectively the face and the tread of the step are adjacent to each other. The rest of the stone is rough-cut, with the exception of the ends, which are cut smooth for the joint in the usual manner. The upper side of each block has three flanges, one large one about 6 inches broad, at the back, the whole length of the stone, and two small polished ones, at right angles to the large one, along the ends. Each of these small flanges, having one side cut flush with the end of the stone, presents a section similar to the half of a Gothic arch. When two stones were joined, these small flanges consequently formed a kind of pent roof over the joint, thus protecting it from the entrance of rain. These small flanges extend all along the ends from the large flange at the back to the face of the step.

On the lower side of each block there is a large groove corresponding in its dimensions to the large flange on the upper side. It passes longitudinally along the stone, and is the same distance from the face that the large flange is from the line marking the boundary of the polished and rough-cut parts of the upper side.

There is a smaller transverse groove passing from the large longitudinal one to the face of the step. These different flanges and grooves are shown in plan and section in figure I.: (1) being a plan of the upper side, (2) plan of the under side, (3) a longitudinal section showing the small flanges and transverse groove, (4) a transverse section showing the large longitudinal flange and groove, and (5) a general view of the whole.

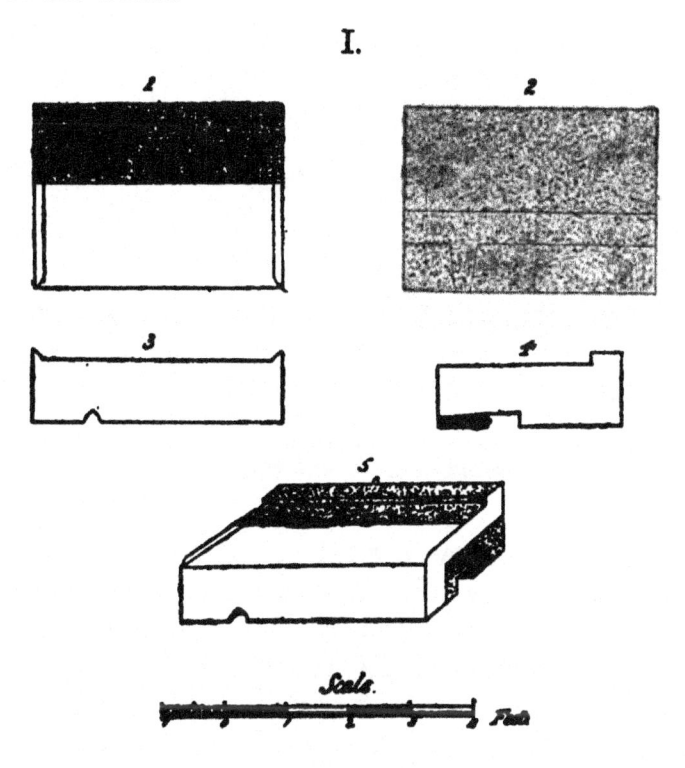

An examination of these will show the purpose of each part, and the manner in which one step has rested on another. The large flange on the upper side fitted into the large longitudinal groove of the under side of the step above, and the smaller transverse groove has been for the reception of the small joint flanges, where they pass along the rough-cut part of the upper side under the step immediately above. Figure II. shows this arrangement: (1) being a transverse section showing the fitting of the large flanges and grooves, and (2) a longitudinal one showing the small ones. From the fact of the transverse groove occurring in every instance towards the middle of the stone, it will be seen that one joint was never placed above another.

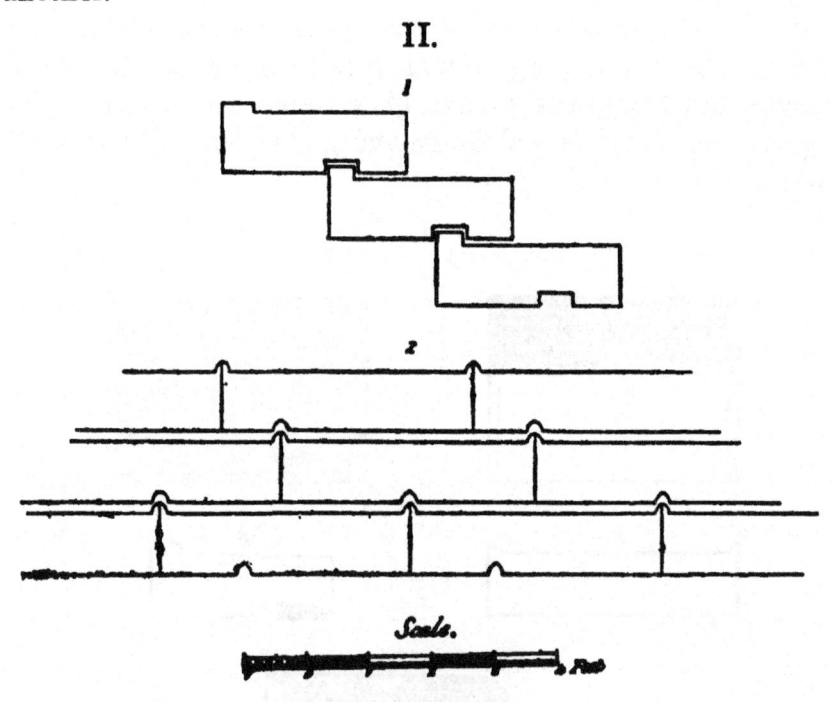

II.

Scale.

This construction was carried out at the corners, as seen from the plans, figure III. By (1), which is the plan of the upper side of a corner-stone, it will be seen that the line marking the boundary of the polished and rough-cut parts consists of two lines meeting at right angles to each other, and each of which is parallel to an edge of the stone. The two faces adjacent to this polished part are, as is naturally to be expected, also polished; thus forming the return of the face of a step, at one of the corners of the pyramid. It will also be seen that the large flange does not extend the whole length of the stone, and the reason is evident; for, if it did, it would come upon the polished part, forming the tread of the step.

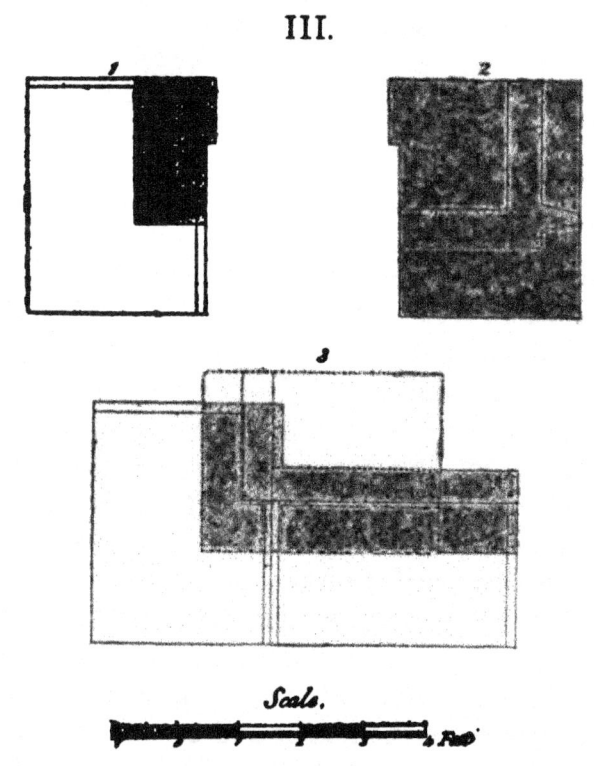

III.

Scale.

The plan of the under side is shown in figure III. (2), by which it will be seen that the large groove returns at right angles to itself, parallel to the face of the step, to fit the return of the large flanges of the stone immediately under. This is shown in figure III. (3), where the lines in black are the plan of the upper side of two contiguous stones at a corner, and the [dotted] lines[1] the plan of the under side of a corner-stone placed upon them.

[1] Red in original drawing.

A general view of this construction is shown in figure IV. The stones of each step have been firmly clamped together with copper.

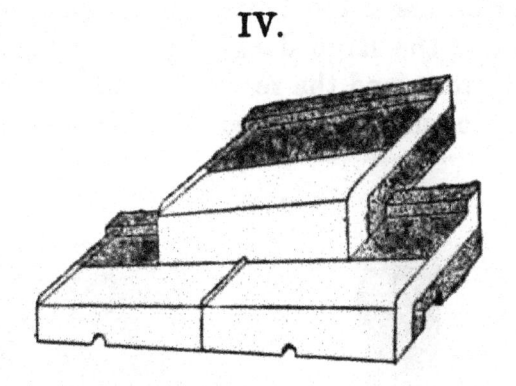

IV.

From what has been said it will be seen that the essential part of the construction of the steps of the pyramid was the fitting of each stone into those above and below it, by large longitudinal flanges and grooves, and the protection of all the joints from water by small joint flanges. These latter being fitted into transverse grooves in the stones immediately above, served another purpose, that of keeping the stones from shifting laterally, as the large flanges and grooves did from motion backwards and forwards.

These steps, however, give not only the construction, but also, when combined with Pliny's account, the size of the pyramid. The measurements of the face and tread of the step give respectively the height and breadth of each, and as we have seen from Pliny that their number was twenty-four, we have the means of finding the three dimensions of the pyramid—viz., its height, its length, and its breadth.

The height is evidently given at once, by multiplying $11\frac{3}{4}$ inches by 24; this gives a result of $23\frac{1}{2}$ feet, to which, however, must be added the height of the *quadriga*.

From the size of the horse which was found among the steps, 14 feet seems a very probable height for the chariot; this, added to the $23\frac{1}{2}$ already obtained, gives a total of $37\frac{1}{2}$ feet, which thus agrees exactly with Pliny's 25 cubits.

In a similar way, from a measurement of the tread of the steps, we arrive at the length and breadth.

This measurement, in all the steps that have been found, is uniformly either 1' 9" or 1' 5". From this it is evident that two opposite sides of the pyramid had 1' 9" and the other two 1' 5", as the breadth of their steps.

That this is the true intèrpretation of the different breadths is shown by the plan of a corner - stone (figure III. 1), in which it will be seen that both these dimensions recur; the breadth of the tread in one direction being 1' 9", and in the other, at right angles to this, 1' 5", thus proving that the breadth of the steps in two adjacent sides of the pyramid was 1' 9" and 1' 5" respectively. This 1' 9" multiplied by 24 will give the horizontal distance of the highest step on one side from the extremity of the base on the same side of the pyramid. This is 42 feet, but, as the distance is the same on the opposite side, we must double this, which gives us a length of 84 feet. To this, however, must be added a considerable length for the chariot-platform on the top. The size of the horse already mentioned gives a probable length of 24 feet. This, added to the 84 feet already obtained, gives the total length of the base of the pyramid as 108 feet.

In the same way from the dimension, 1' 5", we arrive at the breadth. Adding 18 feet for the chariot-platform, we have—

Breadth of base of pyramid

$$= 2 (24 \times 1' 5") + 18$$
$$= 86 \text{ feet.}$$

In the interpretation of the passage I have already quoted from Pliny, modern architects have understood the 63 feet mentioned in it to apply to the whole building, thus making its longest side 63 feet. The *totus circuitus* of 411 feet has in the same way been taken as that of the *peribolus*. But we have seen that the base of the pyramid measured 108 feet by 86 feet, and consequently could not have rested on a building the longest side of which was only 63 feet. We must, therefore, take the 411 feet as referring to the building itself, and the 63 feet as the length of the longer side of the *cella*. An additional proof of the correctness of this interpretation is found in the fact that Hyginus gives the total circumference as upwards of 1300 feet, which we may assume to be that of the *peribolus*.

With these data, the next question is, the distribution of the thirty-six columns with which Pliny says the building was surrounded.

Supposing the stylobate, or step on which the columns rested, projected 3 feet on each side beyond the base of the pyramid, we should have the circumference of the stylobate,

$$= 2 \left\{ 108 + (2 \times 3) + 86 + (2 \times 3) \right\}$$
$$= 2 (114 + 92) = 412 \text{ feet,}$$

which agrees almost exactly with the *totus circuitus* of Pliny. By a few inches alteration in the size of the platform on the top of the pyramid it could, of course, be made to coincide. But such exactness is unnecessary, as, even if Pliny made perfectly accurate measurements, we do not know whether he employed the Greek or Roman foot, both of which differ slightly from ours. The problem now is, to distribute the thirty-six columns over this circumference of 412 feet, keeping the number on each side proportionate to the length, so as to preserve a uniform intercolumniation throughout the building. The arrangement we propose is the one shown in the plan, figure V.

In this way there are eleven columns on the long sides and nine on the shorter ones, or fronts.

In order to find the intercolumniation we must first assume the position of the four corner columns. Supposing the edge of the lowest step of the pyramid to have been just over the centres of the columns, the distances from centre to centre of the four corner columns must be the same as the lengths of the base of the pyramid, or 108 and 86 feet. On the long side of the building, by the proposed arrangement, there are eleven columns, and consequently ten intercolumns.

The space from centre to centre of the columns must therefore be $\frac{108}{10}$ or 10·8 feet. The shorter side having nine columns and eight inter-columns, must therefore be $8 \times 10\cdot8$, or 86·4 feet, added to the 3 feet of projection of the stylobate at each end beyond the centres of the corner columns.

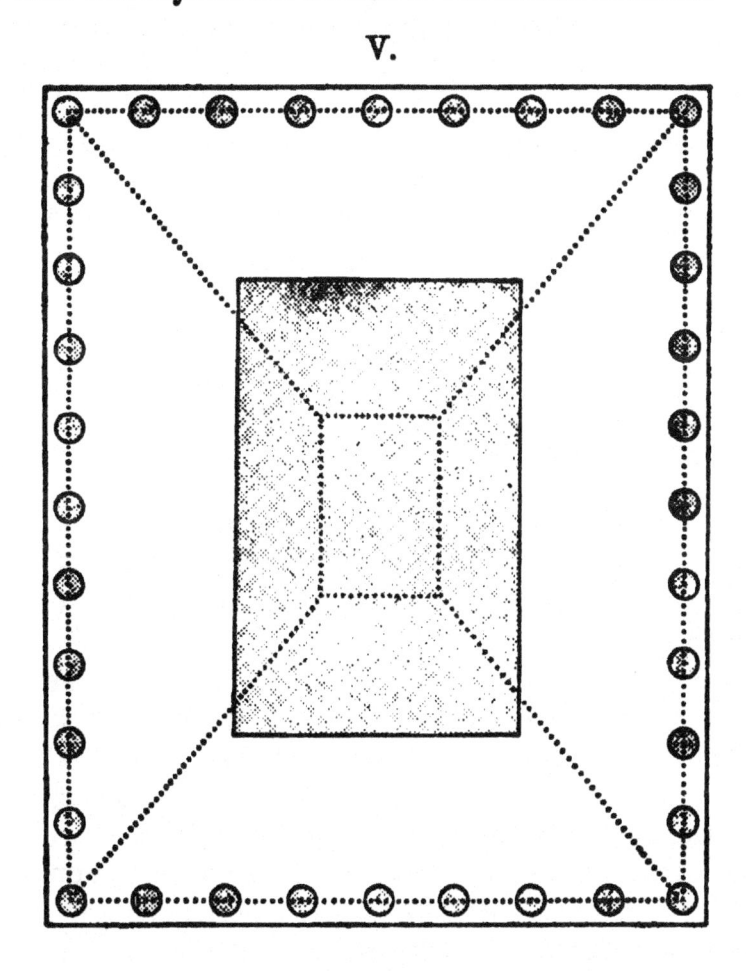

V.

This gives a total length of 92·4 feet, which thus differs only ·4 of a foot from 92 feet, the result formerly calculated from the steps of the pyramid. By adding 18·4 instead of 18 feet for the breadth of the chariot-platform in our former calculation, the two results would exactly coincide.

Taking the diameter of the columns as 3′ 5¼″, which is the result of the measurements of a great many *frusta* that have been discovered in the course of the excavations, we get the intercolumniation in terms of the diameter $= \frac{10\cdot 8' - 3' 5\frac{1}{4}''}{3' 5\frac{1}{4}''} = 2\cdot 12$ diameters, which quite corresponds with that of other Ionic buildings. It is rather a singular coincidence that the actual space between the columns, rather more than 7′ 4″, should be exactly the same as in the Temple of Minerva at Priene, which, in other respects, bears a great resemblance to the Mausoleum, and was built about the same period, and, not improbably, by the same architect. The number of columns on the flanks is also the same as in the proposed plan of the Mausoleum.

It now remains to place the *cella*. Taking its length from Pliny as 63 feet, we should have a space between its walls and the edge of the stylobate of $\frac{114 - 63}{2} = 25\frac{1}{2}$ feet.

As the space would be the same on all sides, by subtracting twice this breadth of 25½ feet from 92 feet, the length of the other side of the stylobate, we get the length of the shorter sides of the *cella*. This gives a result of 41 feet. (See figure V., in which the dotted lines are the plan of the pyramid.)

It may be objected to this plan, that it leaves the unusually large space of 25½ feet from the edge of the stylobate, or 22½ feet from the centres of the columns to the walls of the *cella*; this horizontal breadth of the pyramid being thus left on each side without visible means of support.

This difficulty, however, may be overcome by supposing the pyramid to rest on what is termed a horizontal arch, supported on one side by the columns and on the other by the walls of the *cella*. This means of supporting the pyramid is shown, in section, in figure VI. This arch, it is true, was not, so far as we are aware, used in the construction of Greek temples, but we have examples of it in other buildings prior to the time of Mausolus, thus proving the fact that the builders of that age were not unacquainted with it.

The tomb still standing at Mylasa, the former capital of

VI.

SCALE FEET
1 0 2 4 6 8 10 12 14 16 18 20

Caria, and only a short distance from Halicarnassus, has its pyramidal roof supported on a principle similar to that of the horizontal arch. This tomb in many respects resembles the Mausoleum, being, probably, a copy of that building on a small scale, and is, consequently, frequently referred to by modern architects in writing on the Mausoleum. The arch, springing on one side from the capitals of the columns, and on the other from an equal height in the walls of the *cella*, being concealed from without by the entablature, would not injure in the least the appearance of the building. Besides, an arch of this kind would not, like a radiating arch, require piers or buttresses to withstand the lateral thrust, the pressure being directly downwards.

An examination of the accompanying section will also show that the space between a horizontal plane placed on the capitals of the columns, and the under side of the pyramid, is well fitted for an arch of this kind, the span not being too great for the height of the crown. The wall of the *cella* might be carried up to the steps of the pyramid, and the space between it, the steps, and the arch, filled with masonry.

By this means the part of the pyramid between the columns and the *cella* could be supported, and inside the *cella* there would be no difficulty, as any contrivance which might be made use of would not be seen.

A horizontal dome, similar to the Tomb of Atreus, might be used, or the *cella* itself, like the Pyramids of Egypt, might be a solid mass with chambers.

The Mausoleum being a tomb, and not a temple, this might well be the case. This construction would correspond much better to Martial's phrase, "Aere nec vacuo pendentia Mausolea," than any arrangement in which the pyramid is supported in the usual manner by architraves.

As to the height of the order, we may take Pliny's $37\frac{1}{2}$ feet. The details of the order must afterwards be made out from the several parts which have been discovered, but which were packed and sent on board as they were found. Let the general measurement of Pliny suffice for the present.

This 37½ feet added to the 37½ feet of the pyramid and chariot gives a height of 75 feet. As the total height was 140 feet, this leaves a height of 65 feet below the bases of the columns. This, consequently, must have been occupied by a basement. At first sight this may seem a great height, but on examination, it will be found to correspond with the basements of other tombs, such as the one at Mylasa, the "Souma" in Algeria, referred to by Mr Falkener in his paper on the Mausoleum, and the tombs in Syria, drawn by Sir Charles Fellows. This basement was probably ornamented with one or more friezes, and had statues at intervals, with lions at the corners.

Several fragments of frieze, on a much larger scale than the one of the order, have been discovered in the course of the excavations; thus establishing the fact of a second, if not a third, frieze larger than the other.

The interior of this basement has been built of a kind of green stone, of which a large quantity has been discovered. A great part of the present Castle of Budrum is built of these stones, and we know from the records of the Knights of St John that they ransacked the Mausoleum for building materials. In the castle, also, there is a very large number of polished blocks of marble, which may have been used in the walls of the *cella*, or as a revetment of the basement. One wall of the castle is built entirely of these blocks, and they occur in great numbers in other places.

The site of the Mausoleum which has been excavated is a rectangular space hollowed out in the rock, measuring 126 by 107 feet, thus appearing well adapted for the foundations of a building such as that I have proposed.

I have embodied these results in the elevation of the longer side of the building annexed to the other plans and sections (see figure VII.) Of course it gives no detail, but it may be interesting as showing the general proportions of the building.

These details, as well as the form of the basement, with the distribution of the statues, lions, &c., must be made out

VII.

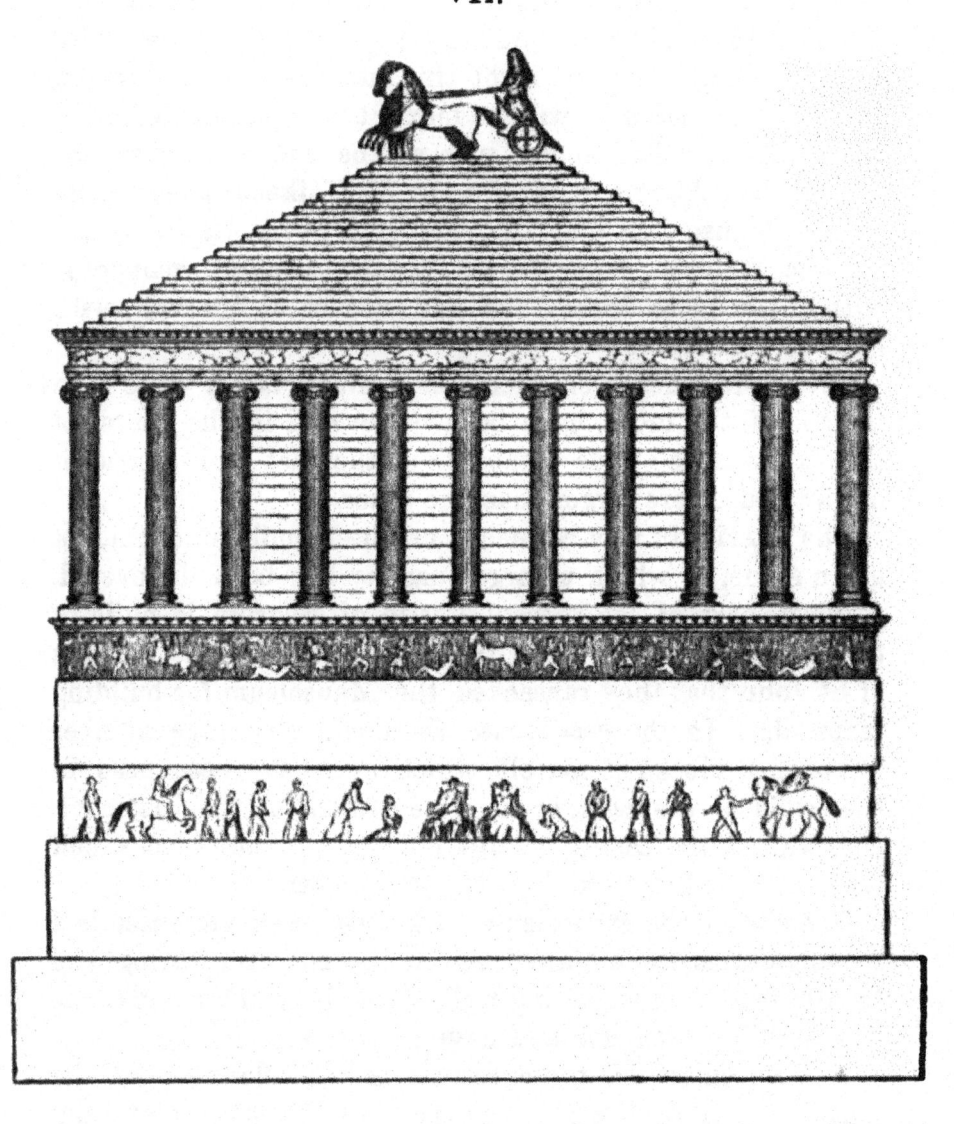

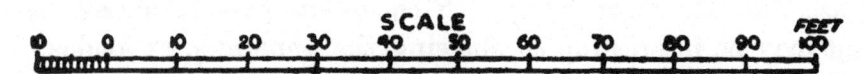

SCALE FEET

by architects, from the study of the different parts of the building, after their arrival in England.—I have, &c.,

R. M. SMITH.

The foregoing report was the basis of the detailed architectural restoration of the Mausoleum by Mr R. P. Pullan, which will be found in Sir Charles Newton's *History of Discoveries at Halicarnassus, Cnidus, and Branchidæ*, vol. ii. pp. 157-185.

INDEX.

Afghan Boundary Commission, 261 note, 296, 300, 301.
Ahurköi, 68, 69.
Alfred, Prince, visits Cnidus and Budrum, 141.
Ali Khan Beg, Kashkai chief, 225.
Alison, Mr Charles, British Minister at Teheran, 223, 224, 252, 259.
Amalgamation of Indo-European and Indian Telegraph Departments, 329.
Amin-es-Sultan (Mirza Ali Askar Khan), 318, 321.
Antiparos, grotto of, 137.
Antiquaries, Society of, of Scotland, 337.
Antoninus Pius, bust of, Cyrene, 184, 346.
Apollo Didymeus, temple of, at Branchidæ, 97.
Apollo, fountain of, Cyrene, 154, 187—temple, 159, 163—statues, 163, 184.
Apollonia (Marsa Sousah), 160, 165, 166, 185, 186.
Arab Hissar, 83.
Arabs, in Cyrenaica, account of, 161 — relations with, 161, 164, 165, 170-172, 176-179, 187-195.
Archippe, statue of, Cyrene, 183.
Arconesus (Orak), 51.
Arsinoë. See Teuchira.
Art, speech on, 337, 343.
Artemisia, discovery of statue of, 57.
Assarlik, 95.

Atabeg Azim. See Amin-es-Sultan.
Athens, 136.
Aurelius, Marcus, bust of, Cyrene, 184—quoted, 346.

Bacchus (Dionysos), statues of, found at Cyrene, 157, 183—statue presented to Edinburgh Museum, 197.
Baghdad, 202, 203, 204, 206, 214, 222, 234, 235, 237, 320.
Baker, Eleanor Katherine. See Smith, Mrs Murdoch.
Baker, Dr James, 250, 251.
Baker, Mrs J. R., 288.
Bakhtiari country, 293, 314.
Bargylia, 64, 96.
Bassadore, 309.
Baturköi, 89.
Beger, M., Russian Minister at Teheran, 255, 256, 272.
Beluchistan, 202, 203, 231, 232.
Benghazi, 149, 151-153, 179, 180-181.
Bou Bakr Ben Hadood, 174, 175.
Branchidæ, 97, 100.
Bridge of Allan, 349.
Brine, Captain, 42.
British Museum, Mausoleum Room, 19, 332—grants by Trustees in aid of Cyrene expedition, 166, 179—sculptures from Cyrene exhibited in, 196—acquires casts of Persepolis sculptures, 314.
Budrum (Halicarnassus), 19, 20, 23-142 *passim*.

INDEX.

Bulwer, Sir Henry, 133, 134.
Burgoyne, Field-Marshal Sir John, 10, 11, 17, 18, 21—letters to, 23-142 *passim*—letter from, 147.
Burne, Sir Owen, 276.
Bushire, 205, 206, 213, 214, 222, 223, 232, 233, 237, 259, 267, 283, 290, 313, 323.
Busrah, 200, 202.

Cables, telegraph: Mediterranean, 181, 196, 201, 202—Red Sea, 201, 202—Persian Gulf, 203, 232, 309.
Campbell, Mr, consul at Rhodes, 77, 135.
Carlingford, Lord, 302.
Caryanda, 96.
Chambers's Encyclopædia, contributions to, 336.
Champain, Sir John Bateman, accompanies Colonel P. Stewart to Persia, 204—associated with Colonel Goldsmid as director, 208—first meeting with Murdoch Smith, 213 — their friendship, 214—reports completion of Persian line, 221—diplomatic success, 227—becomes director-in-chief of Indo-European Telegraph Department, 249—in Persia in 1880, 290—estimate of Murdoch Smith's work, 302 — illness, 307 — last letter to Murdoch Smith, *ib.*—death, 308 — Murdoch Smith's article on, in *R. E. Journal*, *ib.* —picture by, 334—letters to, 266, 267, 272-274, 276, 279, 296, 299, 300, 302, 305—letters from, 227, 251, 307.
Chapar, 211, 260, 265, 266.
Chatham, 6-18.
Chinese War of 1859, 144.
Christmas at Budrum, 103.
Churchill, Mr Sidney, 279, 285, 296, 315.
Clarendon, Lord, 86, 94, 96.
Cnidus, 2, 23, 26, 42, 51, 61, 63, 64, 96, 100, 102, 105-142 *passim*.
Coblenz, 257.
Cockburn Association, 337.
Cole, Sir Henry, 281.
Collins, Sergeant, murder of, 261.

Constantinople, 94, 134, 202, 203, 225, 227, 228, 237, 326.
Conventions, telegraph. *See* Telegraph, Persian; Turkey.
Cowell, Major, 141, 142.
Cox, Captain, 7.
Crimea, Murdoch Smith selected for, 7—departure of sappers for, 8—return from, 14.
Cross, Lord, 311, 326, 328.
Crowe, Mr F., Vice-Consul at Benghazi, 149, 151, 162, 164, 170, 178.
Currie, Mr, 290.
Curzon, Lord, of Kedleston, 239, 270, 309, 320, 336.
Cyclopean masonry at Keramo, 90 —at Assarlik, 95.
Cyrene as a field for exploration, 145—expedition to, proposed by Murdoch Smith and Porcher, 147 —journey to, 150-154—description of, 154—cemeteries, 155—temple and statue of Dionysos, 156—offer of statues to Government, 159—temple and statue of Apollo, 163, 183 — other discoveries of sculpture, 164, 165, 183—embarkation of sculpture, 169—Augusteum, 184—discovery of Imperial portrait busts, 184—end of expedition, 196.
Cyrene, nymph, statues of, 165, 183, 184.
Czar of Russia (Alexander II.), 236.

Danvers, Sir Juland, 302, 311, 314.
Dashtiarjan, 225, 263.
Datscha, 89.
Dehbeed, 266.
Demeter, Temenos of, at Cnidus, 135, 137.
Dennison, Mr W., 179, 186.
Derna, 172.
Dervish, Murdoch Smith's, 246.
Dickson, Sir Joseph, 259.
Dickson, Mrs W. K. *See* Smith, Kathleen Murdoch.
Dieulafoy, Monsieur and Madame, 331.
Dolgorouky, Prince, 320.
Donnelly, Major-General Sir John, 301.

INDEX.

Dufferin, Lord, 311, 317.
Dumaresq, Captain, 143—his monkey, 144.

Edinburgh, life in, 329-350.
Edinburgh Museum of Science and Art, Murdoch Smith appointed director of, 301—history of, 304 —additions to, 330-333—Shah's visit to, 334.
Egyptian War, the Indo-European telegraph and the, 292.
Ellaköi, 115.
Enfield rifle, report on, 10.
Enzelli, 259.

Fahie, Mr J. J., 320, 323.
Falckenhagen concession, 267, 268, 270.
Fao, junction of cable and Turkish line, 203, 204, 206, 207, 234, 235—Turkish fort at, 313.
Fellows, Sir Charles, 30.
Festing, Major-General E. R., C.B., 15, 17.
Findlay, Mr J. R., 337.
Folkestone, 349.
Foreign Office, 96, 97, 138, 146-148, 311.
Frere, Sir Bartle, 232.

Galletly, Mr Alexander, 305, 347.
Gargejek, 83.
Geographical Society, Royal, 335.
Geographical Society, Royal Scottish, 200, 335.
Geronda, 133, 134.
Ghegheb, attack on castle of, 176.
Gibeah, 81.
Giers, M. de, Russian minister, 256.
Glasgow University, 5, 12.
Goldsmid, Major-General Sir Frederic — his book *Telegraph and Travel*, 200 note, 215, 231—mission to Beluchistan, 203—becomes director-in-chief of Indo-European Telegraph Department, 208—describes construction of line, 216-221—negotiates convention of 1865, 229, 230—visits Beluchistan and India with Murdoch Smith, 231, 232—recommendation as to Beluchistan line, 232—returns to England, 233—report on services of telegraph officers, 234—visit to Murdoch Smith at Teheran, 244—letters to, 249, 251, 254, 255, 292.
Göwerjinlik, 64, 65.
Grantown, 344.
Gray, Mr, 297.
Gray, Mrs (Eliza Priest), 288.
Gulahek, 244, 249, 315.
Gümischlu, 82.
Gwadur, 203, 206, 207.
Gymnasium, at Cnidus, 137.

Hadrian, statue of, Cyrene, 164.
Haig, Dr Percy, 266.
Halicarnassus. *See* Budrum.
Hamadan, 205, 228, 282.
Haraköi, 89.
Harkness, Mr, rector of Kilmarnock Academy, 3.
Harness, Colonel, 24.
Hassan Ali Khan, Nawab, 261.
Hauz-i-Sultan, 219, 220.
Hecate, temple of, Lagina, 73, 79-81.
Heddle-Dudgeon collection of minerals, 333.
Helme, Mr Richard, 249.
"Hen," "Year of the," 298.
Horizontal arches, 84, 95, 141, 362.
Hyginus, 87, 93.

Iliats, 210, 224.
Imghernis, 161.
India, projected telegraph to, 201 —Persian Gulf cable, 203—line through Turkey, 204— Eastern Telegraph Company, 237—effects of telegraphic communication with, 239—visits to, in 1866, 232; in 1887, 311. *See* Telegraph, Persian.
Indo-European Telegraph Company, 237.
Ispahan, 205, 216, 223, 228, 231, 255, 264, 266, 267, 290.
Italy, visits to, 143, 344.
Itazad-u-Sultaneh (Ali Kuli Mirza), 227 note.

Jakli, 83, 85.
Jask, 232, 233, 238 — the Jask question, 309, 326 *passim*.

INDEX.

Jenkins, Corporal W., 20, 24, 34, 37, 40, 49, 78, 86, 104, 110, 113, 132, 137-139.
Jiafar Khan, Mirza, 225.
Jones, Sir H., 7.
Julfa, 267.
Jupiter Labrandenus, 82.
Jupiter, Temple of, Labranda, 83.

Kadi Kalessi, 94.
Kalymnos, 51, 85, 97.
Kangawar, 214.
Karachi, 203, 206, 207, 231, 232, 237, 267, 295, 296, 311.
Kara Toprak, 94.
Karowa, 75.
Karun River, 293, 311, 326 — papers on, 335.
Kashan, 216, 220, 228, 295.
K.C.M.G., 328.
Kelvin, Lord, 5, 237.
Kemball, Colonel, 222.
Keramus (Keramo), 88.
Kerbela, 261 note.
Kermanshah, 222, 228, 293, 320.
Khani Khorreh, 266.
Khanikin, 221, 223, 299.
Kilmarnock, 2, 337, 343, 348.
Kinnear, Lord, 337.
Kisalik, 26.
Kiteebas, 171.
Kodja Jallöe, 84, 85.
Kohrud, 214, 216, 220, 266, 291.
Kos, 85 — gulf of, 65, 88.
Krio, Cape (Triopium), 107.
Kum, 216, 217, 228, 295, 296, 347.

Labranda, 83, 86.
Lagina (Laina), 72, 73, 79-81, 86.
Lar, 254, 334.
Latmos, 85.
Lawrence, Lord, 232.
Lees, Very Rev. Dr Cameron, 345.
Legation buildings, British, at Teheran, 253.
Lempriere, Captain, 12.
Leros, 85.
Lighthouse cruise, 305.
Lion, colossal, Cnidus, 118 — removal of, 119-132.
Lioness, St John's adventure with a, 263.
Lothian, Lord, 336.

Lucian, 107.
Lumsden, Sir Peter, 261 *note*, 297, 300.
Lyons, Lord, 63, 97.

M'Cartney, Lance-Corporal, 113.
Macdonald, Sir John (Lord Kingsburgh), Lord Justice-Clerk of Scotland, 337.
Mackenzie, Mr G. S., 293.
Malmesbury, Lord, 119, 133.
Malta, 23, 109, 117, 129, 142, 143, 196, 201.
Man, Mr H., 214.
Manufactures, Board of, 336.
Marcellinus, Cn. C. Lentulus, bust of, Cyrene, 164.
Mars, Temple of, Budrum, 25, 26, 50.
Mather, Mrs. *See* Smith, Jeanie.
Mausoleum at Halicarnassus, 19-20, 25, 29, 33-41, 45-47, 55-60, 75-76, 78, 79, 87, 88, 92-94, 99, 102, 106, 142 — Murdoch Smith's report on, 64, 76-77, 353-367.
Mekran coast, 203, 206, 207, 309.
Mellinet, M., French Minister, 259.
Mendeliah, Gulf of, 65.
Merdj, 150, 154, 174, 180, 182.
Meshed, 258, 297.
Mian Kotal, 263.
Miletus, 97.
Mitchell, Sir Arthur, 337.
Mohammed-el-Adouly, 162, 166.
Moorsom, Captain, 16.
Mosaic pavement found at Budrum, 30, 31.
Mudakhil, 220, 258.
Mughla, 58, 64, 69-72, 76, 98, 106, 109 — pasha of, visits Budrum, 98.
Muir, Sir William, 337.
Mukhber-ed-Dowleh (Ali Kuli Khan), 275, 276, 285, 301, 311, 314, 319, 320, 321.
Murghab, 214.
Murray, Dr A. S., 197.
Muses, temple of, at Cnidus, 137.
Mushir-ed-Dowleh. *See* Yahia Khan.
Mussendom, 206, 233.
Muzaffer-ed-Din Shah, 318, 325.

INDEX. 373

Mylasa (Melassa), 65, 66, 74, 82, 85.
Myndus (Gumishlu), 51, 52, 94.

Nasr-ed-Din Shah, his interest in telegraphy, 228—changes at Teheran during his reign, 243—intended pilgrimage, 258 — purchase of pictures, 270 — gift of sword of honour to Murdoch Smith, 298, 300—regard for him, 303—presentation of band instruments to, 321—gift of diamond snuff-box to Murdoch Smith, 322—audiences of, 285, 300, 316-318, 320-322 — assassination, 325—visit to Edinburgh, 334.
Naval Review of 1856, 9.
Nelles, Francis, 20, 28, 57, 102.
Nelles, Patrick, 20, 28, 107, 120.
Newton, Sir Charles, his first visit to Budrum, 20—published works, 21—expedition to Halicarnassus, Cnidus, &c., in 1856-59, 20-142 *passim* — supports proposed expedition to Cyrene, 147.
Nicolson, Sir Arthur, Chargé d'Affaires at Teheran, 312, 313, 315, 317, 319, 326.

Odeum at Cnidus, discovery of, 114.
Odling, Dr T., 295.
Owen, Sir P. Cunliffe, 282, 283.

Pacha Liman, 96.
Paitschin (Pedasus?), 74.
Palivan, 52-54, 58.
Panizzi, Sir A., 179, 185, 196.
Panmure, Lord, 105.
Paul, Mr Robert, 265.
Pauncefote, Lord, 327.
Persepolis, 295, 314, 336.
Perseus, marble head of, Cyrene, 184.
Persia, physical features, 208, 209—means of communication, 209, 210—inhabitants, 210—national characteristics, 212.
Persian Gulf cable, 203.
Pierson, Lieut., 214, 221, 222, 250, 254, 255.
Pliny, 25, 46, 56, 60, 354.
Ponsonby, Sir Henry, 306.

Pontoon committee, 13.
Porcher, Commander E. A., R.N., 146, 150, 160, 168, 191, 193, 196.
Praxiteles, 109.
Preece, Mr J. R., 200 *note*, 275.
Prince Consort, interest in work at Halicarnassus, 105.
Prinsep, Mr Val, 21, 24, 31.
Ptolemais (Tolmeitah), 175.
Pullan, Mr R. P., 88, 91, 100, 101, 118, 332, 367.

Quarantine troubles, 112.

Racecourse incident, 230.
Railways in Persia, 256, 267, 270.
Ramazan, 62, 66, 69-71, 115, 313, 314.
Rawlinson, Sir Henry, 270, 315.
Red Sea cable, 201, 202.
Reid, Sir George, P.R.S.A., 337.
Reid, Sir William, 24.
Resht, 255.
Rhodes, 32, 42, 133.
Richard, M. Jules, 282, 284.
Roberts, Lord, 325.
Ross, Sir E. C., 265.
Ross, Dr, 25.
"Ross's Platform," Budrum, 25, 49, 55.
Royal Society of Edinburgh, 337.
Russell, Lord John, 147, 150, 165, 185.
Russia, telegraph line opened through, 237—Russian diplomatists, 255, 256, 320—strategy of, 257—railway concession to, 267-270, 273—Penjdeh affair, 297, 298—opposition to England, 273, 294, 320.

Saeed Khan, Mirza, 258.
Sahibkranieh, ceremony at, 320.
Said 'M Rubbut, Sheikh, 189-194—made prisoner, 195.
Said Pasha, Viceroy of Egypt, visits Budrum, 77.
St Giles's Cathedral, Edinburgh, 344.
St John, Sir Oliver, 214, 224, 225, 261 *note*, 263.
Salisbury, Lord, 1, 310, 326, 327, 328, 335.
Sandford, Sir Francis, 301.

374 INDEX.

Sandham, Colonel, 6, 7, 11, 15, 17.
"Sandie," 12.
Schools, R.E. men's, remodelling of, 11.
Science and Art Department. *See* South Kensington, Edinburgh Museum.
Science and Arts, Edinburgh Association of, 337.
Scotsman, quoted, 320, 323, 334.
Sculpture, discoveries of, at Budrum, 20, 30, 32, 33, 36, 41, 55, 57, 59-60, 75, 114—at Stratonicea, 67—at Lagina, 73, 80—at Branchidæ, 97, 100—at Cnidus, 109, 118—at Cyrene, 157, 158, 159, 163, 164-165, 183, 184.
Serjepowtovski, M., Russian secretary of legation, 255.
Shah. *See* Nasr-ed-Din, Muzaffer-ed-Din.
Shiraz, 205, 222, 223, 224, 228, 229, 261, 263, 264, 291, 314.
Shoolgestoon, 266.
Shuster, 293, 314.
Siborne, Major-General, H. T., 199.
Simla, visits to, 232, 311—Shah inquires about, 316.
Smith, Alan Murdoch, 288.
Smith, Archibald Murdoch, 294, 295, 296.
Smith, Mr Cecil, 311, 314.
Smith, Eleanor Murdoch, 294, 295, 297.
Smith, Hubert Murdoch, 294, 295, 296.
Smith, Dr Hugh, 2, 3—letters to, 7, 9, 10, 12, 13, 15—death of, 34.
Smith, Hugh Murdoch, 258, 259, 268, 272, 274, 287, 288.
Smith, Isabel Murdoch, 294, 347, 349.
Smith, Jeanie (Mrs Mather), 3, 294, 343—letters to, 7, 8, 11, 103, 110, 289, 290.
Smith, Jeanie Murdoch, 291.
Smith, Kathleen Murdoch (Mrs W. K. Dickson), 294, 295, 344, 345.
Smith, Sir Robert Murdoch, birth, 3
—schooldays, *ib.*—Glasgow University, 5—gazetted lieutenant in Royal Engineers, 6—home letters from Chatham, 7-17—selected for Crimea, 7—describes naval review, 9—narrow escape, 15-17—selected to accompany Halicarnassus expedition, 18—letters to Sir J. Burgoyne, 23-142 *passim*—excavations, 27 *et seq.*—points out site of Mausoleum, 33—present at Turks' *palivan*, 52—expedition to Mughla, 64—report on Mausoleum, 64, 76, 77, 353-367—at Melassa, 74—returns to Budrum, 75—Lagina, 79—visits Keramo, 90—goes to Cnidus, 106—describes removal of colossal lion, 119-132—on furlough, 135—returns to work, *ib.*—visits Athens, 136—at Malta, 142-149—Cyrene expedition, 149—describes journey, 150-162—excavation of Temple of Apollo, 163—amateur sorcery, 170-172—exploration of Cyrenaica, 172-175—a serious disturbance, 175-179—further excavations at Cyrene, 179—leaves for Benghazi, 180—returns to Cyrene with negroes, *ib.*—awkward incident with Arabs, 182—continued excavations, 183, 184—more difficulties with Arabs, 187-195—expedition returns to Malta, 196—receives appointment in War Office, 198—appointed to Persian telegraph, 200—reaches Teheran, 214—work commences, *ib.*—line open for traffic, 225—made director, 226—military promotion, *ib.*, note, 328—visits Beluchistan and India, 231, 232—returns to Teheran, 233—is visited by Dr Wills, 244—Teheran festivities, 250—marriage, 254—wife's illness, 257—on furlough, *ib.*—at Coblenz, *ib.*—birth of second son, 258—returns to Teheran, *ib.*—journeys of inspection, 260—a chaparing adventure, 264—letters to Colonel Champain, 266-275—influence on Persians, 276, 277—makes purchases for South Kensington Museum, 281-284—domestic

troubles, 287 — thinks of emigrating to New Zealand, 291 — dangerously ill, 292 — goes home, *ib.*—returns, *ib.*—interest in commercial enterprise, 293—wife's death, 294—starts for England with children, 295 — loses three children, *ib.*—returns alone to Teheran, 296—receives a sword of honour, 298—appointed director of Museum of Science and Art in Edinburgh, 302—leaves Persia, *ib.*—lighthouse cruise, 305—succeeds Champain as Director-in-Chief, 308—mission to Persia in 1887, 310-328—audiences of the Shah, 315-318—extension of telegraph conventions, 319, 323, 328—receives present from Shah, 322—K.C.M.G., 328 — retires from army, *ib.*—work in the Museum, 330-333—opens Art Gallery in Kilmarnock, 337-343 — life in Edinburgh, 343 *et seq.*—character, 345—freedom of Kilmarnock, 348—illness, *ib.*—death, 350.

Smith, Mrs Murdoch, engagement and marriage, 251, 254—becomes permanent invalid, 257 — visits Europe, *ib.*—ill with fever, 290—death, 294.

"Smith's Platform," 33.

Smyrna, 43, 77, 94, 100, 101, 135.

Snake-charming, 111.

South Kensington Museum, purchases for, 281, 283, 284—Persian collection at, 284, 287—drawings obtained for, 285 — gifts to, *ib.*—Shah's interest in, 286—lecture at, 336.

Spackman, Corporal, 20, 24, 31, 79-82, 100, 113.

Sparroy, Mr Wilfred, 325.

Spratt, Captain, 25, 50.

Stanhope, Mr, 24, 31.

Stewart, Sir Donald, 261 *note.*

Stewart, Colonel Patrick, takes charge of Indian Telegraph scheme, 204—visits Teheran, 205—death, 207.

Strabo, 83, 85.

Stratford de Redcliffe, Lord, 20, 55, 61.

Stratonicea (Eski Hissar), 67, 72, 81, 82.

Sword of honour, 298, 300.

Symi, gulf of, 89.

Tabriz, 252, 267, 269, 299.

Tanzimat, 113, 274.

Tarleton, Captain, 141, 142.

Tedjrish, 255.

Teheran, 204-326 *passim.*

Tekerinbarek, valley of, 65.

Telegraph and Travel. See Goldsmid, Sir F.

Telegraph, Persian, Convention of 1862, 205-206 — construction of the line, 206, 213-221—political difficulties, 221-225—line opened, 225 — Murdoch Smith becomes Director at Teheran, 226—Convention of 1865, 230—construction of second wire, 233—delay and confusion in transmission, 234 — Indo-European Telegraph Co., 237 — Convention of 1872, *ib.*—prolongation of conventions, 238, 319 — efficiency attained, 238—effect on Persia, 239-241—amalgamation of Indo-European and Indian departments, 329.

Teuchira (Tocra), 174.

Theatricals at Teheran, 249-251, 252.

Tholozan, Dr, 256.

Thomson, Sir Wm. Taylour, British Minister at Teheran, 259.

Tiflis, 267.

Towsey, Captain, 20, 28, 52.

Traquair, Dr R. H., 305.

Tripoli, 149, 157.

Tschinar, 68, 69, 74.

Turkey, telegraph convention with, 202, 205.

Turks, their efficiency as workmen, 30, 78—habits, 43-44—friendliness, 45, 71, 78, 101—*palivan,* 52, 58.

United Service Institution, paper at, 257.

Vallance, Mr D. J., 347.

Vambéry, Professor, 335.

Venus, Temple of, Budrum, 25—